Writing the Digital History of Nazi Germany

Writing the Digital History of Nazi Germany

Potentialities and Challenges of Digitally Researching and Presenting the History of the Third Reich, World War II, and the Holocaust

Edited by Julia Timpe and Frederike Buda

DE GRUYTER
OLDENBOURG

This publication and the workshop from which it derives were made possible by a grant from the Federal Ministry of Education and Research (funding for project: 3D Erfassung der Gedenkstätte U-Boot Bunker Valentin durch Luft-, Boden- und Unterwasserroboter (Valentin3D)).

Free access to the e-book version of this publication was made possible by the 32 academic libraries and initiatives that supported the open access transformation project in History.

ISBN 978-3-11-135591-7
e-ISBN (PDF) 978-3-11-071469-2
e-ISBN (EPUB) 978-3-11-071479-1
DOI https://doi.org/10.1515/9783110714692

This work is licensed under the Creative Commons Attribution 4.0 International License. For details go to https://creativecommons.org/licenses/cc-by/4.0/.

Creative Commons license terms for re-use do not apply to any content (such as graphs, figures, photos, excerpts, etc.) not original to the Open Access publication and further permission may be required from the rights holder. The obligation to research and clear permission lies solely with the party re-using the material.

Library of Congress Control Number: 2021948898

Bibliographic information published by the Deutsche Nationalbibliothek
The Deutsche Nationalbibliothek lists this publication in the Deutsche Nationalbibliografie; detailed bibliographic data are available on the Internet at http://dnb.dnb.de.

© 2023 with the author(s), editing © 2022 Julia Timpe and Frederike Buda, published by Walter de Gruyter GmbH, Berlin/Boston. This book is published with open access at www.degruyter.com.
This volume is text- and page-identical with the hardback published in 2022.
Cover illustration: ©Robotics Team, Jacobs University Bremen

Printing and binding: CPI books GmbH, Leck

www.degruyter.com

Table of Contents

Frederike Buda and Julia Timpe
Chapter 1
Introduction: Writing the Digital History of Nazi Germany —— 1

Part I Digitally Researching the History of Nazi Germany, World War II, and the Holocaust

Sonja Dickow-Rotter and Daniel Burckhardt
Chapter 2
Traces of Jewish Hamburg: A Digital Source Edition of German-Jewish History —— 17

Christiane Charlotte Weber
Chapter 3
Out of the Storage Cabinet and into the World: The Use of State-of-the-Art Digital Technology to Provide Contextualized Online Access to Historical Nazi Documents, as Practiced by the Arolsen Archives —— 39

Part II Digitally Writing the History of Nazi Germany, World War II, and the Holocaust

Sebastian Bondzio
Chapter 4
"At Least He Was Cautioned": Digitally Researching the Gestapo's Ruling Practices —— 57

Mark Dang-Anh and Stefan Scholl
Chapter 5
Digital Discourse Analysis of Language Use under National Socialism: Methodological Reflections and Applications —— 99

Part III Digital Exhibitions and Digital Forms of Commemoration

Andreas Birk, Frederike Buda, Heiko Bülow, Arturo Gomez Chavez, Christian A. Müller, and Julia Timpe
Chapter 6
Digitizing a Gigantic Nazi Construction: 3D-Mapping of Bunker Valentin in Bremen —— 133

Jannik Sachweh
Chapter 7
The National Socialist Prison System and the Illusive Appeal of Digital Maps —— 169

Christian Günther
Chapter 8
Authenticity and Authority in German Memorial Sites —— 181

Further Readings on Writing the Digital History of Nazi Germany and Topics in This Book: A Selection of Academic Scholarship and Online Resources —— 203

Contributors —— 223

Index —— 227

Frederike Buda and Julia Timpe
Chapter 1
Introduction: Writing the Digital History of Nazi Germany

The digital has become ubiquitous in everyday life. Digitization[1] has also impacted the humanities and specifically the field of history: Recent years have seen a plethora of publications that deal with new methods, historical insights, and historiographical opportunities and challenges afforded by digital innovations.[2] This book aims to join this conversation by zooming in on digital history projects

---

[1] The terms "digitization" and "digitalization" are often used synonymously. As editors of this volume, we prefer the term "digitization" in this introduction. In the different chapters, we have preferred to follow the respective authors' usage of either or both term(s).

[2] While acknowledging the new (practical) possibilities afforded by digital approaches, researchers in digital history consistently point out potential methodological and epistemological implications that technical advances might entail for the practice of history; see Wolfgang Schmale, *Digitale Geschichtswissenschaften* (Vienna: Böhlau, 2010), 123; Jörg Wettläufer, "Neue Erkenntnisse durch digitalisierte Geschichtswissenschaft(en)? Zur hermeneutischen Reichweite aktueller digitaler Methoden in informationszentrierten Fächer," *Zeitschrift für digitale Geisteswissenschaften* (2016), accessed October 20, 2020, doi: 10.17175/2016_011; Rüdiger Hohls, "Digital Humanities und digitale Geschichtswissenschaften," in *Clio Guide – Ein Handbuch zu digitalen Ressourcen für die Geschichtswissenschaften*, edited by Laura Busse et al., A.1–1 – B.1–34 (Berlin: Clio-Online and Humboldt-University Berlin, 2018), 22, accessed October 16, 2020, doi: 10.18452/19244; Andreas Fickers, "Digitale Metaquellen und doppelte Reflexivität," in *H-Soz-Kult*, January 26, 2016, accessed October 20, 2020, www.hsozkult.de/debate/id/diskussionen-2954. There are growing calls for greater integration of findings from digital history into the general historiographical discourse; see, for example, Arguing with Digital History Working Group, "Digital History and Argument," white paper, (Fairfax, VA: Roy Rosenzweig Center for History and New Media and George Mason University, 2017), 12, accessed October 16, 2020, https://rrchnm.org/argument-white-paper/. At the same time, digital innovations in the field of history are still sometimes regarded apprehensively or even with strong skepticism, see Sybille Krämer and Martin Huber, "Dimensionen Digitaler Geisteswissenschaften," special issue, *Zeitschrift für digitale Geisteswissenschaften* 3 (2018), section one, accessed October 14, 2020, doi: 10.17175/sb003_013; furthermore, there is an ongoing debate among historians whether "Digital History" should be considered a mere tool in research or should be treated as a stand-alone academic field; see, for example, Hohls, "Digital Humanities"; Arguing with Digital History Working Group, "Digital History and Argument"; Gerben Zaagsma, "On Digital History," *BMGN – Low Countries Historical Review* 128, no. 4 (2013), 14; or Patrick Sahle, "Digital Humanities? Gibt's doch gar nicht!," in "Grenzen und Möglichkeiten der Digital Humanities," ed. Constanze Baum and Thomas Stäcker, special issue, *Zeitschrift für digitale Geisteswissenschaften* 1 (2015), accessed October 17, 2020, doi: 10.17175/sb001_004.

∂ OpenAccess. © 2022 Frederike Buda and Julia Timpe, published by De Gruyter. This work is licensed under the Creative Commons Attribution 4.0 International License.
https://doi.org/10.1515/9783110714692-001

and approaches that focus on the history of Nazi Germany, World War II, and the Holocaust.³ It presents a collection of essays on how the digital can be used to present and analyze topics and sources related to the period of Nazi Germany, written by authors in the light of their own experiences of actually doing so. The book evolved out of papers given at a workshop which took place at Jacobs University Bremen in December 2019.⁴

Working on Nazi Germany as an area of history presents unique issues and challenges. When digital history encounters these features, two points are salient. First, in this field, scrutiny of how best to work (digitally) with historical sources when doing research must be complemented by consideration of how to most effectively and appropriately present and disseminate such sources and the results of related research using new digital formats—be it in the educational settings of schools and universities or in museums, exhibitions, and at memorial sites. This strong public history dimension is especially characteristic of work on Nazi Germany, particularly so in Germany itself, where remembrance of and education about this time period and its crimes, victims, and perpetrators play an important role in contemporary society and politics. Second, and relatedly, there is a specific urgency in this area to pay attention not only to the methodological and heuristic challenges that possibly emerge from digital history approaches, but also to the ethical questions that could likewise emerge. When it comes to remembering and exhibiting the history of Nazi Germany, concerns about appropriateness and suitability are always especially pertinent, and become perhaps even more so when considering employing digital solutions.

An example of such an ethical concern about responsible and appropriate usage of digital solutions arising and then being successfully dealt with is the novel digital visualization employed at the Bergen-Belsen Memorial in Lower Saxony, Germany. Bergen-Belsen was a prisoner-of-war (POW) camp and concentration camp, run by the Nazi regime between 1939 and 1945. Today, the former barracks that once housed 120,000 people have long vanished and only empty

---

3 The history of Nazi Germany, World War II, and the Holocaust is the general historical background considered in this chapter (and this book). However, in the following, to enhance readability, we will use the contracted phrase "Nazi Germany" to refer to this larger context. Also, for the sake of readability, we will use the established term "Nazi" instead of the fuller "National Socialist."
4 The workshop was called "Zeugnisse des Nationalsozialismus, digital – Projekte, Methoden, Theorien" ("Digital Testimonies of National Socialism – projects, methods, theories"). For the conference report, see Friederike Jahn, "Tagungsbericht: Zeugnisse des Nationalsozialismus, digital – Projekte, Methoden, Theorien, 13.12.2019–13.12.2019 Bremen," *H-Soz-Kult*, March 19, 2020, accessed October 16, 2020, www.hsozkult.de/conferencereport/id/tagungsberichte-8695.

heathland remains at the site. But, thanks to digital technology, visitors can now borrow tablets at the Bergen-Belsen museum that allow an Augmented Reality (AR) tour of the site. The tablet screen superimposes representations of the vanished buildings onto a live image of the heath where they once stood. Thus, looking at the tablet is like looking through a window that frames a different time. However, when the project was originally proposed by a former inmate of the camp, there were still serious concerns about the appropriateness of using AR reconstruction. This worry is not unique to Bergen-Belsen; the debate among scholars and historians about employing Virtual Reality (VR) and AR is vigorous, and sometimes even antagonistic. Some voices laud digital tools as the future for Holocaust remembrance,[5] while others strenuously warn that some of these tools could contribute to a "transformation of the Shoah into a [sensationalistic] ghost play [*Geister- und Gespensterstück*]."[6]

For the Bergen-Belsen memorial, such ethical concerns were alleviated when, as Stephanie Billib, head of the project, puts it: "we realized that we weren't dealing with a representation in the style of video games or Walt Disney."[7] The developers of the app decided to render the images in a deliberately simplified and relatively featureless way, so that it makes "buildings become visible again, yet deliberately only in shadowy form."[8] The tension between the use of AR in tandem with somewhat unreal abstract images of the past is cru-

---

5 See, for example, Adam Brown and Deb Waterhouse Watson, "The Future of the Past: Digital Media in Holocaust Museums," *Holocaust Studies* 20, no. 3 (2014), accessed October 20, 2020, doi: 10.1080/17504902.2014.11435374. In general, this discourse on the various forms and best practices of "Digital Holocaust Memory," has produced a growing body of literature. On this, see, for example, the bibliography "Reading about Digital Holocaust Memory" provided by Victoria Grace Walden on the blog Digital Holocaust Memory, accessed October 20, 2020, https://reframe.sussex.ac.uk/digitalholocaustmemory/2020/07/10/reading-about-digital-holocaust-memory/.
6 Micha Brumlik, "Hologramm und Holocaust: Wie die Opfer der Shoah zu Untoten werden," in *Erinnerungskulturen: Eine pädagogische und bildungspolitische Herausforderung*, ed. Meike Sophia Baader and Tatjana Freytag (Weimar: Böhlau, 2015), 27. Specifically, Brumlik refers here to digital, "hologram"-like representations of Holocaust survivors giving testimonies.
7 Jan D. Walter, "Mit dem Tablet durchs KZ," in *Deutsche Welle*, May 5, 2016, accessed October 21, 2020, https://www.dw.com/de/mit-dem-tablet-durchs-kz/a-19230698. (Translated from German by the authors.)
8 Andrea Schwyzer, "Erinnerung digital. Mit der App durch Bergen-Belsen," *NDR*, January 21, 2020, accessed October 28, 2020, https://www.ndr.de/geschichte/chronologie/kriegsende/KZ-Bergen-Belsen-Gedenkstaette-per-App-erkunden,bergenbelsen520.html. (Translated from German by the authors.) See also Memory in the Digital Age, "Bergen Belsen on Site with Augmented Reality," accessed October 28, 2020, http://www.belsen-project.specs-lab.com/summers-fruits-a-new-app-version/.

cial to the project's development. This evolution of the Bergen-Belsen app is a perfect example of how ethical, technical, historical, and educational aspects intertwine and guide considerations in this special field of history. What is technologically possible is not always educationally desirable or ethically appropriate.

New forms of visualization made possible through digitization are also of increasing importance to research work focusing on the history of Nazi Germany.[9] Additionally and as in history overall, digital methods have been applied to deal with big data sets[10] (methods which may, of course, also involve visualization). Some of the chapters in this book will also consider such innovations, as well as related practical, technological, and ethical concerns. The authors featured in this book are all actively engaged in "writing the digital history of Nazi Germany." Some draw in their contributions from their work for online editions of digital sources, archives or museums, where they employ digital solutions to present and disseminate historical sources and knowledge about this period. Others draw from their scholarship on Nazi Germany as part of digital history and digital humanities research projects and programs.

The book is organized in three parts. These are intended to mirror three stages in the process of knowledge production and dissemination with the aid of digital tools and approaches—from a consideration of digital sources, databases, and archives in Part I, through an examination of digital research projects and their findings in Part II, to a discussion of forms of presentation enabled or enhanced by digital technologies as realized in museums and memorial sites in Part III.

Part I, entitled "Digitally Researching the History of Nazi Germany, World War II, and the Holocaust," looks at digital sources, databases, and archives that focus on aspects of the history of Nazi Germany. It begins with a contribution by Sonja Dickow-Rotter and Daniel Burckhardt. Their chapter presents and discusses an online source edition called *Key Documents of German-Jewish History* (*Hamburger Schlüsseldokumente zur deutsch-jüdischen Geschichte*), which is maintained by the Institut für die Geschichte der deutschen Juden in Hamburg.[11]

---

9 Seminal work in this regard has been done by the Holocaust Geographies Collaborative at Stanford University. Its book *Geographies of the Holocaust* (2014) not only utilizes digital methods to produce new insights into various aspects of Holocaust history, but also exemplarily discusses and problematizes the digital methodologies used: Anne Knowles, Tim Cole, and Alberto Giordano, *Geographies of the Holocaust* (Bloomington: Indiana University Press, 2014).

10 For an introduction, see Shawn Graham, Ian Milligan, and Scott Weingart, *Exploring Big Historical Data: The Historian's Macroscope* (London: Imperial College Press, 2016).

11 *Hamburgische Schlüsseldokumente zur deutsch- jüdischen Geschichte* can be found at https://juedische-geschichte-online.net/, last accessed October 28, 2020.

The edition spans 400 years of Jewish history; thus, it also presents Judaism beyond the context of the victimization of the Holocaust. Still, the history of Hamburg's Jews between 1933 and 1945 remains a focal point of the edition. Dickow-Rotter and Burckhardt reflect on best practices and ethical responsibilities when providing digitalized sources about the Holocaust on the internet. For example, since digitizing the sources led to their being mostly decontextualized, the edition seeks to reverse this process by providing topical introductions as well as source interpretations and metadata on the origin of the sources. Dickow-Rotter and Burckhardt give a detailed description of both the historiographical and presentational strategies and the technical issues behind the edition's web presence, revealing how much thought and expertise at multiple levels is necessary to build a digital source edition and put it online. They also see the edition as an example of how a user-friendly website can be built while preserving and highlighting scholarly standards in digitizing sources. Ultimately, this chapter demonstrates that the benefits of an online edition in comparison to a printed one in raising awareness and disseminating knowledge of Jewish history are worth the extra complexity required in producing it. The chapter also highlights the usefulness of online formats in respect to learning about an edition's audience. The availability of online analytic tools can help improve user experience of a digital edition, enhance the edition's responsiveness to its audience and reception, and develop in response to ongoing research findings, in a way that paper editions simply cannot.

In Chapter 3, Christiane Charlotte Weber continues this discussion about best practices and ethical responsibilities in regard to online archives, considering the challenges, pitfalls, and benefits of making sensitive files related to the history of Nazi Germany openly accessible. Weber's chapter focuses on exploring the work of the Arolsen Archives, formerly the International Tracing Service (ITS), which was established by the Allied forces as a tracing service for millions of Displaced Persons during World War II. With holdings of around 30 million documents, this is the world's most comprehensive archive on victims of Nazi persecution. To date, 26 of its 30 million documents have been digitized. In her chapter, Weber describes the benefits of the Arolsen Archives' policy to make documents of Nazi persecution accessible online, a policy grounded in profound commitment to the right to remembrance. She also explains the e-Guide developed by the archives to help with historical contextualization of the online accessible sources.[12] Weber's chapter concludes with some more general reflections on the ways sources change when they are digitized, discussing

---

[12] The e-Guide can be found at https://eguide.arolsen-archives.org/, accessed October 28. 2020.

changes related to their character as well as how they are retrieved and reused, and in regard to their contextualization and users' interaction with them.

The authors of both these first two chapters make strong cases for enabling widely available online access to historical sources. At the same time, they remind us of the sensitive nature of the sources involved. Because of this, the authors of both chapters argue that contextualization is especially urgent: As Weber puts it, when opening the online gate to archives and sources, a "gatekeeper"—possibly itself in digital form—is needed to minimize misuse of the documents and sources that are made freely available on the internet.

The book's second part, "Digitally Writing the History of Nazi Germany, World War II, and the Holocaust," focuses on how digital tools can be used to research the history of Nazi Germany, for example tools such as digital discourse analysis, and digital methods that allow work with big data. In Chapter 4, Sebastian Bondzio explores the work of the Gestapo by analyzing the card index file of the Gestapo's Osnabrück office. The file is made up of index cards generated by Gestapo officers to organize information about individuals, noting biographical information as well as misdemeanors and sanctions issued. Examining this source body in its entirety, he argues, enhances our understanding of the Gestapo's practices and how it tried to implement the ideology of the *Volksgemeinschaft* in German society. However, given the large volume of the Osnabrück index, which comprises about 48,000 file cards, such analysis could only be feasibly achieved by employing digital tools.

Bondzio's chapter is based on his work with a research project at the University of Osnabrück,[13] for which a digital replica of the Osnabrück Gestapo's card index was created. This digitization opened up possibilities for computer-aided simulations of the index's operation and for an analysis of its historical big data with a digital approach in the tradition of Data Driven History. Working with the serial sources of the Osnabrück Gestapo files in this manner, unintentionally inscribed patterns and structures can be made visible, which in turn allow for new insights into the Gestapo's practices. Bondzio's chapter discusses forms, numbers, frequencies, and the duration of punishments noted in the Gestapo file cards, shedding light on the inner workings of the secret police. At the same time, and since the file cards also note agencies and institutions that were cooperating with the Gestapo, the digital data set also allows him to provide new

---

[13] The research project, funded by the German Research Foundation (Deutsche Forschungsgemeinschaft [DFG]) is called "Überwachung. Macht. Ordnung – Personen- und Vorgangskarteien als Herrschaftsinstrument der Gestapo" ("Surveillance. Power. Order. Personal- and Process-Card Indexes as an Instrument of Rule of the Gestapo"); DFG project number: 394480672.

insights into the Gestapo's collaboration with other institutions in Nazi Germany and thus into the Third Reich's larger disciplinary system.

Bondzio's analysis shows that it would be wrong to think of the Gestapo as the center of Nazi terror; rather, the Gestapo has to be seen as an integral part of a larger—center-less—disciplinary network. His chapter also emphasizes how much the Gestapo relied on data gathering and knowledge production, and that its disciplinary actions were closely related to the aim of implementing the Nazi-envisioned "racial community" or *Volksgemeinschaft*, as well as fermenting an intimidating public image.

Bondzio's findings rely on a digital analysis of the Osnabrück Gestapo files, an analysis which would have been impossible or at least much more difficult and time-consuming to conduct in an analog fashion and without the comprehensive digitization of the card index. His chapter thus serves as an example of how digital approaches can enhance our understanding of historical contexts, especially if they are—as in the case study in the chapter—applied in conjunction with a historical critical perspective.

Mark Dang-Anh and Stefan Scholl also work with big data. Their chapter is based on research indebted to Linguistic Social History and focuses on communication in Nazi Germany. It provides two examples of the ways in which digital discourse analysis can enrich our understanding of how German society used language during the Nazi dictatorship from 1933 to 1945. First, analyzing more than 1,000 speeches given by Adolf Hitler and Joseph Goebbels, Dangh-Anh and Scholl show how the concept of *Lebensraum* (living space) was linguistically constructed by central Nazi spokespersons, embedded into German society, and tied to *Volk* (people) and other central (discursive) concepts. The authors discuss the different methodological approaches that led their analysis and argue that, while a digitally driven research process will suggest various possibly fruitful paths, the decision which of these paths to follow demands adequate analytico-hermeneutic decisions by the analysts throughout.

In addition to the rhetoric of Nazi leaders, Dangh-Anh and Scholl look at letters of complaint sent to Nazi officials between 1933 and 1939. The texts in this second sample potentially include more various and complex linguistic elements such as figures of speech or sarcasm. To deal with this complexity, a different method of analysis was applied. The letters of complaint were manually tagged for informative or interesting phrasing, figures of speech, etc. Database tools can then be used to collate and analyze these tags. Even though this part of their project is still ongoing, Dangh-Anh and Scholl can already point to different patterns that appear across the letters—such as the appropriation by complainers of patterns specific to Nazi discourse. Such tagging allows specific patterns to be discerned more quickly and easily than in "traditional" serial reading. However, the authors grant that this method of analysis, to which manual tagging is essential, is rather time-consuming and more fitting for short or medium-length texts.

Similar to Bondzio, Dangh-Anh and Scholl's contribution highlights new research questions and methods that are possible when working digitally on historical source material. However, both chapters make it clear that their analyses would have been incomplete without also applying "traditional" forms of historical methods and source criticism.

In the last part (Part III), this book looks at how digital tools and approaches can innovate and enhance the presentation of the history of Nazi Germany. To that end, it considers across three chapters various types of "Digital Exhibitions and Digital Forms of Commemoration." This section begins with a contribution by the members of the Valentin3D project at Jacobs University Bremen, an ongoing digitization project centered on one particular historical site, namely the large (if never quite completed) Nazi submarine pen Bunker Valentin located in a village near Bremen.[14] This bunker was built by thousands of forced laborers during World War II. Today it houses a memorial and an exhibition. The chapter focuses on technical methods used for 3D-mapping physical remnants. It discusses the complexity and challenges connected with the mapping of a diverse and sometimes dangerous environment. Inaccessible areas of the bunker, such as a flooded basement, have now been explored thanks to solutions provided by the Jacobs Robotics group. The results have been integrated into a 3D-model, which will be available online, allowing research on the bunker to be done remotely from around the world. The chapter also highlights how the exploration and 3D-mapping furthered knowledge about the bunker's history and reflects on the possibilities and challenges data created in this manner present for research and commemoration. The authors also point out that new findings on the history of Bunker Valentin would not have been possible without connecting the exploratory results with traditional analog methods and sources, namely around 400 blueprints, none of which had been analyzed before the project.

In Chapter 7, Jannik Sachweh looks more closely at exhibitions and, specifically, at how digital aids can be used in exhibitions on topics related to Nazi Germany. His chapter focuses on the memorial site at the prison in Wolfenbüttel, Lower Saxony, which provides an exhibition about the history of the prison and

---

14 The project is called "3D Mapping of the U-Boot Bunker Valentin Memorial by Air-, Ground-, and Underwater-Robots" (3D Erfassung der Gedenkstätte U-Boot Valentin durch Luft-, Boden- und Unterwasserroboter)—or Valentin3D—and is funded by the Federal Ministry for Education and Research (Bundesministerium für Bildung und Forschung [BMBF]), accessed October 10, 2020, http://robotics.jacobs-university.de/projects/Valentin3D.

the penal system in Nazi Germany. Sachweh discusses a digital map developed for the memorial's new permanent exhibition. This map depicts places of persecution connected to the Wolfenbüttel prison within the then state of Brunswick. Sachweh's chapter explores the advantages of such a digital map, which allows visitors a more interactive and thus more individualized access to historical information: The map uses digital layers to link background information and, if available, further material such as pictures and historical sources to the locations it depicts. With this digital tool, visitors can more actively curate the input they receive according to their interest. However, Sachweh also highlights the challenges connected to creating such a digital map. Selecting the places to be depicted is not trivial, as he explains in regard to his Wolfenbüttel case study. Following specific definitional frameworks, such as "places belonging formally to Brunswick's state judiciary," would lead to the omission of important information about the complex network and activities of the Wolfenbüttel prison within the larger Nazi penal system. However, to prevent the map becoming too overwhelming or confusing, certain choices must be made. In sum, as Sachweh contends, digital maps in exhibitions can certainly be informative and visually engaging for visitors but will equally unavoidably contain—and sometimes even create—blind spots. While some of this might be already true for analog maps, this danger is plausibly heightened when dealing with digital tools since they seem to suggest to their audience a greater degree of completeness.

The book's final chapter, by Christian Günther, considers again the potentialities and challenges of digital tools used by memorial sites. Less focused on just one particular project, Günther explores the usage of VR and related technologies in German sites that memorialize the crimes of Nazi Germany. His discussion is guided by an examination of the term authenticity and the role it plays at these sites. This is of particular concern when considering the challenges memorials face when introducing immersive technology into their exhibitions and existing modes of presentation on the history of Nazi Germany. Basing some of his considerations on theories from Games Studies, Günther points out that authenticity—one of the major assets of memorials—is created for and by the visitor through communication with the exhibition. That is, the participation of visitors is crucially important. Here, Günther sees an opportunity for digital tools, claiming that they could enhance participatory experience (and, hence, authenticity), as, for example, when visitors are given the chance to enter a dialog with the virtual presentation of a witness giving testimony. Furthermore, the chapter discusses whether visitors should not only be treated as recipients but also as co-creators when implementing VR, and the ramifications of such a move for memorial site professionals.

Through these different contributions, this book, first, wants to shed light on projects that use digital forms and approaches to research and display the history of Nazi Germany from new angles. As any book can highlight only a few projects in detail, the present volume also offers an annotated bibliography listing some digital activities—both concluded and ongoing—related to the history of Nazi Germany. In doing so, the book endeavors to complement the more in-depth insights of the individual chapters with a brief survey that offers some insight into the ever-growing breadth of activities in this field.

Although the different chapters are explicitly about individual projects, a recurring theme permeates the book, as each chapter also considers how these emerging digital approaches and methodologies relate to more traditional forms of researching and displaying topics and sources on Nazi Germany. The different chapters all have in common that they consider whether and how these digital approaches add to our understanding—and learning and teaching —of this history.

In this regard, a first and central question mostly concerns the research side of historians' work. It asks whether and how historians' practices ought to change or adapt in the digital era. Of course, on a general level, all chapters in this book deal with this in that they describe such changes and their potentials through exploring the particular methodological or practical interventions of actual working historians as facilitated by digitization in their individual projects. One clear change is that digitization has certainly led to new ways of dealing with sources; for example, historians can now analyze much larger bodies of sources than previously possible or even imaginable, as is illustrated in Chapter 4 by Bondzio, whose examination of Gestapo files is only realizable because of digital methods, and in Chapter 5 by Dang-Anh and Scholl, who employ a digital discourse analysis of language use in Nazi Germany. So, digitization has generated new forms of research. However, as is pointed out in several instances in this book, it is only in conjunction with "traditional" research methods that these innovations can develop their full potential.[15] Additionally and relatedly,

---

[15] Such calls for the combination of methods can also be found in scholarship dealing more theoretically and epistemologically with digital history. For example, in regard to analyses based on big data, Zaagsma has emphasized that their aim "should not be the replacement of the historian's interpretive and hermeneutic work," demanding rather an "integration of both approaches"; Zaagsma, "On Digital History," 24. Schmale argues in the same vein when he stresses that "there are no quantitative analyses without qualitative analyses in the humanities;" Wolfgang Schmale, "Big Data in den historischen Kulturwissenschaften," in *Digital Humanities: Praktiken der Digitalisierung, der Dissemination und der Selbstreflexivität*, ed. Wolfgang Schmale (Stuttgart: Franz Steiner, 2015), 137. (Translated from German by authors.)

of course, digitization not only affects historians' research methods, but also the "stuff" with which they work: primary sources. They now have to deal with digital sources, a development that has led to calls for historians to more actively consider methods and processes of "digital source criticism."[16] However, as our texts tend to show, digital source criticism can best be understood more as an update to historians' armamentarium than a fundamental transformation of their craft. The traditional practice of source criticism is still applicable, and its application very much required, perhaps even more so than ever.[17] This book illustrates how important digital sources have become, especially for those who work on Nazi Germany with a focus on education and in the field of public history. Here, digital sources afford, in particular, very welcome opportunities to better visualize historical data and contexts. This is very clear in Chapter 7 by Sachweh, but also features in the project discussions provided by the Valentin-3D team and Günther in Chapters 6 and 8.

A second major issue pervading many discussions at the workshop and in this book is particularly prominent in the contributions by both Weber and by Dickow-Rotter and Burckhardt: that of providing sources digitally online and the potential repercussions and drawbacks of such practices. First, there is no doubt that digitizing sources and subsequently making them available via the internet will greatly improve their accessibility. Furthermore, there is a compelling argument that this is inherently beneficial. Thus, the larger range achieved via the open access approach can be considered a step to further democratizing both research and education of history in general and that of Nazi Germany in particular. In the same vein, it certainly can be argued—as in this book by Weber, for example—that both the breadth and strength of remembrance work can be enhanced if archives, museums, and other institutions provide online digital source material on the crimes of Nazi Germany and its victims, as in this manner wider audiences can be reached, unlimited by geography or, to an extent, economic factors. However, there are also some concerns. Enabling such

---

16 See, on this especially, the publications by Andreas Fickers, e.g., Andreas Fickers, "Update für die Hermeneutik. Geschichtswissenschaft auf dem Weg zur digitalen Forensik?," *Zeithistorische Forschungen/Studies in Contemporary History* 17, no. 1 (2020), accessed July 6, 2020, doi: 10.14765/zzf.dok-1765. See also the 2018 dissertation by Pascal Föhr on source criticism in the digital era, Pascal Föhr, "Historische Quellenkritik im Digitalen Zeitalter" (PhD diss, University of Basel, 2018).
17 We have further developed these considerations elsewhere; cf. Frederike Buda, Julia Timpe, and Christiane Charlotte Weber, "Digitale NS-Geschichtsschreibung: Herausforderungen im Umgang mit digitalen Quellen in der Geschichtsforschung und -vermittlung zum Nationalsozialismus," in *Raumdefinitionen –Stadtkonstruktionen –Architekturpraktiken in Mittel-und Osteuropa. Digital Humanities und die "Messbarkeit" des NS-Regime*, ed. Richard Nemec (forthcoming).

(potentially unlimited) access to digital sources on Nazi Germany might also introduce problems. For example, there is the risk of violating the right of privacy of victims on a personal or more collective level. A rather different type of concern is the worry that users accessing the sources would lack the skills and knowledge needed to work properly with the material, so that the result of democratized information access might—through misleading interpretations—generate actual misinformation. While that risk is one of mischance, there is a related risk, especially when it comes to visual sources, that making them available widely might create opportunities for malicious manipulations and de-contextualization.

One way to mitigate such potentially damaging developments would be for archives, online editions, and researchers to act consciously and devise strategies to balance both the opportunities and challenges when providing access to digital sources online. In a sense, they might have to adopt the role of a gatekeeper—that is, taking seriously the role of guiding the public when publishing primary sources and providing historical contextualization. But of course, this has always been the responsibility of historians and, what is more, will only perpetuate the role of memory institutions in safekeeping and "authorizing" knowledge. As Günther points out in his chapter, a better way might include participatory elements that involve visitors/the audience in certain decisions, though this would also entail that archives, museums, and so on change their approach to internal and external communications.

To an extent then, some of the challenges that emerge when looking at newer digital approaches are, on closer inspection, actually older challenges. Differently put, one could speak of an "old wine in new bottles" scenario. This is not meant to dismiss the new challenges and the need to address them. In fact, such considerations are important and beneficial for all historians, regardless of their direct engagement with digital tools, as they allow us to re-calibrate our tasks and methods as historians. Nevertheless, it is useful to recognize that some of the challenges identified in discussions related to (the) digital history (of Nazi Germany) are in fact older concerns which now re-appear connected to digital approaches and sources. Historians have always been—or should always have been—compelled by the argument that increasing access to sources is inherently a good thing, but equally aware of the need to provide contextualization and guidance to that access; digitization does not create, but rather renews this. The sentiment about new wine in old bottles is equally apt, of course, in regard to historians' work with digital sources. As highlighted above, the "old" hermeneutic tool kit is generally well equipped to deal with "new" digital sources. Indeed, one of the most exciting aspects of the projects described in the various chapters is how they demonstrate historians combining their hermeneutic techniques with the possibilities of digital technology. In this regard, as seems to become clear throughout this volume, "writing the digital history of Nazi Germany" is most fruitful when done hand in hand with traditional, analog approaches and principles. As we hope to show in this book, if both approaches align, then more can be learned.

Bibliography

Arguing with Digital History Working Group. "Digital History and Argument," white paper. Fairfax, VA: Roy Rosenzweig Center for History and New Media and George Mason University, 2017. Accessed October 16, 2020. https://rrchnm.org/argument-white-paper/.

Arolsen Archives. "e-Guide." Accessed October 28, 2020. https://eguide.arolsen-archives.org.

Brown, Adam, and Deb Waterhouse Watson. "The Future of the Past: Digital Media in Holocaust Museums." *Holocaust Studies* 20, no. 3 (2014): 1–32. Accessed October 20, 2020. doi: 10.1080/17504902.2014.11435374.

Brumlik, Micha. "Hologramm und Holocaust: Wie die Opfer der Shoah zu Untoten werden." In *Erinnerungskulturen: Eine pädagogische und bildungspolitische Herausforderung*, edited by Meike Sophia Baader and Tatjana Freytag, 19–30. Weimar: Böhlau, 2015.

Buda, Frederike, Julia Timpe, and Christiane Charlotte Weber. "Digitale NS-Geschichtsschreibung: Herausforderungen im Umgang mit digitalen Quellen in der Geschichtsforschung und -vermittlung zum Nationalsozialismus." In *Raumdefinitionen – Stadtkonstruktionen – Architekturpraktiken in Mittel-und Osteuropa. Digital Humanities und die "Messbarkeit" des NS-Regime*, edited by Richard Nemec (forthcoming).

Fickers, Andreas. "Digitale Metaquellen und doppelte Reflexivität." In *H-Soz-Kult*, January 26, 2016. Accessed October 20, 2020. www.hsozkult.de/debate/id/diskussionen-2954.

Fickers, Andreas. "Update für die Hermeneutik. Geschichtswissenschaft auf dem Weg zur digitalen Forensik?" *Zeithistorische Forschungen/Studies in Contemporary History* 17, no. 1 (2020): 157–68. Accessed July 6, 2020. doi: 10.14765/zzf.dok-1765.

Föhr, Pascal. "Historische Quellenkritik im Digitalen Zeitalter." PhD diss., University of Basel, 2018.

Graham, Shawn, Ian Milligan, and Scott Weingart. *Exploring Big Historical Data: The Historian's Macroscope*. London: Imperial College Press, 2016.

Hohls, Rüdiger. "Digital Humanities und digitale Geschichtswissenschaften." In *Clio Guide – Ein Handbuch zu digitalen Ressourcen für die Geschichtswissenschaften*, edited by Laura Busse, Wilfried Enderle, Rüdiger Hohls, Thomas Meyer, Jens Prellwitz, and Annette Schuhmann, A.1–1–B.1–34. Berlin: Clio-Online and Humboldt-University Berlin, 2018. Accessed October 16, 2020. doi:10.18452/19244.

Institut für die Geschichte der deutschen Juden. *Hamburger Schlüsseldokumente zur deutsch-jüdischen Geschichte*. Accessed October 28, 2020. https://juedische-geschichte-online.net/.

Jacobs Robotics. "3D Mapping of the U-Boot Bunker Valentin Memorial by Air-, Ground-, and Underwater-Robots." Accessed October 10, 2020. http://robotics.jacobs-university.de/projects/Valentin3D.

Jahn, Friederike. "Tagungsbericht: Zeugnisse des Nationalsozialismus, digital – Projekte, Methoden, Theorien, 13.12.2019–13.12.2019 Bremen." *H-Soz-Kult*, March 19, 2020. Accessed October 16, 2020. www.hsozkult.de/conferencereport/id/tagungsberichte-8695.

Knowles, Anne, Tim Cole, and Alberto Giordano. *Geographies of the Holocaust*. Bloomington: Indiana University Press, 2014.

Krämer, Sybille, and Martin Huber. "Dimensionen Digitaler Geisteswissenschaften." Special issue, *Zeitschrift für digitale Geisteswissenschaften* 3 (2018): section one. Accessed October 14, 2020. doi: 10.17175/sb003_013.

Memory in the Digital Age. "Bergen Belsen on Site with Augmented Reality." Accessed October 28, 2020. http://www.belsen-project.specs-lab.com/summers-fruits-a-new-app-version/.

Sahle, Patrick. "Digital Humanities? Gibt's doch gar nicht!" In "Grenzen und Möglichkeiten der Digital Humanities," edited by Constanze Baum and Thomas Stäcker. Special issue, *Zeitschrift für digitale Geisteswissenschaften* 1 (2015). Accessed October 17, 2020. doi: 10.17175/sb001_004.

Schmale, Wolfgang. "Big Data in den historischen Kulturwissenschaften." In *Digital Humanities: Praktiken der Digitalisierung, der Dissemination und der Selbstreflexivität*, edited by Wolfgang Schmale, 125–37. Stuttgart: Franz Steiner Verlag, 2015.

Schmale, Wolfgang. *Digitale Geschichtswissenschaften*. Vienna: Böhlau, 2010.

Schwyzer, Andrea. "Erinnerung digital. Mit der App durch Bergen-Belsen." *NDR*, January 21, 2020. Accessed October 28, 2020. https://www.ndr.de/geschichte/chronologie/kriegsende/KZ-Bergen-Belsen-Gedenkstaette-per-App-erkunden,bergenbelsen520.html.

Walden, Victoria Grace, "Reading about Digital Holocaust Memory." Accessed October 16, 2020. https://reframe.sussex.ac.uk/digitalholocaustmemory/2020/07/10/reading-about-digital-holocaust-memory/.

Walter, Jan D. "Mit dem Tablet durchs KZ." *Deutsche Welle*, May 5, 2016. Accessed October 21, 2020. https://www.dw.com/de/mit-dem-tablet-durchs-kz/a-19230698.

Wettläufer, Jörg. "Neue Erkenntnisse durch digitalisierte Geschichtswissenschaft(en)? Zur hermeneutischen Reichweite aktueller digitaler Methoden in informationszentrierten Fächer." *Zeitschrift für digitale Geisteswissenschaften* (2016). Accessed October 20, 2020. doi: 10.17175/2016_011.

Zaagsma, Gerben, "On Digital History." *BMGN – Low Countries Digital Review* 128, no. 4 (2013): 3–29.

Part I **Digitally Researching the History of Nazi Germany, World War II, and the Holocaust**

Sonja Dickow-Rotter and Daniel Burckhardt
Chapter 2
Traces of Jewish Hamburg: A Digital Source Edition of German-Jewish History

German Summary: Dieses Kapitel erläutert, nach einer kurzen Einführung zur jüdischen Geschichte Hamburgs als räumlichen Fokus, den konzeptionellen Rahmen der vom Institut für die Geschichte der deutschen Juden (IGdJ) herausgegebenen digitalen Quellenedition „Hamburger Schlüsseldokumente zur deutsch-jüdischen Geschichte" sowie dessen zentrale Eigenschaften aus der Perspektive der jüdischen Geschichte. Er beschreibt die technische Realisierung und analysiert Umfang, Akzeptanz und Nutzung der Edition seit ihrer Veröffentlichung. Abschließend werden bereits realisierte und noch in Umsetzung befindliche Erweiterungen der Online-Edition an der Schnittstelle zwischen Fachwissenschaft und Public History vorgestellt.

Das jüdische Erbe Hamburgs wurde durch Migration und Vertreibung, am gravierendsten durch die nationalsozialistische Verfolgung, zerstört oder an die unterschiedlichsten Orte weltweit zerstreut. Deswegen hat sich die in diesem Kapitel diskutierte Edition zum Ziel gesetzt, wichtige Teile dieses Erbes digital zusammenzuführen, besser zugänglich zu machen und nachhaltig zu sichern. Seit September 2016 ist das von der DFG geförderte zweisprachige (deutsch/englisch) Digital History-Projekt im Internet frei zugänglich.[1] Ausgehend von mehr als 100 digitalisierten Quellen widmet sich die Edition 400 Jahren jüdischer Präsenz in der Hansestadt, um Veränderungen und Kontinuitäten auch in einer longue durée-Perspektive zu beleuchten. Die Edition setzt einer Verengung der jüdischen Geschichte auf die Zeit des Nationalsozialismus die Vielfältigkeit und Widersprüchlichkeit der jüdischen Vergangenheit entgegen.

In der hypertextuell aufgebauten Edition werden die Quellen als Transkript und digitales Faksimile bereitgestellt und Personen, Organisationen und Orte in den Transkripten und Übersetzungen systematisch mit Normdaten ausgezeichnet. Bei der Digitalisierung, Textauszeichnung und Metadatenerschließung greift die Edition auf etablierte Standardformate digitaler Editionen und der Langzeitarchivierung zurück.

Nutzerfreundlichkeit und Bedienbarkeit sind für die Edition von zentraler Bedeutung. Dazu gehören umfassende Recherche- und Filtermöglichkeiten, mit

---

[1] https://juedische-geschichte-online.net/.

OpenAccess. © 2022 Sonja Dickow-Rotter and Daniel Burckhardt, published by De Gruyter. This work is licensed under the Creative Commons Attribution 4.0 International License.
https://doi.org/10.1515/9783110714692-003

denen Nutzer*innen die Inhalte unter anderem über verschiedene Zugänge (Karte, Zeitstrahl, Themen) abrufen können. Zahlreiche Quellen der Themenkategorie „Judenfeindschaft und Verfolgung" stammen dabei aus dem Zeitraum 1933–1945. Hinsichtlich der Quellengattungen strebt die Edition Vielfalt an. Sie berücksichtigt dabei auch bisher von der Forschung eher vernachlässigte Quellen wie Bild-, Ton-, Videodokumente oder 3D-Repräsentationen von Objekten. Neben einer Vielzahl von neuen Möglichkeiten bietet die digitale Publikationsumgebung jedoch auch Herausforderungen: ein reflektierter Umgang mit der Herauslösung der Quellen aus ihrem Überlieferungszusammenhang – damit verbunden ihre Entkontextualisierung und Entmaterialisierung –, mit dem mehrsprachigen und mehrschriftlichen Quellenmaterial, mit der oft schwer rekonstruierbaren Rechtsnachfolge sowie mit der Notwendigkeit einer gesteigerten Sensibilität bei der Präsentation der Inhalte. Darauf antwortet die Edition mit Interpretations- und Hintergrundtexten, die jede der digitalen Quellen begleiten, in ihre historischen Kontexte einbetten und wichtige Informationen zur Überlieferung, Rezeptionsgeschichte und zu wissenschaftlichen Kontroversen liefern.

1 Introduction

Hamburg's Jewish heritage has been destroyed or scattered all over the world through migration and expulsion, in the most severe way due to National Socialist persecution. The online source edition "Key Documents of German-Jewish History," which is published by the Institute for the History of German Jews (IGdJ) in Hamburg, aims to gather a significant selection of this heritage digitally for wide and easy accessibility and to preserve it in the long term. Since September 2016, the bilingual (German/English) digital history project funded by the German Research Foundation (DFG) has been freely accessible at https://jewish-history-online.net/. Through more than a hundred digitized sources, it covers 400 years of Jewish presence in the Hanseatic city in order to illuminate changes as well as continuities from a longue durée perspective.

Digital projects in the field of Jewish history can be roughly divided into two groups: On the one hand, there are research-oriented projects for digital preservation or metadata generation, on the other hand, there are educational or service projects targeted at a wider audience. The aim of the former, which include projects such as Judaica Europeana or Digibaeck, is to provide the largest possible amount of digitized source material.[2] The latter are projects run primarily by

---

[2] With respect to German-Jewish history, the report by Gerben Zaagsma on a conference held

museums, foundations, and teaching or memorial sites and which are aimed at a broad public and are accordingly attractively presented. Examples include the projects by the Anne Frank Zentrum,[3] the digital offerings of the Jewish Museum Frankfurt[4]—for example, the app "Invisible Places"[5]—as well as "Jewish Places" by the Jewish Museum Berlin,[6] to mention only a few. Such digital projects often focus exclusively on National Socialism as a period of research and do not always integrate the sources into a wider context. In contrast, our edition shows the diversity and contradictions of Jewish history without narrowing it down to this singular period. As the following section on Hamburg, the regional focal point of the edition, aims to illustrate, Jewish history cannot be reduced to victimization and experiences of persecution and extermination alone. However, despite the ambition not to focus on National Socialism alone, current research trends and public debates are ultimately reflected within our edition. As a project that is primarily based on authors volunteering and freely choosing sources related to their fields of study and professional expertise, a significant share of contributions is directly connected to the period 1933–1945.

By explaining the conceptual framework and the central characteristics of the online source edition, this article aims to present the perspective of Jewish history as well as the practical values regarding standardized file formats, normed data, and a strong focus on usability for a platform with a heterogeneous target group at the intersection of academic research and public history.

2 Jewish Hamburg—Past and Present

Recently, Hamburg's rich and multifaceted Jewish history has received some attention beyond the historiographic discourse, as a glance at the regional and national press reveals.[7] Public interest was mainly raised by an initiative

---

seven years ago at the IGdJ is somewhat surprisingly still quite comprehensive: "Tagungsbericht Jüdische Geschichte digital. 13.06.2013–14.06.2013, Hamburg," *H-Soz-Kult*, September 10, 2013, accessed August 25, 2020, https://www.hsozkult.de/conferencereport/id/tagungsberichte-5011.
3 https://www.annefrank.de/en/exhibition-berlin/.
4 https://www.juedischesmuseum.de/en/explore/digital-museum/.
5 https://www.juedischesmuseum.de/en/explore/detail/invisible-places-frankfurt/.
6 https://www.jewish-places.de/.
7 Among others, the following articles have been published on the topic: Insa Gall and Sebastian Becht, "Hamburg will Wiederaufbau der Bornplatzsynagoge unterstützen," *Hamburger Abendblatt*, January 28, 2020, https://www.abendblatt.de/hamburg/article228263907/Hamburg-will-Wiederaufbau-der-Bornplatzsynagoge-unterstuetzen.html; Eva Eusterhus, "Ein Zeichen allein reicht nicht allen," *Welt*, February 10, 2020, https://www.welt.de/regionales/hamburg/ar

from Anjes Tjarks, leader of the party Bündnis 90/Die Grünen in Hamburg's senate and Hamburg state rabbi Shlomo Bistritzky, with support from all major political parties. Tjarks suggested rebuilding the Bornplatz synagogue on today's Joseph Carlebach square in the Grindelviertel area, in the immediate vicinity of the university campus. Before the Shoah, Grindelviertel was the main residential area for Jews living in Hamburg. Inaugurated in 1906, the Orthodox Bornplatz synagogue, home to the Hamburg uniform congregation, provided space for over 1,000 people and was an impressive architectural example of the neo-Romanesque style. The Bornplatz synagogue was not only the largest synagogue in Hamburg, but at that time the largest in Northern Europe. Only 32 years after its inauguration, it was seriously damaged by the National Socialists during the November pogroms of 1938 and demolished in 1939. A feasibility study commissioned by the Hamburg senate is currently examining the general conditions for rebuilding the synagogue.

Another former synagogue in the city has also been brought back to public attention: the New Israelite Temple. Built in 1844, this synagogue hidden in a backyard on Poolstraße is a testimony to the importance of Hamburg in the development of Reform Judaism.[8] The New Israelite Temple association was founded in Hamburg in 1817 as one of the first reform initiatives. Its prayer book of 1818/1819 then represented a widely noticed novelty, as the established liturgy was changed through various revisions, causing protest by the Orthodox denomination. Shortly before the National Socialist "seizure of power," the association relocated to a newly built temple in Oberstraße, inaugurated in 1931 and serving as a place of worship until the November pogroms of 1938. During World War II, the building in Poolstraße was mostly destroyed; today, visitors to Hamburg Neustadt can discover that only a remnant with the apse has been preserved. In the recent past, the history and significance of the temple has been brought to the attention of the public through a number of press articles and events. Due to the objection of the building's owner, however, these events could not take

---

ticle205678747/Synagoge-am-Bornplatz-Ein-Zeichen-allein-reicht-nicht-allen.html; Hanno Rauterberg, "Wie modern muss eine neue Synagoge sein? In Hamburg soll eine Synagoge nach historischem Vorbild rekonstruiert werden. Schon regt sich Protest dagegen," *Zeit Online*, February 19, 2020, https://www.zeit.de/2020/09/synagoge-hamburg-kirchenarchitektur-bau-modernisierung-bornplatzsynagoge; all accessed August 25, 2020.
8 For further information on the New Israelite Temple and the religious pluralization of Judaism see Andreas Brämer, "Religion and Identity," *Key Documents of German-Jewish History*, September 22, 2016, accessed August 25, 2020, https://jewish-history-online.net/topic/religion-and-identity#section-3.

place on the site itself, but only on the sidewalk in front of the building.[9] To date there is no consensus on how to proceed with this ruin.[10]

Despite such debates, many people living in Hamburg may not necessarily be aware that the Jewish history of their city and its former adjacent territories Altona, Harburg, and Wandsbek goes back further than the beginning of the nineteenth century. Moreover, the fact that there have been different congregations and groups with different origins, namely Sephardic and Ashkenazi Jews, in such close proximity to each other yet in different domains already represents a historically notable situation.

With the migration of Jews from Portugal and Spain in the sixteenth century, the Hamburg area developed into an important site of European Jewry. Hamburg profited from this influx, as it boosted the Hanseatic city's international trade.[11] The Jewish cemetery in Altona, built in 1611, points to this history and is today an important cultural monument. In 1867, the municipal statutes of the German-Israelite Congregation Hamburg established the Jewish uniform congregation, a historical exceptional case that united various religious denominations under a single roof. The peculiarity lies in the fact that it formed an umbrella congregation with three religious associations. It was possible to join the congregation without choosing a religious association.

As a port city, Hamburg was also an important transit location for more than half of the over two million Jews who emigrated from Eastern Europe to the United States between 1880 and 1914.[12] After the Shoah, in the second half of the twentieth century, the importance of the Hanseatic city as a place of worldwide trade came back into focus and new Jewish migration routes developed. In this context, the arrival of Persian Jews from Iran from 1950 onwards should be mentioned: For them, Hamburg with its carpet trade became an attractive place to

---

9 Edgar S. Hasse, "Tempel-Ruine in der Neustadt von Einsturz bedroht," *Hamburger Abendblatt*, November 29, 2019, https://www.abendblatt.de/hamburg/article227778695/tempel-ruine-denkmalschutz-judentum-hamburg.html; Moritz Piehler, "Hilferuf einer Ruine," *Jüdische Allgemeine*, December 12, 2019, https://www.juedische-allgemeine.de/gemeinden/hilferuf-einer-ruine/; Andrea Richter, "Wir brauchen eine Synagoge, keine Luxuswohnungen," *Deutschlandfunk Kultur*, December 13, 2019, https://www.deutschlandfunkkultur.de/liberale-gemeinde-in-hamburg-wir-brauchen-eine-synagoge.1079.de.html?dram:article_id=465833; all accessed August 25, 2020.
10 Andreas Brämer et al., *Der israelische Tempel in Hamburg*, Archiv aus Stein. Der jüdische Friedhof Altona 7 (Hamburg: ConferencePoint Verlag, 2020).
11 Michael Studemund-Halévy, "Sephardic Jews," *Key Documents of German-Jewish History*, September 22, 2016, accessed August 25, 2020, https://jewish-history-online.net/topic/sephardic-jews.
12 "Jewish Migration: Location Hamburg," last modified November 16, 2018, https://juedische-geschichte-online.net/ausstellung/migration#intro.

live before most of them moved on to the United States. The Jewish congregation of the post-war period was therefore shaped to a significant extent by these new members, a phenomenon that has hardly been researched so far. Fewer research as well as a lack of visibility in today's city landscape can also be noted for Jewish history before National Socialism. Visible are primarily memorials and commemorative plaques dedicated to the persecution and murder of Hamburg's Jews that took place during the time of National Socialism. On the grounds of the former Bornplatz synagogue, visitors now find the "Synagogue Monument" designed by Margrit Kahl (1942–2009) and inaugurated in 1988 on the occasion of the fiftieth anniversary of the 1938 November pogroms. This monument consists of granite stones left in the ground, which trace the destroyed ceiling vault of the synagogue in original scale.[13] Better known than this early "void" representation[14] are probably the more than 5,800 stumbling stones (*Stolpersteine*) that, since 2002, have been laid across Hamburg, in front of the last known homes of deported Jews.[15] This project is based on an initiative of the artist Gunter Demnig, who has been placing stumbling stones throughout Germany and other European countries since 1992.

But what about those traces of Jewish history—and Jewish presence—that are not as easy to find or recognize? Our digital source edition aims to present, among others, sources and contextualizing interpretation texts on the above-mentioned historical developments and specificities of Jewish Hamburg. In its completeness, the transmission of both written sources (from archives and libraries) and material heritage (in the form of Jewish cemeteries and gravestones) that exist for Hamburg is unique in the German-speaking lands. However, they are located in different places, distributed around the world. Archival records are today divided between Hamburg State Archive and the Central Archives for the History of the Jewish People in Jerusalem.[16] Personal records have been dis-

---

[13] Photo Pavement Mosaic Joseph-Carlebach-Platz (Bornplatz), edited in *Key Documents of German-Jewish History*, accessed August 25, 2020, https://dx.doi.org/10.23691/jgo:source-100.en.v1.
[14] Probably the best-known realization of architectural "voids" in Germany is the building of the Jewish Museum Berlin designed by Daniel Libeskind, cf. "The Libeskind Building," Jüdisches Museum Berlin, accessed August 25, 2020, https://www.jmberlin.de/en/libeskind-building.
[15] "Stolpersteine Hamburg," accessed August 25, 2020, https://www.stolpersteine-hamburg.de/en.php?MAIN_ID=4.
[16] For further information see Björn Siegel, "Verworrene Wege. Die Gründungsphase des IGdJ," in *50 Jahre – 50 Quellen. Festschrift zum Jubiläum des Instituts für die Geschichte der deutschen Juden*, ed. IGdJ (Hamburg: Institut für die Geschichte der Deutschen Juden, 2016), 26–53, accessed August 25, 2020, http://www.igdj-hh.de/files/IGDJ/pdf/hamburger-beitraege/igdj_50jahre-50quellen-festschrift.pdf. In the meantime, a contract was signed between Jerusalem and Hamburg for the digital consolidation of the archival holdings.

persed around the globe. Hence, bringing together scattered written but also visual and audiovisual sources at least virtually on a single site provides a great opportunity for an online project.

3 "Key Documents of German-Jewish History"— Goals, Features, and Challenges

The main goals of our edition are on one hand to impart knowledge about Hamburg's rich Jewish history as briefly outlined above by gathering sources digitally, facilitating access, and thus encouraging new research. Furthermore, it represents a contribution to the preservation and study of Jewish heritage. On the other hand, the sources we selected—we call them "key documents"—provide exemplary insights into historical aspects and events in order to illuminate broader developments and questions in German-Jewish history. The edition aims to address a diverse audience and a wide spectrum of sources. Hamburg always acts as a point of reference, but ideally, every source has the potential to "open doors" to transregional contexts and new questions leading to a better and more vivid understanding of Jewish history beyond the local context.

For the selection of a source to become a "key document" within the edition, it is not important if it was previously published or unpublished. Instead, a source has to fulfill the following criteria
- first, to connect to a broader historical context and pose questions;
- second, to represent a characteristic example from a larger set of sources or tell a "typical" story because of its uniqueness;
- and third, to be clearly identifiable based on extensive information on the source such as time of creation, its author, etc.

Finally, the "key documents" presented in our edition are intended to raise awareness of the long and varied Jewish history of the city of Hamburg, to speak to a diverse target group, and to stimulate new research into the subject. The edition is conceived in such a way that an often-narrow focus on the period of National Socialism is contrasted with the diversity and sometimes contradictory aspects of the Jewish past since the early modern age. Sources from 400 years of Jewish presence in the Hanseatic city are presented to shed light on changes and continuities. In order to explore the full potential of an online edition, "key documents" are not limited to textual sources. Regarding different genres, the edition strives for diversity and therefore explicitly includes sources that have received little attention from the scientific community and the interested public so far, such as images, sound, audiovisual documents, or, currently at a prototype stage, a 3D-model.

Usability was a central aim while implementing the online edition. This includes comprehensive search and filter options. The edition is structured in such a way that users have, in principle, different ways of accessing the contents of the edition—through a timeline, a specific topic, or a map. There is an overview of the fifteen main topics of the edition. Included among these are, for example, "Migration," "Religion and Identity," as well as "Antisemitism and Persecution." The majority of sources from the latter category cover the period of National Socialist reign. Each source can be assigned to up to three different topics by the editors. Alternatively, the sources can be accessed through search, an interactive map, a timeline, or the extensive registers which indexes all the persons, organizations, and places mentioned within the texts. But even though the edition provides all these options for search and access, we should always be aware that an overwhelming majority of our readers do not start their visit to the site by any of these means. Instead, an online search engine, in most cases Google, will lead them directly to their very individual point of departure within the edition. Thus, an online offer like ours must be accessible from any starting point and cannot assume that visitors will follow any of the suggested paths through the site.

Ideally, the production and presentation of digital sources offers the opportunity for new "layers of knowledge" by adding a virtual dimension that allows for time and location-independent access, linkage, and markup. However, the digital publishing environment also presents a set of challenges. These include, first, dealing with the detachment of the sources from their traditional context of creation and transmission—and the associated de-contextualization and de-materialization. In addition, the need to cope with multilingual and multiscriptual source material, with legal successions that are difficult to reconstruct, and with an increased sensitivity in an online presentation of content must also be mentioned. The edition attempts to respond to these issues with interpretation and background texts for each source which, on the one hand, introduce the different topics and, on the other, discuss in detail every digital source. The introductions as well as the source interpretations are informed by current research. The interpretations are intended to re-embed the sources into their historical contexts and provide important information concerning tradition, history of reception, and scholarly debates. At around 1,500 words, they are relatively short and thus well suited for reading online.

As a collaborative project, the edition has many participants, such as the almost one hundred authors who have so far contributed individual or multiple contributions. In addition, there are fourteen editors who oversee the various

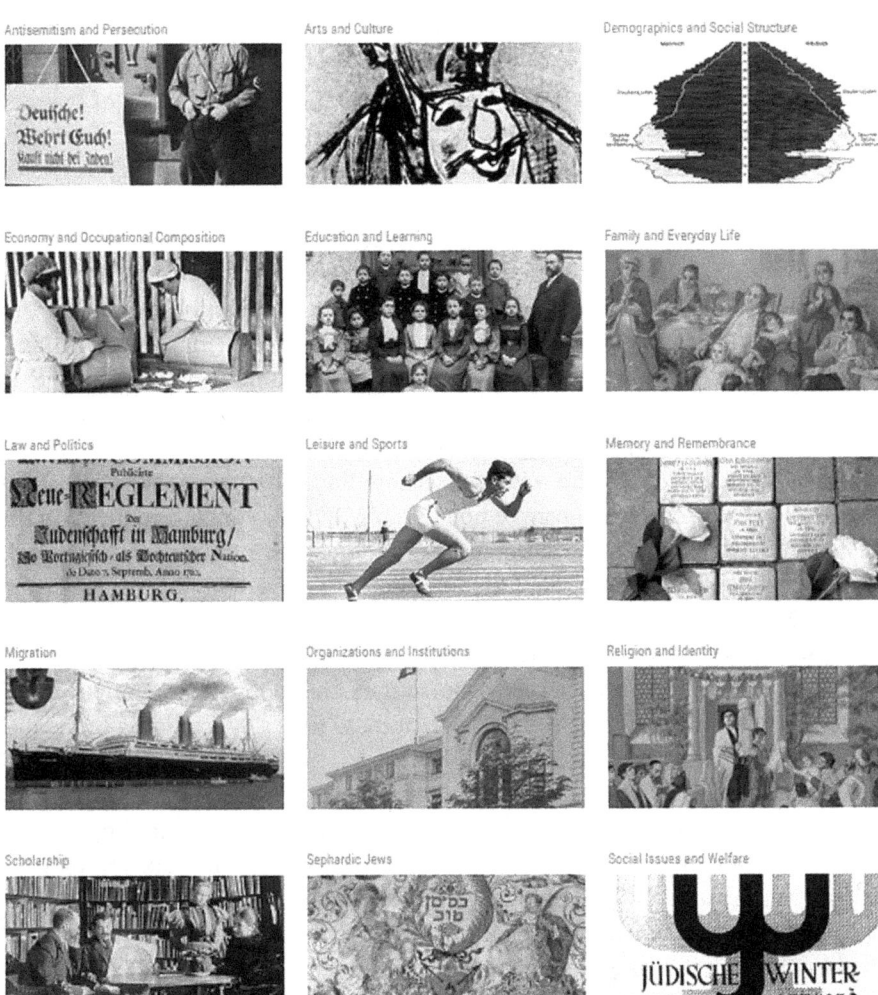

Figure 2.1: Screenshot from the edition's website: https://jewish-history-online.net/topic, accessed September 21, 2021.

subject categories, co-review submissions, and write the introductory texts to their subject area. All editorial texts are provided with a permanent URL under a Creative Commons license (mostly CC BY-NC-ND 4.0: attribution: name of the author, article, in: Key Documents of German-Jewish History, date, URL). An info box next to each source presents detailed information on its creation and its current holding institution. Every contribution has undergone a multi-stage review process by the editors and publishers. The project team[17] regularly meets with its advisory board, which provides crucial feedback and offers thoughtful suggestions on the current focus and new directions of the site.

A further challenge arises from the fact that the edition sees itself as an open platform that strives to explore new modes of presentation. This is the reason why in 2018, the edition started to implement online exhibitions as a new format in addition to the original contributions. Most exhibitions are developed in cooperation with a partner and are presented on the edition's website. The exhibitions are intended to focus on certain themes of the edition and to connect various sources in order to provide an in-depth coverage of specific aspects within a single coherent presentation. Ideally, bringing the various sources together in such a manner will open up new perspectives and questions. To date, six online exhibitions have been realized, on Jewish life since 1945, on the author and scholar Max Salzberg and his wife, the teacher Frida Salzberg, on Jewish migration in Hamburg, on Jewish private photography in the twentieth century, on the history of Jewish school life in Hamburg, and, most recently, on sea travels and the maritime experiences of Ida Dehmel, Joseph Carlebach, and Ernst Heymann in the 1930s and 1940s. Up to now, every digital exhibition has followed the same navigational structure: Vertically arranged chapters present different topics for the users to learn about by scrolling down the exhibition. Horizontally running stations enable an in-depth study of each of these topics by exploring individual aspects and concrete examples.

In collaboration with the HistoriaApp which was developed at Heinrich Heine University Düsseldorf, two city tours along the traces of Hamburg's Jewish past were created: The smartphone app guides a historical walk through the above-mentioned Grindelviertel district as well as a bicycle tour along locations between Neustadt, where Poolstraße is located, and Altona, where traces of Hamburg's Jewish past can be found.[18] Many sites of Jewish life visited on these tours are mentioned in the sources presented on the Key Documents website, so that visitors can find in-depth information about the respective places along their way in the edition's contributions.

The "key documents" target a heterogeneous audience ranging from university teachers and scholars dealing with various topics of Jewish history, to members of an interested lay public. There is an extra module featuring sources particularly suitable for use in high school and college education, complemented by

---

17 https://jewish-history-online.net/about/team
18 For more information on the app, see https://historia-app.de/juedische-geschichte-in-hamburg/, accessed October 18, 2020.

information for students on how to interpret sources. The different offers are intended to connect the supposedly separate areas of academic and non-academic engagement with Jewish history. The possibilities of the digital here serve as an enrichment. With regard to the technical implementation, the different aims and skills of such a wide target group have to be taken into account as well.

4 Technical Implementation

The main goal when implementing the web-based front- and back-end for the Key Documents edition was to combine well-established formats and best practices in digital editing and long-term preservation such es TEI (encoding source transcripts and translations),[19] METS/MODS (description of digitized sources),[20] and DOIs (persistent addressing) with a user-friendly presentation.

The project aimed to demonstrate that digital editing according to scholarly standards as well as guidelines by funding bodies such as the DFG Practical Guidelines on Digitization[21] do not contradict a form of presentation and contextualization that can also be of interest to an audience outside the core of academic research. Following a well-established subset of the TEI/P5, in our case the DTA "Base Format" (DTABf),[22] provided important guidance on how to record the metadata in the TEI header as well as various formal (typographic) and semantic (meaningful) phenomena within our sources. In addition, the DTABf provides a set of freely available tools such as the DTAoX-authoring extension for Oxygen. This plug-in simplifies the markup process especially for newcomers without prior experience in XML editing.[23]

---

[19] "TEI: Text Encoding Initiative," accessed August 25, 2020, https://tei-c.org/. For an extensive introduction by one of the original editors of these guidelines, see Lou Burnard, *What Is the Text Encoding Initiative? How to Add Intelligent Markup to Digital Resources* (Marseille: OpenEdition Press, 2014), accessed August 25, 2020, https://doi.org/10.4000/books.oep.426.
[20] Deutsche Digitale Bibliothek, "METS/MODS für Monografien. Ein Best Practice Guide," accessed August 25, 2020, https://pro.deutsche-digitale-bibliothek.de/downloads/public/bestpracticeguide_metsmods_monografien.pdf.
[21] Deutsche Forschungsgemeinschaft, "DFG Practical Guidelines on Digitisation," last modified December 2016, https://www.dfg.de/formulare/12_151/12_151_en.pdf.
[22] Berlin-Brandenburgische Akademie der Wissenschaften, "Introduction to the DTABf," accessed August 25, 2020, http://www.deutschestextarchiv.de/doku/basisformat/introduction_en.html.
[23] Berlin-Brandenburgische Akademie der Wissenschaften, "Hilfreiche Tools und Anwendungen," accessed August 25, 2020, http://www.deutschestextarchiv.de/doku/basisformat/hilfreicheTools.html.

The presentation of textual sources in the edition consists of a digital facsimile and the transcript, as well as translations into English and—for foreign language sources—into German. Transcriptions and sometimes transliteration—for example, for Yiddish texts originally composed in Hebrew script—not only simplify the reading of hardly legible handwritings, they also provide an important bridge between the facsimile and a translation into modern German or English. The viewer supports switching and parallel presentations between these different levels—that is, the digitized source or the transcription—and can thereby help to trace the editorial steps back to the original document. This makes the process both transparent as well as educational, and—in case a reader disagrees with the edition's preferred reading—a matter of scholarly debate.

Thanks to our site's reliance on TEI and METS, we were able to easily integrate the user-friendly viewer from the MyCoRe-project into our site[24] and provide an integration with the standardized DFG-viewer as required by the founding agency.[25] All relevant metadata and the rights information from the TEI header are provided in the info box next to the viewer. This same information is used again to assign permanent DOIs through the DataCite-API[26] and is made available in machine-readable form according to Open Archives Initiative's Protocol for Metadata Harvesting (OAI-PMH).[27]

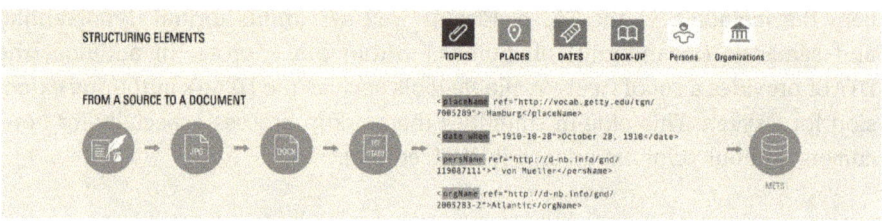

Figure 2.2: From a source to a document: steps leading from an archival source to an online document. Design: Sandra Morath, edelweiss* büro für grafik und design.

---

24 Sebastian Hofmann and Kathleen Neumann, "Bildbetrachter – MyCoRe-Viewer," last modified June 2, 2020, https://www.mycore.de/documentation/frontend/frontend_image_viewer/.
25 "DFG Viewer – the project," last modified July 17, 2020, http://dfg-viewer.de/en/the-project.
26 "DataCite MDS API Guide," last modified March 2020, https://support.datacite.org/docs/mds-api-guide.
27 The edition's OAI-endpoint is https://jewish-history-online.net/oai. For more information on the protocol, see "Open Archives Initiative. Protocol for Metadata Harvesting," accessed August 25, 2020, https://www.openarchives.org/pmh/.

The edition features a hypertextual structure. All persons, organizations, places, epochs, and events mentioned in the transcript, translation, and accompanying texts are systematically encoded with authority data. Thereby, additional information from the Linked Open Data cloud can be integrated into the edition's knowledge graph. Among others, we integrate information on persons and organizations from the Integrated Authority File (GND) of the German National Library[28] as well as geographical information from Getty's Thesaurus of Geographic Names (TGN). Standardized identifiers also provide the basis for mutual linkage with other digital history projects. We both provide GND-BEACON lists and make use of findbuch.net's BEACON service to interlink persons and organizations with a wide range of online initiatives from GLAM institutions and academic research to corresponding Wikipedia entries.[29] In addition, a full bibliography is compiled as a Zotero Group,[30] and linked back and forth from the respective texts. Lesser-known terms are explained and linked to the site's glossary.

Academic offers tend to focus on the quality of their content while all too often neglecting its appearance. By one of TEI's guiding assumptions, the structure of a document can and should be separated from how it is being displayed. But the overwhelming majority of readers of an online edition does not reflect on the form of encoding powering the site. They see the browser's rendition and often decide within a few seconds whether they should look closer at the page or leave immediately.[31] Therefore, a clear message combined with an attractive presentation and an intuitive user experience are key factors needed to draw a heterogeneous group of users deeper into a site. For our project, the decision to involve a professional web designer at an early stage and thus treating content, form, and function equally from conception to initial realization and later adjustments of the project proved to be very beneficial.

---

28 "The Integrated Authority File (GND)," last modified November 26, 2019, https://www.dnb.de/EN/Professionell/Standardisierung/GND/gnd_node.html.
29 Wikipedia, "BEACON," last modified August 11, 2020, https://de.wikipedia.org/wiki/Wikipedia:BEACON, provides an extensive compilation of sites providing BEACON lists, most of which are integrated into the SeeAlso-Service we are using, https://beacon.findbuch.de/#sect-pnd, accessed August 25, 2020. For additional information, see Harald Lordick's case study on the value of BEACON lists for German-Jewish history: "BEACON – 'Leuchtfeuer' für Online-Publikationen," accessed August 25, 2020, https://djgd.hypotheses.org/672.
30 The integration into the front-end makes use of "Zotero Web API v3," last modified June 14, 2020, https://www.zotero.org/support/dev/web_api/v3/start.
31 Jakob Nielsen, "How Long Do Users Stay on Web Pages?," accessed August 25, 2020, https://www.nngroup.com/articles/how-long-do-users-stay-on-web-pages/.

Although online exhibitions by GLAM institutions have found similar acceptance and popularity during the past two decades as scholarly digital editions, no XML format to describe the content of these showings comparable to the TEI has so far been established. Instead, plain HTML or markup and custom tags as defined by the Content Management System (CMS) used by the publishing institution are still the preferred way to implement these presentations.[32] Since this new mode of presentation was integrated into our site at a later stage, we lacked the means to devote ourselves to compiling a proper XML schema for online exhibitions. We thus had to settle on a suboptimal approach with respect to long-term preservation and cross-device presentation by choosing plain HTML-markup according to the site's CSS framework and a JavaScript-library for user interaction.[33]

The code to integrate all these components into a seamless user experience has been written in a popular web application framework and has been published on the GitHub code-sharing platform for inspection and potential reuse.[34] Since certain assumptions of our edition—such as the bilingual presentation, the fifteen main topics, and the decision to provide an interpretation whose function is to "open the door" to every source—are currently part of the code logic, this Open Source publication cannot yet provide a turn-key solution for other scholarly editions. But we are currently busy moving such assumptions from code to configuration and are committed to provide consultation and support to any initiative eager to base their project on this platform.

---

[32] Therefore, little has changed compared to Chapter 6 on "Technical Issues: Markup Languages" in Martin R. Kalfatovic, *Creating a Winning Online Exhibition: A Guide for Libraries, Archives, and Museums* (Chicago: American Library Association, 2002). An otherwise very useful Handbook on Virtual Exhibitions and Virtual Performances published by INDICATE, a European Union FP7 project, in 2012 briefly mentions "static web pages in HTML," "a CMS with dedicated modules software applications designed especially for virtual exhibitions," or "proprietary platforms, which need to install specific plug-ins" as three possible technologies, "Handbook on Virtual Exhibitions and Virtual Performances," last modified August 2012, http://www.dedale.info/_objets/medias/autres/indicate-handbook-on-virtual-exhibitions-and-virtual-performances-751.pdf.
[33] Alvaro Trigo, "fullPage," accessed August 25, 2020, https://alvarotrigo.com/fullPage/.
[34] "Code for the Presentation of the Digital Source Edition Key Documents of German-Jewish History," last modified January 4, 2020, https://github.com/igdj/jewish-history-online.

5 Acceptance and Results

Editions have a long tradition within the sphere of academic research. Printed editions usually appear in heavy and quite expensive volumes. Distribution is thus often limited to the shelves of specialized libraries where only a small circle of specialists is able to take note. Contrary to their claim, they rarely serve as a basis for new research. However, the shift in media from print to freely accessible online publications has fundamentally changed access to editions and to the materials they contain. Sources can now be accessed remotely, transcripts can be searched in full text, and digital facsimiles may be integrated into the collection of sources created on one's personal computer. Internet search, social media, and online encyclopedias make editions visible to a broader public. This has a decisive impact on the user group, more so for topics of wide public interest, as is the case with Jewish history. Beyond collecting, preserving, and documenting, the presentation and dissemination of the material becomes a central aspect of an online edition.

Compared to a printed edition, a digital publication can be analyzed much more easily with respect to its contents and usage. The following short introspective examination of the current contents of our edition as well as an "extrospective" analysis according to the number, composition, and preferences of our visitors aims to demonstrate the value of such insights for the continued improvement of an online presentation.

For an analysis of content, metadata and textual markup can be queried to visualize the focal points and gaps in coverage, both across time as well as with respect to the topics treated by the sources. When looking at the date of creation, we find that from the 119 key documents published so far, fourteen cover the early modern period (1600–1800), another twenty are from the nineteenth century, and six are from the twenty-first. Two-thirds of our sources were thus created in the twentieth century: twenty-five before 1930, eighteen in the second half of the twentieth century, and thirty-five are direct witnesses to the National Socialist period.

Figure 2.3 demonstrates that the edition manages to document over 400 years of German-Jewish history in Hamburg. But this coverage is by no means even or without gaps. For example, for the 1970s as well as for many decades before the 1890s, there is currently not a single source. This uneven temporal focus reveals itself again in the basic biographical information pulled from the 848 persons currently recorded in the edition, a significant percentage of whom were born between 1855 and 1910. Figure 2.4 reflects the sad fact that it

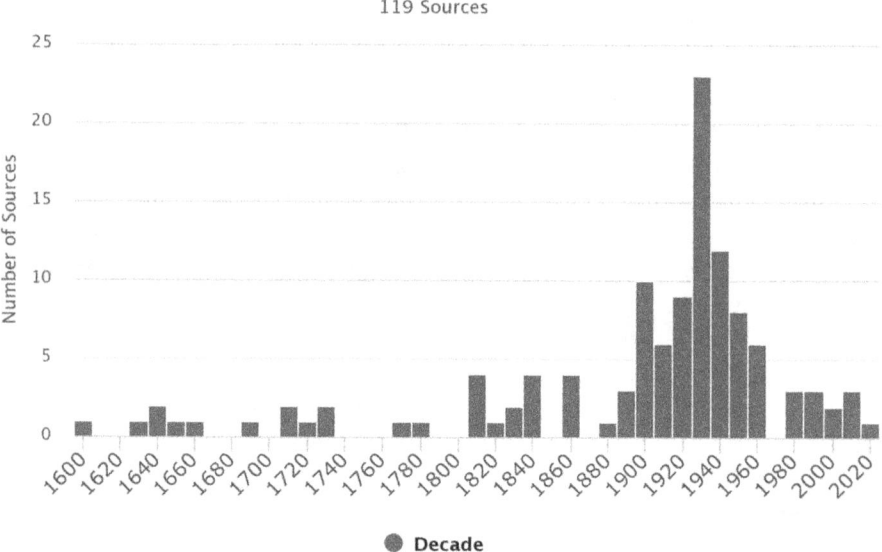

Figure 2.3: Temporal coverage of the sources: number of sources by decade. Graphic created by the authors.

was particularly these older generations of Hamburg's Jews that were deported to and killed in death camps before the end of World War II.[35]

Moving from the temporal to the thematic coverage, it comes as no surprise that the topics most frequently assigned to source interpretation reflect the prominent role of the period from 1930 to 1945 within the edition: Over 30% of the more than one hundred source interpretations deal with "Antisemitism and Persecution," around 27% with the closely related "Law and Politics," followed by "Religion and Identity" and "Organizations and Institutions" (both at 22%). Trailing topics such as "Sephardic Jews" and "Education and Learning" are currently underrepresented.

As important as the inward-looking reflection on what is being presented, is an external perspective as documented by explicit and implicit feedback from actual users. In a striking contrast to printed publications, in-depth reviews of

---

[35] On October 23, 1941, when emigration was prohibited nationwide, Hamburg's Jewish population diminished from almost 20,000 people in the 1920s to only 4,951 people. Of Hamburg's Jews at that time 85% were older than 40, and 55% were above the age of 60, see Miriam Rürup, "Demographics and Social Structure," *Key Documents of German-Jewish History*, September 22, 2016, accessed August 25, 2020, https://jewish-history-online.net/topic/demographics-and-social-structure.

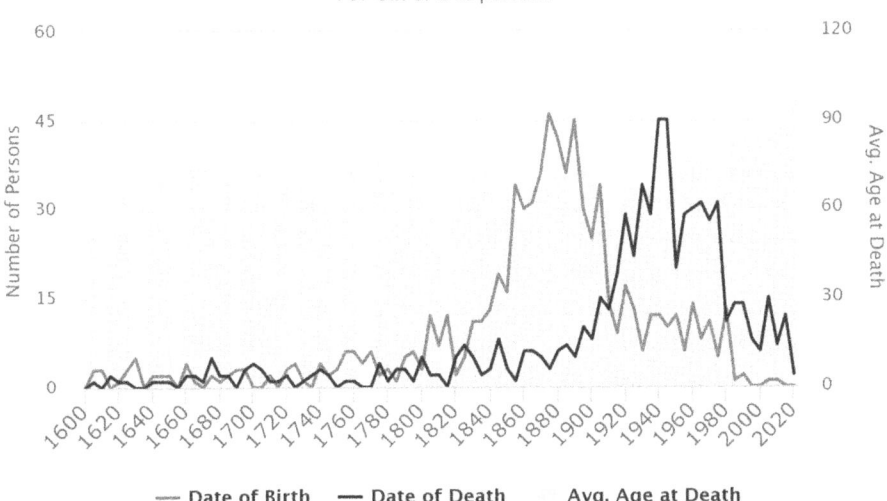

Figure 2.4: Persons recorded within the edition by dates of birth and death. Graphic created by the authors.

digital editions and resources are still a rare exception throughout the humanities.[36] In our case, we were fortunate to receive a review on *H-Soz-Kult* with helpful suggestions for improvements with respect to presentation of the site and the site's search capability.[37] The edition features a contact form and solicits feedback, but only very few users take the effort to fill in a form or write an email. However, the edition's Twitter account (@keydocuments) enables a low-threshold exchange with the users of the edition as well as their feedback. Currently 481 followers are regularly informed about the developments of the project. Moreover, the Twitter account is used for linking the project with related digital offers.

To get an accurate impression on how, by whom, and through which channels an online offer is being accessed, web analytics provide important guidance, even if the reports are fully anonymized as in our local Matomo installation. The

---

[36] A set of helpful "Criteria for Reviewing Scholarly Digital Editions" have been formulated by Patrick Sahle in collaboration with George Vogeler and the members of IDE, a review journal for digital editions and resources, last modified June 2014, https://www.i-d-e.de/publikationen/weitereschriften/criteria-version-1-1/.

[37] Jonas Jung, review of *Hamburger Schlüsseldokumente zur deutsch-jüdischen Geschichte. Eine Online-Quellenedition*, H-Soz-Kult, June 3, 2017, accessed August 25, 2020, https://www.hsozkult.de/webreview/id/rezwww-171.

strongest indicator of the continued demand and increasing acceptance of our site is the constantly rising number of visitors. The number of monthly visits steadily increased from a mere 600 in October 2016, the first month our site was publicly available, to over 6,000 in June 2020. While such numbers might appear minor when compared to commercial online publishers, this number reflects a growing public visibility that a small research institute such as the IGdJ could hardly ever achieve through traditional research and outreach efforts.

The steady rise is mostly due to visitors being directed there by search engines, which are responsible for around three-quarters of all visitors coming to the site. Referrals from social networks such as the edition's Twitter account, Facebook shares, and links from a wide variety of third parties—ranging from the institute's homepage, Wikipedia, or course platforms at various universities and high schools from around the world—constitute a relatively minor share of initial visitors (below 10%). However, due to their explicit interest in the specific links, these users are often much more engaged than users coming from a general search engine. While the latter will often press the back button immediately to leave the site, users coming from www.igdj-hh.de on average stay almost seven minutes and open seven pages during their visit. This is significantly more than the overall average across all visitors: Visits are usually slightly below two minutes long and include the opening of two pages.

For a bilingual offer that spends a considerable amount of time and money on translations, it is important to know if this effort is being honored. Currently, 70% of the site's visits come from Europe (primarily from Germany, followed by Austria, the UK, and Switzerland), while 24% come from North America, and another 5% from Asia and Oceania. Visits from Africa and South America are barely visible. If we differentiate by language, we can see that visitors with a German-language browser (55.8%) visit slightly more frequently than those with an English one (38.8%). For all the other languages recorded (French, Spanish, Dutch, Hebrew, Russian, Italian, Chinese, and Polish), the number of visits is below 1% each. Corresponding to the regional distribution and the language preferences, about two-thirds of the pages visited are in German, one-third in English. There are also significant differences between the sections being viewed: The fifteen thematic overviews constitute the most popular section in English (35% of all English-language page views), where, for example, the overview "Antisemitism and Persecution" by Werner Bergmann serves as an often-referenced introduction for English readers without a specific regional interest. On the other hand, German-language visitors are not as much interested in survey texts; this section ranks sixth in German (10% of all German-language page views). Instead, source interpretations (21%) is the section most viewed, hinting that German speaking users look more closely into the various questions raised by the "key documents" and the source interpretations. Non-German speakers, on the other hand, seem to appreciate that our site does not only offer sources, but also thematic overviews and introductions.

Online analytics also provide crucial insights into the devices used by visitors to view the site. While the majority of visits still come from a desktop computer (63%), smartphone usage is becoming increasingly prominent (32%)—more than a doubling compared to four years ago, when the site was initially launched (14% of visitors used a mobile device at that time). Mobile usage was explicitly supported from the foundation of the site through a responsive framework, but some sections such as the exhibitions do not yet work on smaller screens. By noticing such trends, it becomes clear that this and similar shortcomings need to be addressed and that regular testing cannot be limited to the project staff's workplace computers.

6 Outlook and Conclusion

The recent past, so significantly shaped by the COVID-19 pandemic, has clearly demonstrated the necessity and potential of digital offerings for research and education. At times when even libraries had to close, online resources were still available independent of the time and location of potential users. At the same time, it is important to reflect critically on how to approach the de-contextualization and de-materialization of the sources when detaching them from their conventional—analog—context of creation and transmission.

Digital projects have the advantage that they are in a state of constant flux and can flexibly react to the current demands of the academic community and the interested public. In our case, online exhibitions were introduced at a later stage to address some of the shortcomings mentioned above. In contrast to the individual sources, which stood at the center of the original edition, an exhibition provides the opportunity to present sources in a synopsis and thus emphasizes mutual connections, developments, and dependencies. The attractive visual presentation can appeal to users who do not have much previous knowledge and guides them through a specific topic. At the same time, the exhibitions can specifically present additional source material that has received little coverage so far—in our case, for example, realized by the exhibitions "History of Jewish School Life in Hamburg" and "Jewish Life since 1945." In a similar way, the city tours in collaboration with HistoriaApp were developed in order to fuse the virtual with traces of Jewish history still visible on-site and thus, at least partially, re-contextualize and re-materialize some aspects of the sources presented online.

Currently, a new format is being developed in order to present extensive source material or entire collections of sources as opposed to the shorter extracts we selected as "key documents." It will initially be launched with a thematic dossier on the diaries of Martha Glass, written during her time in the Terezín ghetto (1943–1945) to where she was deported from Hamburg at the age of 63. Her digitized diaries will be accompanied by transcripts, their translations, and a comprehensive collection of additional material. An introduction provides an overview of the history of the Terezín ghetto as well as of the role of ego-documents in times of persecution and Nazi terror. As with the regular contributions, all texts and transcripts will be encoded in TEI and tagged with metadata.

These new undertakings demonstrate how our edition tries to question itself critically and sees itself as an open platform that aims to continuously explore new formats of research and education. If the online publication is taken seriously as a presentation medium, there can no longer be a fixed format. Rather, as the project progresses, both the presentation and the selection of the materials must be constantly questioned and reinvented. If corresponding resources are available, such openness offers a great opportunity.

Bibliography

Alvaro Trigo. "fullPage." Accessed August 25, 2020. https://alvarotrigo.com/fullPage/.
Anne Frank Zentrum. Accessed October 16, 2020. https://www.annefrank.de/en/exhibition-berlin/.
Berlin-Brandenburgische Akademie der Wissenschaften. "Hilfreiche Tools und Anwendungen." Accessed August 25, 2020. http://www.deutschestextarchiv.de/doku/basisformat/hilfreicheTools.html.
Berlin-Brandenburgische Akademie der Wissenschaften. "Introduction to the DTABf." Accessed August 25, 2020. http://www.deutschestextarchiv.de/doku/basisformat/introduction_en.html.
Brämer, Andreas. "Religion and Identity." *Key Documents of German-Jewish History*, September 22, 2016. Accessed August 25, 2020. https://jewish-history-online.net/topic/religion-and-identity#section-3.
Brämer, Andreas, Ulrich Knufinke, Mirko Przystawik, Miriam Rürup, and Christoph Schwarzkopf. *Der israelitische Tempel in Hamburg*. Hamburg: ConferencePoint Verlag, 2020.
Burnard, Lou. *What Is the Text Encoding Initiative? How to Add Intelligent Markup to Digital Resources*. Marseille: OpenEdition Press, 2014. Accessed August 25, 2020. https://doi.org/10.4000/books.oep.426.
"Code for the Presentation of the Digital Source Edition Key Documents of German-Jewish History." Last modified January 4, 2020. https://github.com/igdj/jewish-history-online.
"DataCite MDS API Guide." Last modified March 2020. https://support.datacite.org/docs/mds-api-guide.

Deutsche Digitale Bibliothek. "METS/MODS für Monografien. Ein Best Practice Guide." Accessed August 25, 2020. https://pro.deutsche-digitale-bibliothek.de/downloads/public/bestpracticeguide_metsmods_monografien.pdf.

Deutsche Forschungsgemeinschaft. "DFG Practical Guidelines on Digitisation." Last modified December 2016. https://www.dfg.de/formulare/12_151/12_151_en.pdf.

"DFG Viewer – the project." Last modified July 17, 2020. http://dfg-viewer.de/en/the-project.

Eusterhus, Eva. "Ein Zeichen allein reicht nicht allen." *Welt*, February 10, 2020. Accessed August 25, 2020. https://www.welt.de/regionales/hamburg/article205678747/Synagoge-am-Bornplatz-Ein-Zeichen-allein-reicht-nicht-allen.html.

Gall, Insa, and Sebastian Becht. "Hamburg will Wiederaufbau der Bornplatzsynagoge unterstützen." *Hamburger Abendblatt*, January 28, 2020. Accessed August 25, 2020. https://www.abendblatt.de/hamburg/article228263907/Hamburg-will-Wiederaufbau-der-Bornplatzsynagoge-unterstuetzen.html.

Hamburger Schlüsseldokumente zur deutsch-jüdischen Geschichte: Eine Online Quellenedition. https://juedische-geschichte-online.net/.

Hasse, Edgar S. "Tempel-Ruine in der Neustadt von Einsturz bedroht." *Hamburger Abendblatt*, November 29, 2019. Accessed August 25, 2020. https://www.abendblatt.de/hamburg/article227778695/tempel-ruine-denkmalschutz-judentum-hamburg.html.

HistoriaApp by HHU. Accessed October 18, 2020. https://historia-app.de/juedische-geschichte-in-hamburg/.

Hofmann, Sebastian, and Kathleen Neumann. "Bildbetrachter – MyCoRe-Viewer." Last modified June 2, 2020. https://www.mycore.de/documentation/frontend/frontend_image_viewer/.

INDICATE. "Handbook on Virtual Exhibitions and Virtual Performances." Last modified August 2012. http://www.dedale.info/_objets/medias/autres/indicate-handbook-on-virtual-exhibitions-and-virtual-performances-751.pdf.

"Jewish Migration: Location Hamburg." Last modified November 16, 2018. https://juedische-geschichte-online.net/ausstellung/migration#intro.

Jewish Places. Accessed October 17, 2020. https://www.jewish-places.de/.

Jüdisches Museum Berlin. "The Libeskind Building." Accessed August 25, 2020. https://www.jmberlin.de/en/libeskind-building.

Jüdisches Museum Frankfurt. "Digitales Museum." Accessed October 18, 2020. https://www.juedischesmuseum.de/en/explore/digital-museum/.

Jung, Jonas. Review of *Hamburger Schlüsseldokumente zur deutsch-jüdischen Geschichte. Eine Online-Quellenedition. H-Soz-Kult*, June 3, 2017. Accessed August 25, 2020. https://www.hsozkult.de/webreview/id/rezwww-171.

Kalfatovic, Martin R. *Creating a Winning Online Exhibition: A Guide for Libraries, Archives, and Museums*. Chicago: American Library Association, 2002.

Lordick, Harald. "BEACON – 'Leuchtfeuer' für Online-Publikationen." Accessed August 25, 2020. https://djgd.hypotheses.org/672.

Nielsen, Jakob. "How Long Do Users Stay on Web Pages?" Accessed August 25, 2020. https://www.nngroup.com/articles/how-long-do-users-stay-on-web-pages/.

"Open Archives Initiative. Protocol for Metadata Harvesting." Accessed August 25, 2020. https://www.openarchives.org/pmh/.

Piehler, Moritz. "Hilferuf einer Ruine." *Jüdische Allgemeine*, December 12, 2019. Accessed August 25, 2020. https://www.juedische-allgemeine.de/gemeinden/hilferuf-einer-ruine/.

Rauterberg, Hanno "Wie modern muss eine neue Synagoge sein? In Hamburg soll eine Synagoge nach historischem Vorbild rekonstruiert werden. Schon regt sich Protest dagegen." *Zeit Online*, February 19, 2020. Accessed August 25, 2020. https://www.zeit.de/2020/09/synagoge-hamburg-kirchenarchitektur-bau-modernisierung-bornplatzsynagoge.

Richter, Andrea. "Wir brauchen eine Synagoge, keine Luxuswohnungen." *Deutschlandfunk Kultur*, December 13, 2019. Accessed August 25, 2020. https://www.deutschlandfunkkultur.de/liberale-gemeinde-in-hamburg-wir-brauchen-eine-synagoge.1079.de.html?dram:article_id=465833.

Rürup, Miriam. "Demographics and Social Structure." *Key Documents of German-Jewish History*, September 22, 2016. Accessed August 25, 2020. https://jewish-history-online.net/topic/demographics-and-social-structure.

Sahle, Patrick, in collaboration with Georg Vogeler and the members of IDE. "Criteria for Reviewing Scholarly Digital Editions." Last modified June 2014. https://www.i-d-e.de/publikationen/weitereschriften/criteria-version-1-1/.

Siegel, Björn. "Verworrene Wege. Die Gründungsphase des IGdJ." In *50 Jahre – 50 Quellen. Festschrift zum Jubiläum des Instituts für die Geschichte der deutschen Juden*, edited by IGdJ, 26–53. Hamburg: Institut für die Geschichte der deutschen Juden, 2016. Accessed August 25, 2020. http://www.igdj-hh.de/files/IGDJ/pdf/hamburger-beitraege/igdj_50jahre-50quellen-festschrift.pdf.

"Stolpersteine Hamburg." Accessed August 25, 2020. https://www.stolpersteine-hamburg.de/en.php?MAIN_ID=4.

Studemund-Halévy, Michael, "Sephardic Jews." *Key Documents of German-Jewish History*, September 22, 2016. Accessed August 25, 2020. https://jewish-history-online.net/topic/sephardic-jews.

"TEI: Text Encoding Initiative." Accessed August 25, 2020. https://tei-c.org/.

"The Integrated Authority File (GND)." Last modified November 26, 2019. https://www.dnb.de/EN/Professionell/Standardisierung/GND/gnd_node.html.

Wikipedia. "BEACON." Last modified August 11, 2020. https://de.wikipedia.org/wiki/Wikipedia:BEACON.

Zaagsma, Gerben, "Tagungsbericht Jüdische Geschichte digital. 13.06.2013–14.06.2013, Hamburg." *H-Soz-Kult*, September 10, 2013. Accessed August 25, 2020. https://www.hsozkult.de/conferencereport/id/tagungsberichte-5011

Christiane Charlotte Weber

Chapter 3
Out of the Storage Cabinet and into the World: The Use of State-of-the-Art Digital Technology to Provide Contextualized Online Access to Historical Nazi Documents, as Practiced by the Arolsen Archives

German Summary: Grundlegender Umbruch, Paradigmenwechsel, Neubeginn – die Bezeichnungen der aktuellen Entwicklungen deuten klar in eine Richtung: Archive und ihre Bereitstellung von Dokumenten wurden durch die digitalen Techniken in ihren Möglichkeiten revolutioniert. Nutzer:innen können nun theoretisch selbst kleinste Bestände finden und von anderen Kontinenten aus darauf zugreifen. Für die Thematik der nationalsozialistischen Verfolgung ist dies besonders wichtig, da zum einen akademische Forschung dazu nicht nur in Deutschland oder Europa betrieben wird, aber zum anderen auch, weil die Überlebenden nach dem Krieg auswanderten und heute Nachkommen weltweit mehr über das Schicksal ihrer Familienangehörigen erfahren möchten.

Seit einigen Jahren öffnen sich daher die Arolsen Archives und ihre Vorgängerorganisation, der International Tracing Service (ITS), damit ein möglichst breites Publikum auf die dort verwahrten Dokumente zugreifen kann. Bereits heute sind ca. 26 Millionen Dokumente im Online-Archiv zugänglich. Dabei werden verschiedene digitale Ansätze angewandt, um auf das Schicksal und die Verfolgungswege von KZ-Häftlingen, Zwangsarbeiter*innen und Displaced Persons aufmerksam zu machen. Neben dem Online-Archiv gibt es mit dem e-Guide ein digitales Tool, das die Dokumente in ihren historischen Kontext beschreibt.

Die Vorstellung und Einordnung der beiden Projekte im vorliegenden Kapitel zeigen beispielhaft, wie NS-Dokumente aus einem analogen in ein digitales Archiv transferiert werden können. Die sich dabei stellenden grundlegenden und für alle Archive geltenden Fragen werden als Ausblick von verschiedenen Seiten beleuchtet: Verändern sich – und wenn ja wie – Dokumente bei diesem Wechsel? Weisen digitale Quellen im Gegenzug zu analogen andere Charakteristika auf?

∂ OpenAccess. © 2022 Christiane Charlotte Weber, published by De Gruyter. [CC BY] This work is licensed under the Creative Commons Attribution 4.0 International License.
https://doi.org/10.1515/9783110714692-004

1 Introduction

When a central tracing service for the victims of Nazi persecution back in the early 1940s first began to be organized, it seems safe to assume that none of the Allied agencies involved at the time were expecting things to develop in the way they have. For the founding fathers and mothers of the International Tracing Service (ITS)—the predecessor organization of the Arolsen Archives[1]—it will have been impossible to imagine that some 30 million documents now help clarify the fates of concentration camp prisoners, Western and Eastern European forced laborers, and Displaced Persons (DPs), let alone that these documents can now be accessed from all over the world. But thanks to digital technologies, the documents that have been collected and filed away in storage cabinets in the small North Hessian spa town of Bad Arolsen since 1946 are now only a click away. Mario Glauert, Head of the Brandenburg State Archives (BLHA), called this far-reaching change that all archives—no matter what size, type, or jurisdiction—currently have to face "the beginning of a new era of archive use."[2] It is a fundamental shift: Instead of users coming to the documents, the documents come to the users—24/7 all over the world.[3]

A few years ago, the Arolsen Archives reacted to this change by publishing their holdings in an online archive with only a few exceptions.[4] Thus, the circle of potential users expanded to include anyone with an internet connection. However, when making documents available in digital form, their immediate availa-

---

[1] The Arolsen Archives are an international center on Nazi persecution with the world's most comprehensive archive on the victims of National Socialism. The collection is listed on UNESCO's Memory of the World register and is the result of work carried out by the International Tracing Service (ITS). The organization changed its name from ITS to Arolsen Archives in May 2019 to reflect the changing priorities of the organization. Information on its current activities can be found online at: "Arolsen Archives," accessed May 31, 2020, https://arolsen-archives.org/en/. For an overview of the history of the institution, see Henning Borggräfe, Christian Höschler, and Isabel Panek, *A Paper Monument: The History of the Arolsen Archives* (Bad Arolsen: self-published, 2019). The exhibition catalogue is available free of charge at the following link: https://arolsen-archives.org/content/uploads/aa_catalogue_en.pdf (accessed May 31, 2020).
[2] See Mario Glauert, "Archivbenutzung im Digitalen Zeitalter," *Brandenburgische Archive* 33 (2016): 3.
[3] Glauert speaks of "user to content and content to users." "Archivbenutzung," 3.
[4] Documents with particularly sensitive content, such as medical records and the files of the Child Tracing Service, are excluded.

bility⁵ to the user is not the only major consideration. "Just" making the documents available in digital form is by no means enough. Contextualizing the documents at various levels is equally important.

This is what prompted the Arolsen Archives to create the e-Guide, a tool that enables users to research the historical context of documents online and to give them the means to better interpret what happened to the people mentioned on the cards and files.[6] Both the online archive and the e-Guide have their origins in certain peculiarities of the ITS/Arolsen Archives. These will be outlined at the beginning of the next section, followed by a description of the considerations behind the online archive and the e-Guide. This article closes with a discussion of a more general nature because all digital projects raise one central question: What happens to sources when they are taken out of the storage cabinet and made available in digital form?

2 Unique Characteristics of the Arolsen Archives

2.1 The Nature and Structure of the Holdings

The collections of the Arolsen Archives contain over 30 million documents that were collected by the International Tracing Service—formerly the Central Tracing Bureau (CTB)—after the end of World War II. The documents themselves are quite diverse. They mainly consist of cards and forms that were filled out for inmates in concentration camps, documents concerning civilian forced laborers in the German Reich that were created by companies, registry offices, and police authorities, and materials that were produced in connection with the care and emigration of DPs by two UN relief organizations: the United Nations Relief and Rehabilitation Administration (UNRRA) and the International Refugee Organization (IRO). Some of the documents were collected in the liberated concentration camps, while others were sent to the ITS by German authorities and companies

---

[5] The availability of documents—whether analog or digital—always depends on the degree of indexing, cataloguing and the quality of archival descriptions. In the case of the Arolsen Archives, this is a work in progress.
[6] The online archive (https://collections.arolsen-archives.org/en/search/) currently holds about 26 million documents. The Arolsen Archives aim to make their entire holdings available online within the next few years and to index them in full. The e-Guide (https://eguide.arolsen-archives.org/en/) explains the most common documents in the archive in their historical context. By 2021, the e-Guide will be partly available in Russian, Polish, and French in addition to the complete versions in German and English, which are already provided.

on the orders of the Allies or transferred directly to the institution from DP camps. The intention was for them to be used to help trace victims of Nazi persecution.[7]

Four special characteristics of the collection were of central importance in determining the current structure of both the analog and the digital archive. The first special feature is connected with the mission of the ITS as described above: The documents were arranged for the purposes of the tracing service, and not in accordance with the principles applied in conventional archives. In order to make it quicker to search for information about a person, collections were broken up and the documents rearranged. In archiving terms, the collections can currently be said to be organized according to the principle of pertinence rather than that of provenance. Many documents on DPs that came to the ITS from various organizations were sorted into a common card file in alphabetical-phonetic order, for example. This postwar card file (*Nachkriegszeitkartei*) now contains 3.5 million documents. This made it easier to search for information about a specific person as the search only needed to be made in one large card file instead of in a number of smaller ones. However, it also meant that the contexts of individual collections are no longer evident and that the origins of some documents are now unclear. The ITS individual document envelopes are another interesting example that deserves consideration in this context:[8] After the liberation of the concentration camps, various card files that had been used for the management of the prisoners in the camps found their way to Arolsen. These were card files from the camp's registry offices, effects storage rooms, sick bays, political departments etc. In Arolsen the ITS employees went through the individual card files, collected all the cards that had been created for one person within a concentration camp, and put these in envelopes. These envelopes were used from the beginning of the 1960s on, and the various types of documents—prisoner registration card, personal effects card, or post control card, for example—were pre-printed on their front (see Fig. 3.1). Employees noted how many documents of each different type were contained inside an envelope as best they could. However, it was not always possible to classify documents entirely correctly as the contexts of the collections were sometimes no longer known.

---

[7] About 20,000 inquiries are still submitted to the Arolsen Archives each year. Researchers and journalists are not the only people who submit inquiries; the majority come from the relatives of persecutees. Seven decades down the road, the Arolsen Archives are continuing to fulfill the task that they first took up in the 1940s of clarifying victims' fates.

[8] For a detailed description of the envelopes, see "e-Guide," accessed May 31, 2020, https://eguide.arolsen-archives.org/en/archive/details/1/.

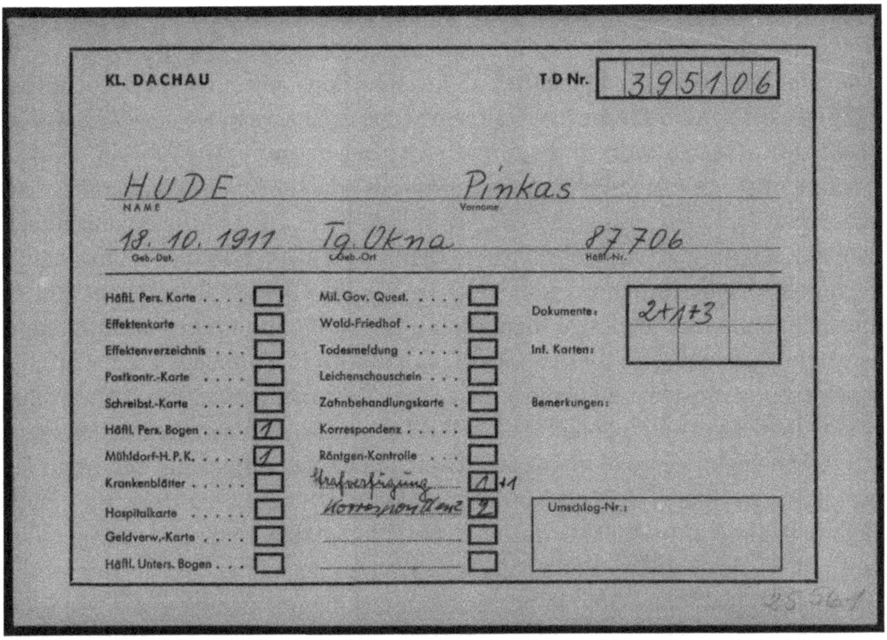
KL. DACHAU
T D Nr. 395106
HUDE
NAME
Pinkas
Vorname
18. 10. 1911
Geb.-Dat.
Tg. Okna
Geb.-Ort
87706
Häftl.-Nr.
Häftl. Pers. Karte
Effektenkarte
Effektenverzeichnis
Postkontr.-Karte
Schreibst.-Karte
Häftl. Pers. Bogen 1
Mühldorf-H. P. K. 1
Krankenblätter
Hospitalkarte
Geldverw.-Karte
Häftl. Unters. Bogen
Mil. Gov. Quest.
Wald-Friedhof
Todesmeldung
Leichenschauschein
Zahnbehandlungskarte
Korrespondenz
Röntgen-Kontrolle
Strafverfügung 1+1
Korrespondenz 2
Dokumente: 2+1+3
Inf. Karten:
Bemerkungen:
Umschlag-Nr.:

Figure 3.1: ITS individual document envelope, 1.1.6/10099249/ITS Digital Archive, Arolsen Archives.[9]

The second special feature of the archive is the kind of documents that were collected. This is of particular importance for the structure of the e-Guide as described below. In many cases, the documents are of an administrative nature, which means that their structure is identical.[10] For example, the Arolsen Archives hold 186,000 registry office cards from the Dachau concentration camp and 2.1 million so-called DP 2 cards that were used to register Displaced Persons in the camps.[11] Such documents all follow the same pattern, which means that users can decode them themselves once they have understood the basic structure. This characteristic was a prerequisite for the development of the e-Guide.

---

9 For the documents on Pinkas Hude created in the Dachau concentration camp and stored in the envelope, see "Online Archive," accessed May 31, 2020, https://collections.arolsen-archives.org/en/archive/10099248/?p=1&s=Pinkas%20Hude&doc_id=10099249.

10 During the conference, Sebastian Bondzio (University of Osnabrück) applied the term "serial documents," which is a very accurate description, cf. also Bondzio's chapter in this book.

11 For information on how the registry office cards and the DP 2 cards were used, see "e-Guide," accessed May 31, 2020, https://eguide.arolsen-archives.org/en/archive/details/7/ and https://eguide.arolsen-archives.org/en/archive/details/162/.

2.2 Few Legal and Technical Obstacles

The remaining two special features of the collections reflect the basic conditions that were important for the development of the online archive per se and will remain critical for the work of the Arolsen Archives in future. The Arolsen Archives are one of the few archives that can make their documents available online relatively easily. Firstly, this is due to the international nature of the organization.[12] The Arolsen Archives are not subject to German archive law, which imposes strict regulations and restrictions that must be fulfilled before a document can be published in either analog or digital form. The situation of the Arolsen Archives is rather different: The International Commission that oversees their work has given them a very clear mandate to make their documents available online.[13] Secondly, there is the simple fact that 85% of the collection has already been digitized. This high degree of digitization, which few other archives of this size have managed to achieve, stems from the fact that the ITS began digitizing their holdings at the end of the 1990s already, in order to be able to answer tracing inquiries more quickly. Instead of having to search for documents in the archive one by one, ITS staff were able to access them in a digital database very early on. Therefore, both the legal and the technical groundwork required for the online archive was already in place and presented no barrier to its realization.[14]

---

[12] For information on the International Commission that oversees the work of the Arolsen Archives and the legal basis, see "Who We Are," accessed July 15, 2021, https://arolsen-archives.org/en/about-us/who-we-are/.

[13] An exception was made for the medical files of Displaced Persons, which will not be made available online because of the very personal nature of the information they contain. However, it remains possible to view them in Bad Arolsen or on the premises of copyholders, such as the United States Holocaust Museum in Washington, DC, or the Wiener Holocaust Library in London. Relatives and people who are directly affected themselves also have the right to object to the online publication of specific documents.

[14] In this connection, there is a limitation that affects the findability of the documents in the online archive. Many of the individual documents—i.e., many of the cards and forms produced for an individual person—can be found very easily in the online archive as they have already been indexed for the database of the tracing service. However, in order to find people included on arrival lists or transport lists from concentration camps—i.e., in cases where a document contains more than one name—ITS employees began to develop the Central Name Index (CNI) back in the 1940s, an analog system that, however, cannot be used in digital form. They used small index cards to note the name, the date of birth, and, in the case of concentration camp prisoners, the prisoner number of the person concerned along with the reference code under which the list can be found in the archive. It is only recently that names have begun to be indexed at the document level. The consequence is that although these documents are available in the online archive, they cannot be found by searching for the name of a person. The Arolsen Archives are

3 Aspects of Digital Access— Provision, Contextualization, and Presentation of Historical Sources

As well as being important to the descendants of persecuted people on every continent, Nazi persecution is a topic that attracts attention from researchers from all over the world. To put it another way, interest in the documents of the Arolsen Archives is not restricted to users from a specific locality. On the contrary, the inquiries submitted to the archive show that documents on Nazi victims are relevant beyond regional boundaries. Most of those interested in the documents would not have the opportunity to search the database in person in Bad Arolsen or on the premises of one of the copyholders like the Archives Nationales in Paris-Pierrefitte or the Wiener Holocaust Library in London. The online archive was created in response to interest at the global level, out of the profound belief that the collection is an important source of knowledge for today's society and because making the documents available is a crucial part of the institution's international mandate. Therefore, the Arolsen Archives see it as their obligation to provide low-threshold access to the documents to as many people as possible.

3.1 In Use All over the World: The Online Archive

In 2015, the Arolsen Archives—or the ITS, as the institution was known at the time—made some of their holdings available online for the first time under the name "Digital Collections Online." The documents concerned belonged to individual collections that had been particularly well indexed. The card file of the Reich Association of Jews, geo-referenced materials on the death marches, and files from the Care and Maintenance program run by the IRO were some of the

---

currently working hard to change this. The crowdsourcing project "#everynamecounts" is one of the approaches they are using to tackle this issue. See "#everynamecounts," accessed May 31, 2020, https://arolsen-archives.org/en/learn-participate/interactive-archive/every namecounts/. The effects of crowdsourcing initiatives are obvious, and the approaches are integrated into more and more projects. The topic is also making its way into academic debates, see e. g. the online workshop "Transcribing – Encoding – Annotating: New Approaches of Technology and Methodology for Historical Sources in Crowd Sourcing and Citizen Science" from November 2020 (see Daniel Haas, "Conference Report," accessed July 12, 2021, https://hsozkult. de/conferencereport/id/tagungsberichte-8991).

materials chosen. Those responsible for making this selection did so in response to a structural peculiarity of the collection which has only been mentioned in passing so far: the varying degrees of cataloging. Some holdings, and those mentioned above are a case in point, are very broadly indexed and can be filtered and searched for a multitude of different pieces of information. Other collections could not be indexed to the same degree because of the sheer number of documents they contain. The postwar card file, for example, counts over 3.5 million documents in total, and until recently, only about every twenty-fifth card in this file had been indexed with digital metadata for the name of the person on the card. In the database used by the staff of the Arolsen Archives for researching tracing inquiries, employees conducted manual searches for the right person in the alphabetical-phonetic structure within this framework. Conversely, however, this would have meant that twenty-four out of twenty-five cards would not have been findable directly in the online archive because they had not yet been indexed. Hence the initial focus was on those collections that had already been adequately indexed.

When the next phase of the project began in June 2019, the Arolsen Archives made a decision that set it apart from other archives: They took advantage of the exceptionally high level of digitization with the goal of gradually putting as many documents as possible online—regardless of the level of cataloging.[15] The online archive was launched with 13 million documents, most of which concerned concentration camp prisoners. However, some emigration lists were also included. The documents could be searched for names and, to a limited extent, topics. Since then, the online archive has been growing continuously and now contains 26 million documents. Work is continuously being done to improve and complete the metadata.

An important aspect is that the online archive is linked to Google, and entering names there also searches the metadata of the documents in the online archive. In his welcome speech at the opening of the 18th Brandenburgische Archivtage Mario Glauert concluded: "Angesichts der zunehmenden (nur noch) digitalen Recherche werden [...] Offline-Archive nicht mehr wahrgenommen, sie werden zu den Verlierern des Digitalen Zeitalters werden" (In the face of increasing (entirely) digital research, offline archives will no longer be noticed,

---

15 According to Glauert, digitization itself is not the main obstacle that keeps archives from publishing their holdings online: "Das Teure ist dabei weniger das Scannen selbst. Der Aufwand für die technische Vorbereitung des Archivgutes, die fachgerechte und standardisierte Erschließung seiner Informationen sowie die Verwaltung und Sicherung der entstehenden Images und Metadaten übersteigen die einmaligen Kosten für die technische Erstellung von Digitalisaten ('Scannen') um ein Vielfaches." Glauert, "Archivbenutzung," 4.

they will become the losers of the digital age).¹⁶ The technical functionality of linking the archival data to search engines or other portals is crucial because many relatives—and many researchers too—do not (yet) know of the existence of the Arolsen Archives. It would never occur to them to search for documents there. The online search results help users find their way to the archive.¹⁷

One of the issues that gave rise to the most heated debate—and will surely continue to shape the development of the online archive in the years (and decades) to come—is the question of the sensitive nature of the sources. It is beyond question that information about a person's persecution by the Nazis or about the path their life took after the end of the war is personal and can also sometimes be difficult to deal with at an emotional level. While this leads some archives and some individuals to the conclusion that the documents should not be made accessible online, the Arolsen Archives place particular emphasis on the right to remembrance.¹⁸ They hold the view that it should be possible to find the documents so that the person who suffered persecution can be remembered. Consequently, the special nature of the sources is brought to the attention of users of the online archive before they are allowed to access them. The notification window that opens before they are given access to the online archive contains the following text:

> Please note that this portal on victims of Nazi persecution contains sensitive data on identified and identifiable persons. As a user of this portal, you are personally responsible for respecting privacy rights and other laws, the interests of third parties and other persons concerned, and generally recognized practices relating to personal data.¹⁹

Users are required to check a box to confirm a declaration of consent in which they undertake not to misuse the sensitive data.

---

16 Glauert, "Archivbenutzung," 5.
17 This point was discussed at length during the conference and it was pointed out that this technical solution may involve risks. Relatives who innocently enter the name of a family member in a search engine may well come upon unfiltered information for which they are entirely unprepared.
18 See "Risks and Opportunities of an Online Archive," accessed July 15, 2021, https://arolsen-archives.org/en/about-us/statements/online-archive/.
19 "Online Archive," accessed May 31, 2020, https://collections.arolsen-archives.org/en/search/.

3.2 Sharing Knowledge: The e-Guide

Arolsen Archives' e-Guide is an important tool which can be used in connection with the online archive. The documents that users find in the digital and/or analog archive of the Arolsen Archives contain a wealth of information which is by no means self-explanatory. Furthermore, most of the documents are in German and difficult to understand for non-native speakers. Thus, relatives, researchers, and other users have questions that need to be answered. Hence the e-Guide provides historical contextualization for the most common document types: Who used the documents on concentration camp prisoners, DPs, and forced laborers, when were they used, and what were they used for? What do the abbreviations on the cards mean, and what else can be found out about the fate of the person in question? The e-Guide is available online in a number of different languages. It is free of charge and can be accessed by anyone who is interested in using it. It is also suitable for use in schools and other educational contexts.[20]

Unlike the online archive whose principal aim is to make the documents accessible online in the first place, the main task of the e-Guide is their historical contextualization. When people visit the archive in person, staff are always at hand to answer their questions. But in the digital world, it is the e-Guide that takes on the role of the gatekeeper that was traditionally performed by archival staff and consists of providing answers to any questions that may arise when people work with the documents. The documents themselves remain the same, but the way they are presented is different: In the online archive, the main issue is to find exactly the document you are looking for on a specific person. In the e-Guide, the focus is on explaining that document with the aid of a sample document. This democratizes the "elite" knowledge held by the archive, empowers the users, and invites them to participate by sharing their own observations and knowledge in return. This interaction is what Kate Theimer calls the "participatory archive."[21] Furthermore, because the e-Guide is a digital tool, new information can be incorporated and updated with ease.

---

[20] For more information on how the e-Guide works, see Christiane Weber, "Von der analogen Quelle zum digitalen 'Schlüssel'. Der e-Guide der Arolsen Archives als Beispiel einer Informationsressource 2.0," in *Entgrenzte Erinnerung. Erinnerungskultur der Postmemory-Generation im medialen Wandel*, ed. Anne-Berenike Rothstein and Stefanie Pilzweger-Steiner (Berlin: De Gruyter 2020), and Christiane Weber, "Der e-Guide der Arolsen Archives als digitales Tool der aktiven historischen Wissensvermittlung," in *Funktion und Aufgabe digitaler Medien in Geschichtswissenschaft und Geschichtsunterricht*, ed. Krešimir Matijević (Gutenberg: Computus, 2020).
[21] Kate Theimer, "Partizipation als Zukunft der Archive," *Archivar* 1 (2018): 10, accessed July 19, 2021. https://archive20.hypotheses.org/files/2018/03/Aufsatz-Theimer.pdf.

When it came to implementation, it was important for the e-Guide to be able to adapt to the needs of individual users. One of the major ways this was achieved was by incorporating overlays—that is, markers that users can actively choose to click on in order to find out what a certain piece of information on a document really means. On the one hand, this enables users to find the answers they are looking for without being overwhelmed by the sheer wealth of information available, while on the other hand, it makes the e-Guide suitable for users with different levels of knowledge. This is because users only click on those overlays that are important for their own understanding, and this is dependent on their own prior knowledge. So, the sources that are shown in the e-Guide are intended to make knowledge transfer simple and accessible to all. The quintessential nature of these sources is used to that effect.

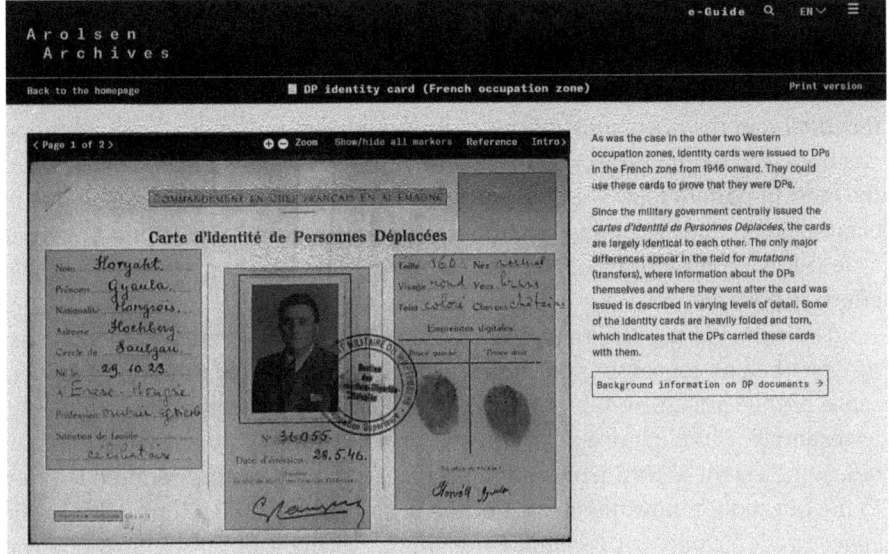

Figure 3.2: Screenshot of the e-Guide: https://eguide.arolsen-archives.org/en/archive/details/dp-identity-card-french-occupation-zone/, accessed September 21, 2021.

4 General Considerations: How Do Analog Sources Change When They Are Moved to the Digital World?

One of the fundamental questions that remains to be addressed can be expressed in the following terms: Do documents change if they are no longer provided in analog form, but are available in digital form instead—and if so, how? Current developments touch on at least five areas where changes are evident: document retrieval, the character of the documents, the possible reuse of documents, interaction, and contextualization.

Online archives are always the easiest way—and sometimes the only way—to find a document. At the Arolsen Archives, this is particularly true for the relatives of people who were persecuted by the Nazis. A perfectly ordinary process, a Google search, for example, leads them to an archive which, despite its importance, still remains unknown to many people today. A total of 17.5 million people are mentioned in the documents of the Arolsen Archives, but to date the institution has only received inquiries about 3.5 million people. The online archive is one of the most important tools with the power to change this and to make it possible to commemorate the remaining 14 million people. However, if the online archive is to fulfill its promise, it must be possible to find documents online with as little effort as possible.

The switch to digital can also bring about changes in an area that might best be described as concerning the character of the documents in the very broadest sense of the term. The e-Guide highlights the serial character of the documents, for example. Although one card still stands for the life of an individual human being, the extent of Nazi persecution becomes clear when consideration is given to the question of how often cards of the same type were filled out in a specific concentration camp or DP camp. For example, in the Arolsen Archives one can find approximately 110,000 personal effects cards[22] that were created in Buchenwald concentration camp. That information is clearly given in the e-Guide—in the question "How common is the document?"—while it is lost in the analog archive because in the latter the cards are stored individually in the aforementioned document envelopes for each former prisoner.

The character of a document also changes in another way. The document does not stand alone as a source of information, but is complemented by meta-

---

[22] "e-Guide," accessed October 10, 2020, https://eguide.arolsen-archives.org/en/archive/details/39/.

data. As the description of the online archive given in section 3 made clear, in the digital world, a document is only as "good" as the metadata that goes with it. One simply cannot find a document in the online archive until it has been indexed and until the necessary metadata has been created. This constitutes an expansion in that the digital data set exists in addition to the document, which is also available in analog form.

For many, the crucial difference between digital and analog sources is that digitized documents can be reused—there is almost no limit to the number of times a document can be reused. Of course, this can be viewed in a negative light and the horrific scenario of documents from concentration camps appearing on cups or tea towels can be painted in the most lurid of colors. However, the reproducibility of documents can—and most of the time does—have a positive twist. Digital sources can be integrated into new contexts, projects, or social media posts, thus, finding their way to new interested audiences.

Documents that are available online also make it possible to explore new ways of interacting with users via the documents. The online archive of the Arolsen Archives includes a chat function,[23] and the e-Guide displays the e-mail address at numerous locations accompanied by text encouraging users to get in touch. In the online archive in particular, relatives make use of this opportunity to provide further information about the members of their family whose documents they have found.

The contextualization of the documents, to come to the final point, has always been of vital importance. Although it would be a mistake to believe that it was possible to have more control over users' understanding of the documents when they visited the archive on site, it has to be said that the number of people who come into contact with the documents used to be much smaller than it is now—as banal as this may sound. So, the question of whether the contextualization of documents will be of greater importance in digital projects in the future is certainly one that deserves consideration. Because greater numbers of users with different levels of prior knowledge now come into contact with the documents, knowledge about the documents must be provided as directly as possible.

---

[23] One needs to keep in mind that a chat function like this is resource intensive as—in the case of the Arolsen Archives—several trained people are needed to post answers in less than a day.

5 Conclusion

Digital approaches throw the doors of archives wide open to the interested public. Documents that may well never normally have been found during research can be made more accessible in digital form. This enables archives to fulfill one of their most central tasks: to provide easy access to knowledge and clear the way for new insights into Nazi persecution.

In general, there are, of course, various approaches to the question of how to present sources digitally. Many different strategies are conceivable—ranging from searching through large quantities of documents as is the case in the online archive of the Arolsen Archives, to the study of individual documents that have been prepared in very great detail.[24] The interplay between the approach chosen, the collection of documents involved, and the objective that is being pursued will continue to offer further scope for discussion and experimentation in the future.

There is no conflict between digital tools like the online archive or the e-Guide of the Arolsen Archives and knowledge that is disseminated in analog form; digital tools merely disseminate such knowledge in a differentiated manner by making it more easily accessible from all over the world. The e-Guide demonstrates this particularly clearly: It would have been perfectly conceivable to publish the source material in traditional book form. However, digital presentation brings numerous advantages—ranging from clarity to the fact that the content can be accessed on any smartphone. The digital use of sources should not be seen as breaking with traditional forms, but as enhancing them.

Bibliography

Arolsen Archives. "Arolsen Archives." Accessed May 31, 2020. https://arolsen-archives.org/en.
Arolsen Archives. "e-Guide." Accessed May 31, 2020. https://eguide.arolsen-archives.org/en/.
Arolsen Archives. "#everynamecounts." Accessed May 31, 2020. https://arolsen-archives.org/en/learn-participate/interactive-archive/everynamecounts/.

---

[24] Cf. in particular the online source edition: Institut für die Geschichte deutscher Juden, "Hamburger Schlüsseldokumente zur deutsch-jüdischen Geschichte," accessed June 2, 2020, https://juedische-geschichte-online.net/, which is presented in this volume by Sonja Dickow. The Hamburg Source Edition and the offerings of the Arolsen Archives were discussed together in a panel at the conference, and the fact that their approaches are so fundamentally different made it possible to demonstrate the range of different ways in which documents can be presented online as well as the specific conditions that apply in each case.

Arolsen Archives. "Online Archive." Accessed May 31, 2020. https://collections.arolsen-archives.org/en/search/.
Arolsen Archives. "Risks and Opportunities of an Online Archive." Accessed July 15, 2021. https://arolsen-archives.org/en/about-us/statements/online-archive/.
Arolsen Archives. "Who We Are." Accessed July 15, 2021. https://arolsen-archives.org/en/about-us/who-we-are/.
Borggräfe, Henning, Christian Höschler, and Isabel Panek. *A Paper Monument: The History of the Arolsen Archives*. Bad Arolsen: self-published, 2019. Accessed May 31, 2020. https://arolsen-archives.org/content/uploads/aa_catalogue_en.pdf.
Glauert, Mario. "Archivbenutzung im Digitalen Zeitalter." *Brandenburgische Archive* 33 (2016): 3–9.
Haas, Daniel. "Conference Report." Accessed July 12, 2021. https://www.hsozkult.de/conferencereport/id/tagungsberichte-8991?title=transcribing-encoding-annotating-new-approaches-of-technology-and-methodology-for-historical-sources-in-crowd-sourcing-and-citizen-science&recno=9&q=&sort=&fq=&total=8694.
Institut für die Geschichte deutscher Juden. "Hamburger Schlüsseldokumente zur deutsch-jüdischen Geschichte." Accessed June 2, 2020. https://juedische-geschichte-online.net/.
Theimer, Kate. "Partizipation als Zukunft der Archive." *Archivar* 1 (2018): 6–12. Accessed July 19, 2021. https://archive20.hypotheses.org/files/2018/03/Aufsatz-Theimer.pdf.
Weber, Christiane. "Der e-Guide der Arolsen Archives als digitales Tool der aktiven historischen Wissensvermittlung." In *Funktion und Aufgabe digitaler Medien in Geschichtswissenschaft und Geschichtsunterricht*, edited by Krešimir Matijević. Gutenberg: Computus, 2020.
Weber, Christiane. "Von der analogen Quelle zum digitalen 'Schlüssel'. Der e-Guide der Arolsen Archives als Beispiel einer Informationsressource 2.0." In *Entgrenzte Erinnerung. Erinnerungskultur der Postmemory-Generation im medialen Wandel*, edited by Anne-Berenike Rothstein and Stefanie Pilzweger-Steiner. Berlin: De Gruyter, 2020.

Part II **Digitally Writing the History of Nazi Germany, World War II, and the Holocaust**

Sebastian Bondzio
Chapter 4
"At Least He Was Cautioned": Digitally Researching the Gestapo's Ruling Practices

German Summary: Seit sich die Geschichtswissenschaft in den 1990er und frühen 2000er Jahren intensiv der Gestapo gewidmet hat, sind die Schleier der sie umgebenden Mythen nach und nach gelüftet worden. Die enge Verflechtung der deutschen Gesellschaft mit der nationalsozialistischen Geheimpolizei trat sichtbar hervor, stellte Gewissheiten und Exkulpierungsstrategien der deutschen Nachkriegsgesellschaft in Frage und beförderte die intensive Auseinandersetzung mit diesem Aspekt der nationalsozialistischen Vergangenheit.

Die Gestapo selbst wurde in diesem Prozess historisiert und verlor ihr Image einer allmächtigen, allwissenden, und allgegenwärtigen Institution. Gleichwohl blieben interne Mechanismen und zentrale geheimpolizeiliche Praktiken weiterhin unerforscht. Bis heute erscheint das Innenleben der Gestapo deshalb als Blackbox. Während die historische Forschung Informationszuträgerschaft und Opfer – also gewisser Maßen Input und Output – der NS-Geheimpolizei fest im Blick hat, blieben die Mittel, mit denen die Gestapo die Bevölkerung systematisch terrorisierte, weitgehend unverstanden.

An diesem Punkt setzt dieses Kapitel an: Um die Terrorherrschaft der Gestapo zu begreifen, um also zu verstehen, wie sie es schaffte, die deutsche Gesellschaft im Sinne der nationalsozialistischen Volksgemeinschaft zu durchherrschen, untersucht dieser Beitrag die Sanktions- und Strafpraktiken der NS-Geheimpolizei. Empirische Grundlage dafür bildet das digitale Replikat der Osnabrücker Gestapo-Kartei. Als einzige digitalisierte Quelle ihrer Art erlaubt das maschinenlesbare Volldigitalisat eines zentralen geheimpolizeilichen Wissensspeichers die historische Simulation des Karteibetriebs, als historical Big Data ermöglicht sie der historischen Forschung eine äußerst differenzierte Analyse der Handlungen der Gestapo.

Zu diesem Zweck haben wir einen Workflow entwickelt, mit dem aus den sog. ‚Sachverhalten' systematisch die Sanktionsprofile der Gestapo herausgearbeitet werden können. Sie verweisen auf die institutionellen Regelmäßigkeiten, die bei der Verhängung von Sanktionen und Strafen für bestimmte ‚Vergehen' existierten. Die weiterführende Interpretation dieser Befunde lässt drei zentrale Herrschaftspraktiken der Gestapo hervortreten: 1.) Wird die immense Bedeutung von Wissensproduktion als basale Tätigkeit auch bereits der vordigitalen NS-

 OpenAccess. © 2022 Sebastian Bondzio, published by De Gruyter. This work is licensed under the Creative Commons Attribution 4.0 International License.
https://doi.org/10.1515/9783110714692-006

Geheimpolizei ersichtlich. 2.) Deutet sich an, dass es verkürzt wäre, die Gestapo als singuläre Instanz des NS-Terrors zu denken. Vielmehr war sie Teil eines umfassenderen Disziplinarsystems, in dem unterschiedliche NS-Institutionen gemeinsam an der Disziplinierung von Andersdenkenden, ‚Volksgenossen' und Zwangsarbeiter:innen arbeiteten. Diese ‚Arbeitsteiligkeit des Terrors' war Bedingung der Möglichkeit ihrer Effizienz. 3.) Zielte die Gestapo mit ihren Sanktions- und Strafpraktiken über ihre unmittelbaren Opfer hinaus. Sie nutzte ihr einschüchterndes Image bewusst, um bei jeder Interaktion mit einem Individuum zugleich auch eine Botschaft in die Gesellschaft zu senden und so ihren disziplinierenden Wirkungskreis zu vergrößern.

1 Introduction

Johann Heinrich Weustink first appeared on the Gestapo's radar in 1937. Fifty years earlier, he was born in the small Dutch border town of Nieuw-Schonebeek. As a citizen of the German Reich, he lived in Neuenhaus within the County of Bentheim, only about 20 kilometers from his birthplace. In Neuenhaus he worked as a bricklayer, got married and fathered six children. The latter was information the Gestapo (Geheime Staatspolizei; transl. Secret State Police) usually did not record, but in this case was considered particularly noteworthy and was therefore explicitly mentioned on Weustink's index card.[1] On August 25, 1937, the Gestapo produced this index card and recorded the personal information on Weustink it deemed relevant.

A small detail in this information deserves attention: The record proves that Weustink's birthplace was considered less important than his current address. The Nazis' secret police recorded the information about his residence very precisely in three lines. In contrast to this, it noted his birthplace only as "Neuschonebeck," a Germanized version of the Dutch town's name, which was presumably recorded phonetically. One could think of this as a triviality, but it already reveals an important characteristic of the secret police's practices in knowledge production.[2] While the Gestapo would have been able to identify Weustink as a

---

[1] See NLA OS Rep 439 No. 46464.
[2] For more information on the topic of knowledge production by the Gestapo, see: Sebastian Bondzio and Christoph Rass, "Allmächtig, allwissend, allgegenwärtig: Die Osnabrücker Gestapo als Massendatenspeicher und Weltmodell," *Osnabrücker Mitteilungen* 124 (2019), 230–50; Sebastian Bondzio, "Doing 'Volksgemeinschaft'. Wissensproduktion und Orndungshandeln der Gestapo," in *Geschichte und Gesellschaft* (forthcoming in 2021). This paper advocates a concept of a history of knowledge that goes beyond a history of science and scholarship and also incor-

person with the help of the phonetic and Germanized version of his place of birth, it was essential to know his exact whereabouts in order to be able to maintain a hold on him.[3] These procedures have to be taken as a premise when researching the Gestapo's ruling practices (*Herrschaftspraktiken*)[4] by analyzing the secret police's repository of knowledge.

Weustink had become of interest to the Gestapo the moment it learned the following: "W. soll sich in letzter Zeit abfällig über Einrichtungen und Erziehungsmethoden der Jugend im dritten [sic] Reich geäussert haben"[5] (W. is said to recently have made disparaging remarks about the institutions and educational methods of the youth in the Third Reich). The cautious formulation of the *Sachverhalt*[6] in the form of indirect speech, which is rather atypical for the Gestapo, suggests that the 50-year-old bricklayer was the victim of a denunciation. However, we do not know the fullness of these details. By assuming that there was a denunciation, we already go beyond the information provided by the source. The personnel file to which Weustink's index card refers, and which was kept by Department II/3 of the Gestapo's Osnabrück Office, would certainly

---

porates other stocks of knowledge. See Simone Lässig, "The History of Knowledge and the Expansion of the Historical Research Agenda," *Bulletin of the German Historical Institute* 59 (2016): 29–58; Jakob Vogel, "Von der Wissenschafts- zur Wissensgeschichte: Für eine Historisierung der 'Wissensgesellschaft,'" *Geschichte und Gesellschaft* 30, no. 4 (2004): 639–60.

3 See Bondzio and Rass, "Allmächtig, allwissend, allgegenwärtig," 252.

4 I'm applying a concept of praxeology that connects individual actions and societal structures and was outlined by Anthony Giddens in his structuration theory: Anthony Giddens, *Die Konstitution der Gesellschaft: Grundzüge einer Theorie der Strukturierung* (Frankfurt am Main: Campus, 1984); Thomas Welskopp, "Die Dualität von Struktur und Handeln: Anthony Giddens Strukturierungstheorie als 'Praxeologischer' Ansatz der Geschichtswissenschaft," in *Struktur und Ereignis*, ed. Andreas Suter and Manfred Hetting (Göttingen: Vandenhoeck & Ruprecht, 2001), 99–119.

5 NLA OS Rep 439 No. 46464.

6 I will retain the German term *Sachverhalt* in this paper. It refers to a specific field the Gestapo used on its index cards, which recorded information on what the person referred to was blamed for by the Gestapo. By not translating *Sachverhalt*, I want to point to the process of objectivization of information that took place, when the Gestapo stored information in its knowledge repository, and which, in an administrative sense, gave it the epistemological state of "truth." For this see a related process: Christopher Kirchberg, "'… Die Elektronisch erzeigte Schuldvermutung?' Die Auseinandersetzung um das 'Nachrichtendienstliche Informationssystem' des Bundesamtes für Verfassungsschutz," in *Welche 'Wirklichkeit' und wessen 'Wahrheit'? Das Geheimdienstarchiv als Quelle und Medium der Wissensproduktion*, ed. Thomas Großbölting and Sabine Kittel (Göttingen: Vandenhoeck & Ruprecht, 2019), 127; Constantin Goschler, Christopher Kirchberg, and Jens Wegener, "Sicherheit, Demokratie und Transparenz. Elektronische Verbundsysteme in der Bundesrepublik und den USA in den 1970er und 1980er Jahren" in *Wege in die digitale Gesellschaft. Computernutzung in der Bundesrepublik 1955–1990*, ed. Frank Bösch (Göttingen: Wallstein, 2018), 79–80; Bondzio, "Doing 'Volksgemeinschaft.'"

have elucidated the circumstances and how the information was obtained. Unfortunately—like all other personnel files in Osnabrück—it was destroyed meticulously by the Gestapo towards the end of the war.[7] All that remains in regard to sources from the former administrative district of Osnabrück, which was the Gestapo's Osnabrück Office's area of responsibility, is the Osnabrück Gestapo card index. It has survived almost in its entirety with about 48,000 index cards.[8]

The Gestapo utilized individual index cards to briefly record what made a person relevant. After the Third Gestapo Law of 1936, which largely deregulated the Secret State Police, the Gestapo officers recorded even minor misdemeanors and vigorously persecuted the people involved in these infractions.[9] In the name of the National Socialist idea of *Volksgemeinschaft*[10] the Gestapo was able to act at its own discretion and to take disciplinary sanctions.

Against this backdrop, Weustink's alleged statements on the education of the youth in the Third Reich were suspicious. The fact that Weustink was the father of six made it even more relevant. Since the Nazi regime was very aware of the role of youth in the long-term stabilization of its reign and the necessity of the younger generations for the planned expansion policy, the information about Weustink's number of children provided important information. Evidently, the Gestapo was not willing to tolerate the upbringing of six children in a household that publicly criticized Nazi pedagogy.

In order to get to the bottom of the matter, the Gestapo conducted its own investigation. The individual steps of this process left no paper trail. We do not know who the Secret State Police questioned and what it did beyond that. However, the Gestapo clearly recorded the result: "Die Ermittlungen führten jedoch

---

7 See Sebastian Weitkamp, "Die Kartei der Politischen Polizei / Gestapo-Stelle Osnabrück 1929–1945," *Niedersächsisches Jahrbuch für Landesgeschichte* 89 (2017): 109; Volker Eichler, "Die Frankfurter Gestapo-Kartei. Entstehung, Struktur, Funktion, Überlieferungsgeschichte und Quellenwert," in *Die Gestapo. Mythos und Realität*, ed. Gerhard Paul, Klaus-Michael Mallmann (Darmstadt: Primus, 2003), 178–99.
8 Only six of the approximately 200 formerly nationwide existing card indexes of the Nazis' secret police slipped through the thorough process of destruction, either in whole or in part. See Weitkamp, "Die Kartei," 110–11.
9 See Bondzio and Rass, "Allmächtig, allwissend, allgegenwärtig," 227–29.
10 This core concept of National Socialism can be roughly translated as "people's community." For more on the concept and its discussion, see Dietmar von Reeken and Malte Thießen, "'Volksgemeinschaft' als soziale Praxis? Perspektiven und Potenziale neuer Forschungen vor Ort," in *'Volksgemeinschaft' als soziale Praxis. Neue Forschungen zur NS-Gesellschaft vor Ort*, ed. Dietmar von Reeken and Malte Thießen (Paderborn: Ferdinand Schöningh, 2013), 9–33; Michael Wildt, "'Volksgemeinschaft' – eine Zwischenbilanz," in von Reeken and Thießen, *'Volksgemeinschaft'*, 355–69; Michael Wildt, *Die Ambivalenz des Volkes. Der Nationalsozialismus als Gesellschaftsgeschichte* (Berlin: Suhrkamp, 2019), 23–46.

zu keinem positiven Ergebnis"[11] (The investigations did not lead to a positive result). The suspicion against Weustink could not be substantiated, nothing incriminating had been brought to light, the accusations had proven to be unfounded. Weustink was to be considered innocent.

The last part of the *Sachverhalt* on Weustink's index card is therefore remarkable. Although the Gestapo had established that there had been no—in its view— "positive result," it concluded the section with the statement: "Immerhin wurde er verwarnt"[12] (At least he was cautioned). So, although the investigation had been without any result and no wrongdoing was found, the Nazi's secret police sanctioned Johann Heinrich Weustink nevertheless. No trace of a presumption of innocence. Instead, the insertion of the adverb "*immerhin*" (at least) expresses the exact opposite: a fundamental mistrust accompanied by a system-inherent presumption of guilt that pre-structured the Gestapo's perspective on and perception of the world.[13] Irrefutable and at the same time extremely potent, this presumption was enough to let Weustink experience the power of the Gestapo and—without any doubt—made this contact with the Secret State Police an unforgettable experience.

Paradoxically, the Secret State Police was able to count its warning as a successful sanction. For, regardless of whether Weustink had made the statements of which he had been accused or not, the Gestapo did not have to deal with Weustink again. His index card shows no further record. Until the end of the Nazi regime, Weustink did nothing that made him suspicious again. From the Gestapo's perspective the *staatspolizeiliche Warnung* (state police's warning)— even though Weustink might never have said what he was blamed for—clearly had worked.

It is difficult to estimate what exactly the "state police's warning" against Weustink contained. What is clear is that it was a routine sanction of the Gestapo. It was explicitly noted 3,291 times in the card index of the Gestapo's Osnabrück Office, making it the secret police's most frequent sanction. The warning was often only the last in a series of routine actions that the Gestapo itself sometimes described as "staatspolizeiliche Maßnahmen"[14] (state police's sanctions). Warnings were issued to anyone who had previously been arrested, interrogated, and instructed. The "state police's warning" was the penultimate step in a process that ended in release from Gestapo custody. On the personal index cards, the

---

11 NLA OS Rep 439 No. 46464.
12 NLA OS Rep 439 No. 46464.
13 On the topic of the perception of reality by the Gestapo, see: Bondzio, "Doing 'Volksgemeinschaft.'"
14 For example: NLA OS Rep 439 No. 25991.

Gestapo noted one or more of these five elements of the standard procedure. Nevertheless, while listed individually, they belonged together and, in combination, formed the way in which the Gestapo most frequently interacted with the population.

Even if the precise content of the "state police's warnings" remains obscure, their meaning becomes very clear on another level: Each time this sanction was exerted, the Gestapo also promoted its intimidating presence, stabilized its self-propagated[15] image of being omnipotent, omniscient, and omnipresent,[16] and through this, violently projected its power into society.[17]

Identifying such ruling practices, which can be derived from the sanctions and punishments recorded in the Gestapo's card index, motivated me to write this chapter. Under the question which sanctions and punishments the Gestapo took or imposed and what this tells us about its ruling practices, I will analyze the card index of the Gestapo's Osnabrück Office as a body of knowledge. Beforehand, it is necessary to reflect upon the challenges that come with wanting to analyze the Gestapo's sanctions in the card index as well as to explain the idea of an exploratory digital historiography and the theoretical and methodical thoughts behind it. After that, I will conduct four empirical steps of research: (1) A general overview of the state police's sanctions will be provided by analyzing the general sanctions profile of the Gestapo's card index. (2) The general findings will be differentiated systematically, first by time, (3) then in correlation to categories of *Sachverhalte* the Gestapo recorded. (4) I will point out phenomena I call *fringe cases*, relevant for the identification of ruling practices, which do not show in a strictly systematic analysis.

In this chapter, I will limit my analysis to the cards of one of the Abteilung II: Politische Polizei (department II: Political Police). It was this department that was responsible for terrorizing the population in the name of the National Socialist idea of the *Volksgemeinschaft*, in the first place. While the Gestapo's Abteilung III: Abwehrpolizei (department III: Defense Police) was concerned with

---

15 See Klaus Michael Mallmann and Gerhard Paul, "Die Gestapo. Weltanschauungsexekutive mit gesellschaftlichem Rückhalt," in *Die Gestapo im Zweiten Weltkrieg*, ed. Klaus Michael Mallmann and Gerhard Paul (Darmstadt: Primus, 2000), 612.
16 For the myth see: Robert Gellately, "Allwissend und allgegenwärtig? Entstehung, Funktion und Wandel des Gestapo-Mythos," in *Die Gestapo. Mythos und Realität*, ed. Klaus Michael Mallmann and Gerhard Paul (Darmstadt: Primus, 2003), 42–72; Bondzio and Rass, "Allmächtig, allwissend, allgegenwärtig."
17 Formerly, Gestapo research focused on *Schutzhaft* as the Gestapo's main instrument of terror. See Klaus Hesse and Andrej Angrick, *Topographie des Terrors. Gestapo, SS und Reichssicherheitshauptamt in der Wilhelm- und Prinz-Albrecht-Straße; eine Dokumentation; Katalogband zur gleichnamigen Präsentation*. 3rd ed. (Berlin: Stiftung Topographie des Terrors, 2010), 147–55.

tasks of defense intelligence until 1941 and has been largely forgotten in the shadow of the Amt SD-Ausland (Foreign Intelligence Service) of the Reichssicherheitshauptamt (RSHA) (Reich Main Security Office), Abteilung II is the department directly associated with the horror of the Gestapo and has become virtually synonymous with the entire Gestapo as a criminal organization.[18]

This is also reflected in the composition of the Osnabrück Gestapo card index as a source: 19,530 of all 23,101 sanctions recorded in the entire card index were noted on the 24,564 index cards of the Political Police department. In contrast, only 3,751 sanctions were recorded on the 24,203 index cards of the Abwehrpolizei. Thus, with roughly the same number of index cards produced, 85% of the recorded sanctions are found in the card index of the Political Police. The card indexes of the two Gestapo departments had been kept separately until 1944 and were only then merged into the card index of department II[19] on orders from the RSHA—three years after department III had largely ceased producing cards.[20]

Both departments of the Gestapo thus had rather different areas of responsibility. This led to a high degree of disparity between the bodies of knowledge the two departments produced. Both factors are decisive reasons for a separate analysis of the sanctions and ruling practices of the Gestapo's Political Police department.

2 The Challenge of Analyzing Gestapo Sanctions

As the Nazis' *Weltanschauungsexekutive* (ideological executive force), the political department of the Gestapo was directly involved in the implementation of the National Socialist *Volksgemeinschaft*[21]—a concept that was not static and whose

---

[18] Forgetting Abteilung III is nonetheless very problematic. It had an essential function in protecting and stabilizing the Third Reich. Only a few times was this department explicitly the topic of research: Justus Jochmann, "Abwehr. Die nachrichtendienstliche Tätigkeit der Abteilung III der Staatspolizeistelle Trier am Beispiel Luxemburgs," in *Die Gestapo Trier. Beiträge zur Geschichte einer regionalen Verfolgungsbehörde*, ed. Thomas Grotum (Cologne: Böhlau Verlag, 2018), 203–4. Nonetheless, its relevance became obvious in the production of knowledge of Abteilung III. See Bondzio and Rass, "Allmächtig, allwissend, allgegenwärtig," 237.
[19] See Weitkamp, "Die Kartei," 115.
[20] See Bondzio and Rass, "Allmächtig, allwissend, allgegenwärtig," 237–39.
[21] Main ideologist in the RSHA, Werner Best, praised the Gestapo as an "Arzt am deutschen Volkskörper." See Carsten Dams and Michael Stolle, *Die Gestapo. Herrschaft und Terror im Dritten Reich* (Munich: Beck, 2012), 42.

interpretation was subject to certain dynamics during the 12 years of Nazi rule.[22] The Gestapo surveilled[23] and punished in its name and thereby contributed to the implementation of this ideological construct. Aware of the relevance of such *doings*[24] of the National Socialist *Volksgemeinschaft*, Michael Wildt recently called for the concept to be operationalized in a praxeological way.[25] For Gestapo research this means reassuring itself of its own social historical traditions, reflecting on them through new paradigms, thinking ahead in innovative ways, and ultimately using digital workflows productively to gain new empirical insights.

If we research National Socialist ruling practices on the basis of a secret police's repository of knowledge, it is clear that we can only observe a small part of the communitization (*Vergemeinschaftung*) of the main ideological concept. It is therefore necessary to reflect on the epistemic horizon of the source: By looking into the Gestapo card index, we see the society of the administrative district of Osnabrück from the perspective of an administrative institution that is closely entwined with the government. With the help of the medium of the card index, this society was described according to National Socialist ontologies. Attributions that were considered correct for ideological reasons were verbalized on the index cards and, beyond that, did not become the object of any further reflection. This way, information became part of the secret police's body of knowledge that was generated under the premises of the National Socialist *episteme*.[26] The complex institutional and power structures at play made the information *the truth*. In this form it could then be mobilized by an empowered Gestapo to order society in accordance with the imaginations of the *Volksgemeinschaft*.[27]

This awareness of the nature of the card index is a *conditio sine qua non* for working with the medium. It fundamentally calls into question the information stored on the index cards to the extent that it can no longer *not* be understood as an expression of the Gestapo. With this, source-positivist approaches become more difficult to justify; instead, the Gestapo's card index in its entirety becomes

---

22 See Reeken and Thießen, "Soziale Praxis?," 20–21; Bondzio, "Doing 'Volksgemeinschaft.'"
23 For an overview of the field of historical surveillance studies see: Sven Reichardt, "Einführung: Überwachungsgeschichte(n): Facetten Eines Forschungsfeldes," *Geschichte und Gesellschaft* 42, no. 1 (2016): 5–33.
24 This *doing* refers to the performative power of the Gestapo's practices in regard to the *Volksgemeinschaft*.
25 See Wildt, *Die Ambivalenz des Volkes*, 40.
26 "Episteme" describes the societal a priori of knowledge and discourse. See Michel Foucault, *Die Ordnung der Dinge* (Frankfurt am Main: Suhrkamp, 2003), 22.
27 See Bondzio, "Doing 'Volksgemeinschaft.'"

a source for researching the secret police. An analysis of the Gestapo's sanctions and punishments must be carried out under these preconditions. Findings must be interpreted with reference to the Gestapo itself. The possibility of this new perspective is a real gain. With the support of digital tools, it is now possible to examine the Gestapo's ruling practices in detail on a broad empirical basis.

2.1 Data Driven History

Since the 1980s the card index of the Gestapo's Osnabrück Office has often been discussed. For the last decades historiography has studied it from different angles.[28] However, its value as a historical source has been largely negated beyond its potential for individual case studies or the investigation of specific aspects of the Gestapo's victims.[29] Only in recent years has there been a growing awareness of the potential of the card index as a source for an empirical analysis of the inner functioning of the Gestapo itself.[30] Nevertheless, as late as 2017, Weitkamp still criticized that none of the surviving card indexes had been systematically cataloged, let alone researched.[31]

To react to this desideratum was the initial motivation of the research project *Überwachung. Macht. Ordnung – Personen- und Vorgangskarteien als Herrschaftsinstrument der Gestapo* (*Surveillance. Power. Order. Personal- and process-card indexes as an Instrument of Rule of the Gestapo*).[32] It has been conducted at the University of Osnabrück since 2018 and is funded by the German Research Foundation. For this project, a Gestapo card index was for the first time digitized in its entirety with the help of artificial intelligence and other algorithms. This digitization went beyond the production of image files and the collection of metadata. The information on the cards was extracted, made machine-readable, pre-

---

28 For example: Claudia Bade, *"Die Mitarbeit der gesamten Bevölkerung ist erforderlich!": Denunziation und Instanzen sozialer Kontrolle am Beispiel des Regierungsbezirks Osnabrück 1933 bis 1949*, Osnabrücker Geschichtsquellen und Forschungen 50 (Osnabrück: self-published, 2009); Claudia Bade, "Die Osnabrücker Gestapo-Kartei," *Historical Social Research / Historische Sozialforschung* 26, no. 23 (96/97) (2001): 235–38; Herbert Wagner, *Die Gestapo war nicht allein: Politische Sozialkontrolle und Staatsterror im Deutsch-Niederländischen Grenzgebiet 1929–1945*, Anpassung – Selbstbehauptung – Widerstand 22 (Münster: LIT, 2004); Rainer Hoffschild, *Die Verfolgung der Homosexuellen in der NS-Zeit: Zahlen und Schicksale aus Norddeutschland* (Berlin: Verlag Rosa Winkel, 1999).
29 See Bade, "Osnabrücker Gestapo-Kartei," 236–38.
30 See Weitkamp, "Die Kartei," 108.
31 See Weitkamp, "Die Kartei," 110–11.
32 DFG project number: 394480672.

processed, and in this form stored in relational databases.[33] Thereby, a digital replica of the card index was created, which enables the computer-aided simulation of the card index's historical operation. This means that for any point between 1929 and 1945, the period of the card index's operation, its particular state can be reconstructed with little effort. Thus, a differentiated study of one of the Gestapo's central repositories of knowledge was made possible.

Such databases can no longer be evaluated analogously in a reasonable way. Too much information has to be included and processed at the same time. In order to be able to use the database in its entirety in historical research, we therefore developed a digital approach that stands in the tradition of other *Data Driven Histories* (DDH).[34] The basis of our particular DDH is an exploratory approach that allows the analysis of "historical big data" that is extracted from serial sources. It is not primarily concerned with so-called *close reading* of the sources. Instead, it critically examines the contexts in which the sources were created and considers their research a prerequisite for the analysis of "historical big data."

Due to their high degree of formalization, serial sources are particularly suited for this form of digital evaluation. With our workflow entire archives of these administrative mass sources of the modern age can be made machine-readable and then be included in historical research. Such mass sources include inventories of registers of civil status,[35] military medical examination documents,[36] application forms,[37] and so on, but also, as in the present case, entire card indexes.

As process-generated sources, they are the product of administrative action in the face of a social phenomenon that was perceived as a challenge. Thus, at the same time they are (1) an expression of a consciousness of a particular his-

---

33 For a more detailed description of this process of digitization, see Sebastian Bondzio and Christoph Rass, "Data Driven History: Methodische Überlegungen zur Osnabrücker Gestapo-Kartei als Quelle zur Erforschung datenbasierter Herrschaft," *Archiv-Nachrichten Niedersachsen* 22 (2018): 132–34.
34 Peter Haber coined the term "Data Driven History" in 2010 but did not provide a systematic methodology: https://www.hist.net/archives/4895 (accessed May 25, 2021). For information on our specific approach to DDH as an exploratory method, see Bondzio and Rass, "Data Driven History," 134–36. Also: https://www.nghm.uni-osnabrueck.de/data_driven_history/data_driven_history.html (accessed August 31, 2020).
35 See Sebastian Bondzio, *Soldatentod und Durchhaltebereitschaft: Eine Stadtgesellschaft im Ersten Weltkrieg*, Krieg in der Geschichte 113 (Leiden: Brill, 2020), 29–37.
36 See Christoph Rass, *'Menschenmaterial': Deutsche Soldaten an der Ostfront. Innenansichten einer Infanteriedivision 1939–1945* (Paderborn: Ferdinand Schöningh, 2003), 28–29. For a short exploration of the possibilities of this kind of source in digital approaches: https://nghm.hypotheses.org/467 (accessed August 31, 2020).
37 See https://transrem.arolsen-archives.org/maps/ (accessed August 31, 2020).

torical society and its attribution of relevance, (2) historical repositories of knowledge, and (3) detailed protocols of the chosen coping strategies.

In our Data Driven History we apply digital tools to large sets of structured historical data to make such complexes researchable, to test existing hypotheses, and to generate new ones. By doing so, we hope to contribute to the progress of the larger field of *digital history*. In the case of the Gestapo card index, one of the central challenges is not to succumb to the temptation of data-positivist misconceptions, but to design questions and methods in such a way that they produce findings and bring insights that stand up to critical epistemological scrutiny.

2.2 Theoretical and Methodical Reflection

For the perspective of the larger research project and especially for this study, the preliminary considerations pose a significant challenge. Simply drawing conclusions about the historical reality of the described phenomena in the knowledge produced by the Gestapo seems problematic. We do not know if the actions the Gestapo recorded as *facts* ("*Sachverhalte*") and used as a basis for sanctioning people actually happened. The goal of historical source criticism should not be to point out the contingent, historical circumstances of the source under investigation and then, nonetheless, use the information mediated in it uncritically. Rather, source criticism leads to an awareness of the epistemic potential of the source—that is, a knowledge about which statements and conclusions based on a source are valid and which are not.

Strictly speaking, the Gestapo's knowledge only provides insight into the process of knowledge production of the Gestapo itself. The analysis of the card index initially only provides findings about the genesis of the card index. For an analysis of the sanctions and punishments meted out by the Gestapo, this first means that we can only determine when the Gestapo made a note of which sanctions and punishments, how they relate to each other or to other information in the Gestapo's card index, and which ontology of categorizations the institution used at a specific point in time. Every other statement—whether it relates to the secret police's world view or their ruling practices—then includes at least one step of interpretation. In a certain way, this already transcends the demands of the strict empiricist approach of early social history, as it crosses the border towards hermeneutics and thus to more comprehensive interpretations of the findings.

There are various ways of dealing with this historiographical practice. With an appropriately sophisticated awareness, in which the steps of interpretation remain transparent, I consider mixing empiricist and hermeneutic perspectives to be legitimate and even necessary to produce relevant historical knowledge. After all, the Gestapo's card indexes are the largest coherent corpora of sources of the Nazis' secret police available for research. In these files, the Gestapo has inscribed traces of their ruling practices. In order to work these practices out, it is necessary to productively overcome radical empirical positions (such as radical constructivism) in such a way that an equally post-positivist and post-constructivist position can emerge, which—in the awareness of both positions—emphasizes and operationalizes pragmatic aspects.[38]

Ultimately, the Gestapo's card index—as is true for every other stock of historical big data—contains patterns and structures, which are inherent to it[39] and have been inscribed unwittingly by the producer. In contrast to other Gestapo sources, in which the Gestapo itself designed the outlines of its image by using propaganda, these patterns were generated unintentionally and have not already been transformed narratively by intentions of self-portrayal. As traces of past practices, these phenomena are of particular interest for the analysis at hand and can be carved out with the help of exploratory methods.[40] In concrete terms, this means that we are able to apply the exploratory approaches of the so-called *Knowledge Discovery in Databases*[41] to the sanctions and punishments recorded in the Gestapo's card index.

3 Crunching the Numbers

Before we step into the detailed analysis of the Gestapo's sanctions and punishments, it makes sense to provide some basic numbers on the Gestapo's card

---

38 The goal is to operationalize in an empirical way theoretical neo-pragmatist approaches as they were laid out by Richard Rorty. Rorty opposed the assumptions of epistemic representationalism. This way, statements of the Gestapo lose their appearance as describing some sort of objective reality and instead can be understood as intersubjective, contingent, and historical expressions. The Gestapo described things it considered as real and recorded its own reaction towards it. For Rorty's position, see: https://plato.stanford.edu/entries/rorty/#2 (accessed June 30, 2020).
39 See Bondzio, *Soldatentod und Durchhaltebereitschaft*, 27–28.
40 See Rob Kitchin, "Big Data, New Epistemologies and Paradigm Shifts," *Big Data & Society* 1, no. 1 (2014): 1–12; Irving John Good, "The Philosophy of Exploratory Data Analysis," *Philosophy of Science* 50, no. 2 (1983): 283–95.
41 Usama Fayyad, "Data Mining and Knowledge Discovery in Databases: Implications for Scientific Databases," in *9th International Conference on Scientific and Statistical Database Management: Proceedings August 11–13, 1997, Olympia, Washington*, ed. Yannis Ioannidis and David Hansen (Piscataway, NJ: IEEE: 2000), 2–11.

index: As mentioned in Section 1 of this chapter, the 24,564 index cards of the political department contain about 19,530 sanctions, which account for 85% of all the sanctions recorded in the card index. On the cards, they are part of a free text field the Gestapo has overwritten with the objectifying term *Sachverhalte*. In the Osnabrück Gestapo card index, a total of 40,934 *Sachverhalte* have been recorded. Of these, 32,778 (80%) can be found on the index cards of the Political Police. Not every *Sachverhalt* therefore contains a sanction. At the same time, a *Sachverhalt* can contain more than one sanction. For example, on the index card of the Prague-born locksmith Emil M., who was forced to work at a construction site of the Osnabrück Klöckner-Werke, the Gestapo recorded in May 1943:

> M. wurde in Hannover festgenommen, weil er seine Arbeitsstelle eigenmächtig verlassen hat, er wurde am 23.4.43 der hies. Dienststelle überstellt. Da M. bislang noch nicht in Erscheinung getreten ist, wurde er nach scharfer Zurechtweisung, Belehrung u. Warnung am 29.4.43 seiner alten Arbeitsstelle wieder zugeführt.[42]

> M. was arrested in Hanover because he left his workplace unauthorized, on 4/23/1933 he was transferred to the local Gestapo office. Since M. had not made an appearance yet, he was returned to his old workplace on 4/29/1943, after sharp rebuke, instruction and warning.

A total of seven sanctions are included in this *Sachverhalt:* Emil M. was arrested, transferred to the Gestapo's Osnabrück Office, sharply reprimanded, instructed, and warned. After being held in police custody for seven days, he was returned to his former job.

He escaped harsher punishment in a concentration camp or a so-called *Arbeitserziehungslager* (AEL) (Labor Education Camp) only because he previously had behaved inconspicuously. The fact that his index card contains no further records after this *Sachverhalt* indicates that after the incident Emil M. preferred to bow to the inhuman and brutal forced labor rather than to be "sharply reprimanded" once again. Given that this phrase must be understood as a euphemism hiding nothing less than violent mistreatment and torture by the secret police, this comes as no surprise.[43]

---

42 NLA OS Rep 439 Nr. 26540.
43 See Lothar Gruchmann, *Justiz im Dritten Reich 1933–1940: Anpassung und Unterwerfung in der Ära Gürtner* (Munich: Oldenbourg Wissenschaftsverlag, 2009), 705–9.

3.1 State Police Sanctions—An Overview

The case of Emil M., with its seven recorded sanctions, however, was an exception. Table 4.1 shows that less than 1% of the *Sachverhalte* contain more than three sanctions. In fact, more than half of all *Sachverhalte* do not include any sanction. For the most part, they report general information about the person described in the index card or note a Gestapo-internal reference or procedure. Of those *Sachverhalte* that did indeed contain information on a sanction, the vast majority only stated one or two.

Table 4.1: Number of sanctions in the "Sachverhalte" of the Osnabrück political department (n = 32,778).

Number of sanctions in a *Sachverhalt*	Count	Share of count
0	18,316	55.88%
1	10,647	32.48%
2	2,791	8.51%
3	823	2.51%
4	177	0.54%
5	20	0.06%
≥ 6	4	0.01%

What can be said for the sanctions also applies to the recorded punishments. They, too, were noted in the text field of the *Sachverhalte*. In about half of the cases the exact sentence was recorded by the Gestapo in the *Sachverhalt* to which the punishment was related. Others stated no sentence or took the form of August Thüner gen. Steffmann's index card:

> in Schutzhaft gen.[ommen] am 12.7.33 wegen erhebl.[icher] Störung der öffentl.[ichen] Sicherheit u.[nd] Ordnung durch sein Verhalten in einer Wirtschaft in Bohmte (Absingen von komm.[unistischen] Liedern [,] Aeusserungen über die nat.[ionalsozialistischen] Regierung usw.), wird in Konz[entrations]-Lager überführt.[44]

> taken in preventive custody on 12/7/33 because of considerable disturbance of public safety and order by his behavior in a bar in Bohmte (singing of communist songs, statements about the National Socialist government, etc.), will be transferred to a concentration camp.

The ideological motivation for the Gestapo's actions in this case is very clear. Immediately after the National Socialists came to power, the Gestapo fought

---

[44] NLA OS Rep 439 No. 42830.

hard against communists and expressions of communist attitudes. At the same time, there is a lack of clarity: This *Sachverhalt* does not provide any information about the duration of Thüner gen. Steffmann's concentration camp imprisonment. This information is only found in the next *Sachverhalt* and thus requires us to calculate the duration of the sentence by hand. There it states: "released on 9/30/33,"[45] meaning that Thüner gen. Steffmann spent two-and-a-half months in a concentration camp.

Without considerable effort, an efficient, digital evaluation on this basis is not possible. However, in 9,230 cases the sentence was noted directly in the *Sachverhalt* that also contained the sanction. This enables us to correlate the duration of prison sentences or the size of fines with the sanctions and *Sachverhalt* of the same records.

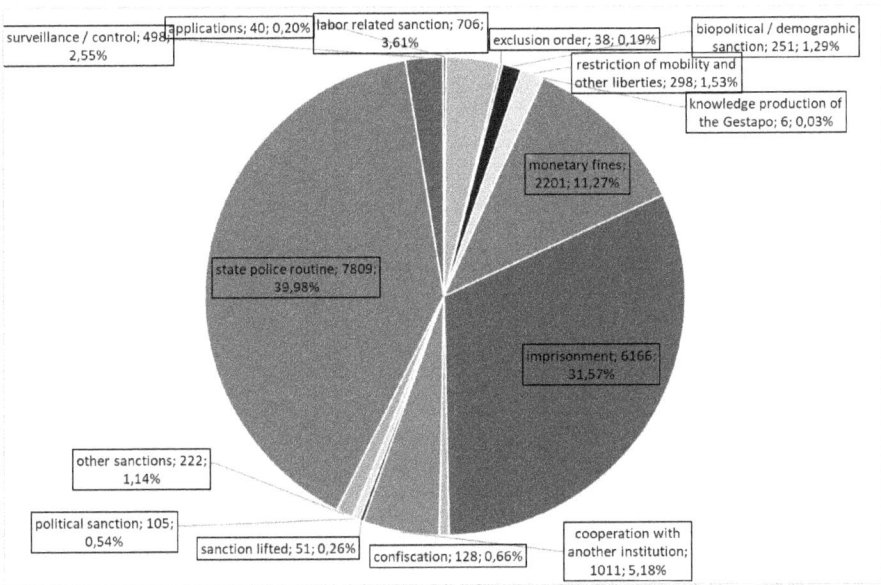

Figure 4.1: General sanction profile in the card index of the political department of the Gestapo in Osnabrück (n = 19,530). Graphic created by the author.

In recording its sanctions and punishments the Gestapo used a total of 3,921 different categories. In order to analyze them meaningfully, they needed to be classified by applying an abstracting ontology. Figure 4.1 displays the general frequency distribution of the Gestapo's sanctions, which I call the *general*

---

45 NLA OS Rep 439 No. 42830.

sanction profile of the card index of the political department of the Gestapo in Osnabrück. As indicated above, the most frequent form of interaction between the secret police and the population of the administrative district of Osnabrück consisted of *staatspolizeiliche Routinen* (state police routines). This category comprises 7,809 entries, which in turn fall into eighteen subcategories. The three most frequent of these were 3,228 *staatspolizeiliche Warnungen* (warnings by the Gestapo), 1,448 arrests, and 938 interrogations.

The next most frequent are 6,166 notes of imprisonment. In 2,337 cases, this imprisonment was not further qualified, but in 1,717 instances imprisonment in a so-called Labor Education Camp (AEL) was imposed; in 989, concentration camp imprisonment; and in 827, imprisonment in *Schutzhaft* (preventive custody) was recorded. It should be noted, however, that the Gestapo did not make a clear distinction between *Schutzhaft* and concentration camp imprisonment in its card index. A lot of concentration camp prisoners were actually *Schutzhäftlinge* (prisoners in preventive custody), while prisoners in *Schutzhaft*—especially when the period of imprisonment was shorter—frequently spent their incarceration, for example, in police prisons.

Table 4.2: Penalties for prison sentences in the Political Police files (n = 5,647).

Penalties	Quantity	Share of total
Up to 1 day	169	2.99%
2 days to 1 week	859	15.21%
8 days to 1 month	830	14.70%
1 to 6 months	3,179	56.30%
6 to 12 months	215	3.81%
1 to 2 years	186	3.29%
2 to 3 years	93	1.65%
3 to 4 years	28	0.50%
4 to 5 years	17	0.30%
5 to 10 years	31	0.55%
≥10 years	11	0.19%
Until further notice	29	0.51%

Table 4.2 shows how broad the spectrum of detention periods was that the Political Police recorded. Some people were held in police custody for only one day, but in most cases longer sentences were imposed. Often, they ranged between one and six months. The case of Kasimir R. shows, however, that in individual cases sentences could be much longer. On March 19, 1943, the Gestapo noted that it had arrested Kasimir R. because he allegedly had "mit der deutschen Hau-

sangestellten T[...] geschlechtlich verkehrt"[46] (sexual intercourse with the German domestic worker T[...]). In other cases of sexual acts with a German woman, *Sonderbehandlung*—that is, execution—would have been administered immediately.[47] But because of his *Eindeutschungsfähigkeit*[48] Kasimir R. was initially taken into *Schutzhaft* for one year and deported to the SS's special concentration camp Hinzert.[49] Meanwhile, the RSHA in Berlin continued to work his case and in February 1944 ordered that Kasimir R. should be transferred to the concentration camp Buchenwald for a period of 25 years.[50] The absence of Kasimir R.'s name in the death books of the Buchenwald[51] and Mittelbau-Dora[52] concentration camps gives reason to hope that he did not fall victim to the brutal working conditions there. If he survived until the liberation in April 1945, he had spent a good part of two years in the concentration camp.

The actual duration of Kasimir R.'s imprisonment can no longer be exactly determined. However, this information is not necessary to understand the punishment practices of the National Socialist disciplinary system. For an understanding of what the Nazi regime considered appropriate punishment, the information in the Gestapo card index is sufficient, as it shows the National Socialists' draconian methods and can be interpreted accordingly.

Figure 4.1 shows that the third largest category of sanctions were "monetary fines." A total of 3,608 times the Gestapo mentioned a concrete amount of money in a *Sachverhalt*. Included are also two cases in which bail money expired. Again, the Gestapo used a broad range of penalties. The most common one was between 5 and 50 Reichsmarks (RM), fines of up to 250 RM also were not unusual, and in a few cases they were even higher than 100,000 RM.

Heinrich Maschmeyer from Schüttorf, for example, was first taken into *Schutzhaft* for five days on October 9, 1939, because he was accused of sabotaging

---

46 NLA OS Rep 439 No. 35472.
47 See for example the case of Joseph Grzeskowiak: NLA OS Rep 439 No. 13089.
48 *Eindeutschungsfähigkeit* is a racist term: After heterosexual sexual intercourse between what the Gestapo considered to be a *Volksgenossin* (female) and a *Gemeinschaftsfremder* (male), in cases of pregnancy the Gestapo checked if the child could be considered as German. Decisive was if the male was *eligible* for *Germanization*, which means that it was checked, if the male could be considered as part of the "Nordic race." These sanctions shed some light onto the biopolitics of the *Volksgemeinschaft*. See Felix Klormann, "'Eindeutschungs-Polen' im SS-Sonderlager/Konzentrationslager Hinzert: Zur Praxis des 'Wiedereindeutschungsverfahrens,'" in Grotum, *Die Gestapo Trier*, 116.
49 See Klormann, "Eindeutschungs-Polen," 117–18.
50 See NLA OS Rep 439 No. 35472.
51 See http://totenbuch.buchenwald.de/names/list (accessed August 31, 2020).
52 See http://totenbuch.dora.de/ (accessed August 31, 2020).

Table 4.3: Fines recorded in the card index of the Political Police (n = 3,608).

Penalties	Quantity	Share of total
1–4 RM	259	7.18%
5–9 RM	483	13.39%
10–24 RM	1,683	46.65%
25–49 RM	411	11.39%
50–99 RM	241	6.68%
100–249 RM	226	6.26%
250–499 RM	92	2.55%
500–999 RM	76	2.11%
1,000–1,999 RM	73	2.02%
2,000–2,999 RM	19	0.53%
3,000–3,999 RM	13	0.36%
4,000–4,999 RM	2	0.06%
5,000–9,999 RM	13	0.36%
10,000–49,000 RM	12	0.33%
50,000–99,999 RM	2	0.06%
≥100,000 RM	3	0.08%

his brother's business. Two years later, the Gestapo dealt with him again and noted that he had been sentenced "vom Sondergericht wegen Devisenschiebung zu 5 Jahren Zuchthaus und 5 Jahren Ehrenverlust [...] und Geldstrafe von 180000 Rm"[53] (to 5 years in jail and 5 years loss of honor and fined 180,000 RM by the 'special court' for foreign exchange fraud").

In some other cases, the Gestapo granted the possibility of paying a certain amount of money as a substitute for imprisonment. The amount of the daily rate varied considerably. At the beginning of Nazi rule, it usually amounted to 10 RM, from December 1940 onwards it was reduced to 5 RM. This change can be understood as a necessary step to relieve detention institutions, which saw a doubling of prisoners between 1939 and the end of 1940.[54] By reducing the size of the daily rate, more people were able to pay the fine. This way, not only would the prisons and concentration camps be less overcrowded, but additional funds for the state

---

53 NLA OS Rep 439 No. 26607.
54 See Ulrich Herbert, Karin Orth, and Christoph Dieckmann, "Die Nationalsozialistischen Konzentrationslager: Geschichte, Erinnerung, Forschung," in *Die Nationalsozialistischen Konzentrationslager: Entwicklung und Struktur*, ed. Ulrich Herbert, Karin Orth and Christoph Dieckmann (Göttingen: Wallstein, 1995), 29; Andrea Löw, *Die Verfolgung und Ermordung der europäischen Juden durch das nationalsozialistische Deutschland 1933–1945*. Vol. 3, *Deutsches Reich und Protektorat September 1939–September 1941* (Munich: Oldenbourg Wissenschaftsverlag, 2012), 30.

would be generated. Monetary fines thus also became a way for the Gestapo to manage the detentions system's intake capacity.

To conclude discussion on the general frequency distributions, two further relevant categories of sanctions will be analyzed to expose a second level of National Socialist ruling practices: Both the cooperation of the Gestapo's Osnabrück Office with other institutions of the Nazi regime and the many *arbeitspolizeiliche Maßnahmen* (sanctions enforced by the Gestapo that were related to labor) indicate that the Gestapo was embedded in a more comprehensive system, in which various institutions of the Nazi state collaborated to brutally discipline the German population as well as those sentenced to forced labor.

The main achievement of social historical research on the Gestapo in the 1990s and early 2000s was to point out the close interrelation between the National Socialist secret police and German society.[55] In doing so, historical researchers were able to show the importance of denunciations and undercover informants for acquiring new information.[56] Another branch of research focused on the Gestapo's cooperation with other police departments, the SS, and Nazi party organizations. Dams and Stolle called these institutions "eine Art Reserve-Gestapo zur besonderen Verwendung"[57] (a kind of reserve Gestapo for special use) and pointed out that administrative cooperation by other authorities was an integral part of the Gestapo's calculus.[58] With this focus, research on the Gestapo was able to discover the carefully created network of persecution during the Third Reich. The Gestapo, sat at the center of this web, was able to expand its range considerably, and, with the help of the network, acquire knowledge for its card indexes.[59]

However, this perspective, which focuses very strongly on the Gestapo and thus simultaneously reproduces the image of a centrally acting institution of terror, predetermined the interpretation of the findings. Historians conceived the

---

55 See Mallmann and Paul, "Die Gestapo."
56 See Dams and Stolle, *Die Gestapo*, 69–94; Bade, *Denunziation*; Claire M. Hall, "An Army of Spies? The Gestapo Spy Network 1933–1945," *Journal of Contemporary History* 44, no. 2 (2009): 247–65; Herbert Dohmen, *Denunziert: Jeder tut mit; Jeder denkt nach; Jeder meldet* (Vienna: Czernin, 2003); Katrin Dördelmann, *Die Macht der Worte: Denunziationen im nationalsozialistischen Köln*, Schriften des NS-Dokumentationszentrums der Stadt Köln 4 (Cologne: Emons, 1997); Karl-Heinz Reuband, "Denunziation im Dritten Reich: Die Bedeutung von Systemunterstützung und Gelegenheitsstrukturen," *Historical Social Research* 26, no. 2 (2001): 219–34; Dieter W. Rockenmaier, *Denunzianten: 47 Fallgeschichten aus den Akten der Gestapo im NS-Gau Mainfranken* (Würzburg: Richter, 1998).
57 Dams and Stolle, *Die Gestapo*, 94.
58 See Dams and Stolle, *Die Gestapo*, 94.
59 See Dams and Stolle, *Die Gestapo*, 94–102.

network of other institutions as serving the Gestapo. As a result, the predominant topics were the secret police's output, namely surveillance, persecution, and deportation.[60]

But in addition to that, the Gestapo was also part of another, second system. Its traces have left their mark in the Gestapo's card index. Until now, however, historical scholarship has mainly only assumed its existence and marked the empirical investigation of the network a desideratum.[61] For just as the Gestapo's working practices and internal mechanisms remained a black box due to the desperate lack of sources, what can be described as the *disciplinary system* of the Third Reich, of which the Gestapo was a part, also remained largely invisible.

In his 2016 article, Roth urged that this institutional network had to be researched—that is, that the system the Gestapo formed with other police forces, justice, internal administration, tax authorities, labor administration, or communes should be investigated.[62] In a way, Roth continues to follow the tradition of focusing on the network of persecution that Dams and Stolle pointed out. But by removing the Gestapo from the center, he takes a crucial step and creates the possibility of understanding the Nazi secret police in relation to other parts of a more comprehensive, non-hierarchically ordered network and—unlike a system that is directed towards the Gestapo—to focus on the mutual interactions between the institutional agents.

This system's goal was to discipline people who behaved in ways deemed deviant by punishing them. Concentration camps, *Arbeitserziehungslager*, police prisons, and other places of detention were as much a part of it as were investigative authorities, internal administrations, labor offices, and the judiciary system. No clear center can be identified in this disciplinary system. Rather, it resembles a rhizome.[63] Each of its parts fulfilled a specific function in order to realize the intended greater task of the system. All the actors worked together in ways that formed a comprehensive state mechanism that aimed to rule over society and to implement the National Socialist *Volksgemeinschaft*. The identification of this functional apparatus locates the Gestapo at a new place inside the

---

60 See Dams and Stolle, *Die Gestapo*, 103–32.
61 See Thomas Roth, "Die Gestapo Köln: Ansätze weiterer Forschung. Überlegungen zu einem Projekt des NS-Dokumentationszentrums der Stadt Köln," *Geschichte in Köln* 63, no. 1 (2016): 252; Lena Haase, "Die Gestapo in der Gesellschaft: Quellenlage und Forschungsfelder zur Geschichte Der Staatspolizeistelle Trier," in Grotum, *Die Gestapo Trier*, 24.
62 See Roth, "Die Gestapo Köln," 252.
63 See Gilles Deleuze, Félix Guattari, and Dagmar Berger, *Rhizom*, Internationale marxistische Diskussion 67 (Berlin: Merve-Verl., 1977), 16.

Third Reich and sheds some light on the *division of labor* that Nazi terror required.

In the Osnabrück Gestapo card index, more than a thousand references to cooperation with other institutions and around 700 work-related sanctions expose those parts of the disciplinary system that go beyond the Gestapo itself, the concentration camps, and the prison system. Three-quarters of the recorded labor-related sanctions were in fact acts in which the Gestapo noted that a person had been transferred either to an employer or—more frequently—to a labor office (*Arbeitsamt*) to assign them to a new place of forced labor.[64]

The labor offices in the administrative district of Osnabrück played a central role at the junction between the forced labor and disciplinary system. The index card of the Dutchman Bernardus B. from Rotterdam is an example of the institution's position in the Nazi regime:

> B. wurde am 11.2.43 festgenommen, weil er seine Arbeitsstelle eigenmächtig verlassen hatte. Da die Arbeitserziehungslager wegen Seuchenverdachts nicht aufnahmefähig sind, wurde B. dem Arbeitsamt in Osnabrück am 3.11.43 überstellt.[65]
>
> B. was arrested on 11/2/1943, because he had left his workplace unauthorized. Since the work education camps are not receptive due to suspicion of epidemic disease, B. was transferred to the employment office in Osnabrück on 11/3/1943.

After his arrest, Bernadus B. would actually have been deported to an AEL. Due to external circumstances, however, this was not possible, so this disciplinary step was skipped. Instead, B. was to be directly forced back to work. The Osnabrück Labor Office took over his new placement.

Other actors in the disciplinary system can also be identified through the Gestapo's card index. In about 200 cases it is clear that there was collaboration with another institution, but the Gestapo did not record the details. In 471 cases, the Gestapo noted that it had handed over a case to the judicial system. The public prosecutor's office or district attorney's office in Osnabrück then took over the case, made further investigations, and, if the results were sufficient, brought the case before a judge who ruled in accordance with National Socialist law.[66] In

---

64 The special significance and interdependence of the labor administration in the Third Reich was already emphasized by Henry Marx in his study of the *Reichsarbeitsministerium*. See Henry Marx, *Die Verwaltung des Ausnahmezustands: Wissensgenerierung und Arbeitskräftelenkung im Nationalsozialismus* (Göttingen: Wallstein, 2019), 114–20.
65 NLA OS Rep 439 No. 5097.
66 For the National Socialist concept of law and justice see Herlinde Pauer-Studer and Julian Fink, eds., *Rechtfertigungen des Unrechts: Das Rechtsdenken im Nationalsozialismus in Original-*

other cases, the Gestapo handed over cases directly to the *Sondergericht* (special court) in Hanover.[67] On 212 occasions the political department of the Osnabrück Gestapo handed a case over to another Gestapo office, while seventy-two cases were handed over from other Gestapo offices to the office in Osnabrück. In twenty-seven instances, a case was transferred to another police department, the *Schutz-* or *Kriminalpolizei*, for reasons of authority.

Thus, while some of the actors in the disciplinary system were already part of the Gestapo's persecution network, this brief overview makes it clear that the disciplinary system must be thought of as more comprehensive. Its full extent, as well as mechanisms and points of intersection, have yet to be explored in greater detail. This way, the system's structure becomes recognizable as an important condition[68] of the violence imposed by the Third Reich.

The five categories mentioned above (state police routines, imprisonment, fines, cooperation with other institutions, labor-related sanctions) encompass 92% of all sanctions in the Political Police card index in Osnabrück. Two central ruling practices of the National Socialist regime can be identified at this general level:

1. The significance of the routines of the Secret State Police as projections of power becomes visible. As the Gestapo's most frequent form of interaction with the population, they were an essential practice for dominating and disciplining German society. Not only people's direct interaction with the Gestapo, but, beyond that, the communication about these encounters in the social space—which Nazi propaganda had prepared discursively[69]—worked in favor of the Nazi's secret police.
2. Analyzing the Gestapo's records reveals that concentrating exclusively on the Gestapo does not do justice to the disciplinary system created by the Nazis. It was far more comprehensive, consisted of a range of interacting institutional agents, and gained its efficiency through a clear division of tasks. The Gestapo's exact position in this system and its relationship to other actors have yet to be determined precisely. However, the insight provided here already

---

texten (Berlin: Suhrkamp, 2014); Werner Konitzer, ed., *Moralisierung des Rechts: Kontinuitäten und Diskontinuitäten Nationalsozialistischer Normativität* (Frankfurt: Campus, 2014), 7–9.

67 On the topic of people from Osnabrück at the *Sondergericht* in Hannover see Raimond Reiter, "'Heimtücke' und 'Volksschädlinge': Osnabrücker vor dem Sondergericht Hannover in der NS-Zeit," *Osnabrücker Mitteilungen* 103 (1998): 267–77.

68 Based on Kant's concept of the *Bedingung der Möglichkeit*, which aims for the circumstances that are necessary for something to happen.

69 Mallmann and Paul pointed to the public relations work of the Gestapo in creating its intimidating image. See Mallmann and Paul, "Die Gestapo," 612–13.

makes it clear that it is relevant to further research this systemic level of the totalitarian state in order to better understand the tyranny imposed in the name of the National Socialist *Volksgemeinschaft*.

3.2 Differentiating the Gestapo's Sanctions

In addition to such general findings digital analysis enables the production of differentiated findings to almost any degree. A productive way to obtain more detailed findings is through multidimensional database queries. In these queries, several attributes that have a meaningful relationship to each other are evaluated together. This way, for example, temporal progressions or correlations in the data can be made visible.

3.2.1 Time

Figure 4.2 shows the dynamics of the sanctions imposed by the Political Police in Osnabrück between 1933 and 1945. As can be expected, the five most frequent categories already identified become particularly visible in this context. The increase in these five sanctions in the 1940s is striking. However, given the Gestapo's increasing knowledge production during this period, which has already been pointed out in another paper,[70] and the insight that this knowledge related primarily to forced laborers who were disciplined, this is not a particularly surprising finding.

New insights into the practices of the Gestapo during Nazi rule are rather to be found in the details of the graphic. The developments already identified above can now be located temporally and be differentiated throughout time. For example, the boom in state police routines began before 1940. Even before more and more forced laborers were harassed and terrorized by the Gestapo, an increase in this particular practice can be observed. While from 1933 on these measures had already been the most common ones taken, cases increased drastically from 1937 onwards. From 1936, the aforementioned Third Gestapo Law had made it much easier for the Political Police department to take people into custody on the slightest suspicion, to interrogate them, and, if it seemed necessary, to torture them.

---

70 See Bondzio and Rass, "Allmächtig, allwissend, allgegenwärtig," 247–51.

80 — Sebastian Bondzio

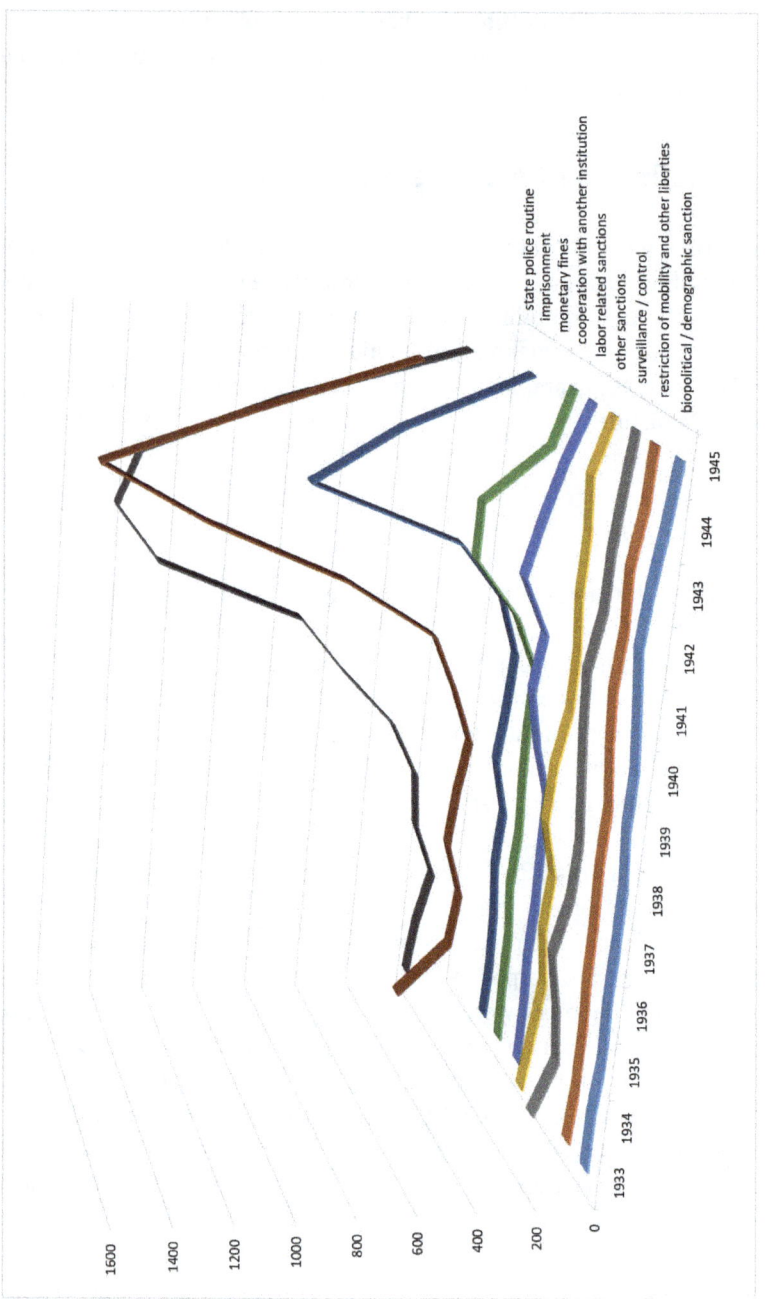

Figure 4.2: Sanctions recorded in the card index of the Gestapo's political department in Osnabrück by year. Graphic created by the author.

This was accompanied by a short boom in prison sentences. While in a first wave in 1933 about 300 mainly KPD and SPD members were incarcerated,[71] there was a second wave of arrests in 1936 and 1937. This time, being characterized as having an attitude classified as a threat to the state was enough to be excluded from society for some time, without any trial and, for example, to be imprisoned in a concentration camp. The third wave then eclipsed everything that had gone before: Following the beginning of the war, the number of imprisonments increased and reached its peak in 1943 with 1,525 cases. Whereas previously it was mainly Germans who were to be disciplined in the sense of the National Socialist *Volksgemeinschaft*, in the third phase increasingly forced laborers, whose resistance to their enslavement was to be broken, were imprisoned. Frequently, however, their deviant behavior was not only punished with a prison sentence. Additional fines were quite common for forced laborers.

During the same period, the disciplinary system took on its threatening shape. Labor-related sanctions increased as early as 1939 and the number of collaborations with other institutions increased nearly ten-fold between 1940 and 1942, from 33 to 291. This increase cannot be explained on a monocausal basis. Due to the rising number of intimate contacts between forced laborers and *Volksgenossen*,[72] which became quite common given the masses of forced laborers present in Germany, the Gestapo increasingly transferred cases to the *Sondergericht* in Hanover. At the same time, however, help from the Osnabrück public prosecutor's office and district attorney's office, who held hearings locally, was more frequently called for.

This system of disciplinary institutions, which to some extent already existed prior to 1941 and was mobilized between twenty to thirty times a year, was used more frequently between 1941 and 1943. This strengthened the system's importance and impact. In 1944, however, the number of collaborations suddenly dropped to sixty-eight. Because the number of *Sachverhalte* in the card index of the Political Police, which referred to forced laborers, did not decrease to the same extent,[73] it stands to reason that by establishing the AEL Ohrbeck near Osnabrück in 1944 the Gestapo gained some independence from the disciplinary system. With this new resource, it could imprison people without having to collaborate with any other institution. Once more, the Gestapo's power had increased.

---

[71] See Bondzio and Rass, "Allmächtig, allwissend, allgegenwärtig," 242–45; Dams and Stolle, *Die Gestapo*, 103–10.
[72] This racist Nazi term referred to individuals who were considered worthy members of the *Volksgemeinschaft*.
[73] See Bondzio and Rass, "Allmächtig, allwissend, allgegenwärtig," 237.

3.2.2 Deviance and Punishment

In order to provide deeper insights into the Gestapo's penal practices, a combined analysis of the sanctions and *Sachverhalte*[74] needs to be conducted. Unfortunately, the depiction of the entire correlation matrix resulting from this step of the analysis goes beyond the possibilities of this publication. I will therefore limit myself to discussing specific sanction profiles and describing relevant findings in the text. Basically, such a matrix shows which sanctions the Gestapo took in relation to a certain category of *Sachverhalt* and how often (in absolute and relative numbers) it did so. In this way, patterns of distribution and frequency become discernible, which subsequently can be interpreted with regard to the practices of the secret police.

It is a rather obvious finding that different categories of *Sachverhalte* have been sanctioned differently by the Gestapo. The sanction profiles of the individual categories of *Sachverhalte* differ from the general sanction profile of the general population—that is, the correlation of sanctions and *Sachverhalte* in the whole card index of the political department of the Osnabrück Gestapo, as shown in Figure 4.1. Significant deviations of sanction profiles from the general profile refer to distinct penal practices.[75]

For example, a total of 3,115 sanctions have been recorded in connection with labor offenses (which were often, but not always, related to forced laborers). Of these sanctions, 46% provided information on imprisonment and 41% referred to state police routines. Both sanctions frequently occurred in the same *Sachverhalt* and show that the Gestapo predominantly imposed prison sentences for labor offenses such as the refusal to work, so-called *Arbeitsvertragsbrüche* (violations of labor contracts), and what in the eyes of the Gestapo was considered inadequate performance of work.

But *Sachverhalte* that can be related directly to forced labor have a clearly distinguishable profile of sanctions. While state police routines also accounted for 41%, 25% of the sanctions were prison sentences and 21% were fines. Apparently, it was part of the secret police's practices to fine forced laborers for certain offenses in addition to imprisonment or, if a deviant behavior was considered minor, to impose a fine as an alternative to incarceration in order to maintain the working power of a forced laborer.

---

[74] For the categorization of the *Sachverhalte* see Bondzio and Rass, "Allmächtig, allwissend, allgegenwärtig," 240–41.
[75] The figures once again at a glance: State police routine 40%; imprisonment 32%; fines 11%; cooperation with other institutions 5%; labor police measure 4%; supervision/control 3%.

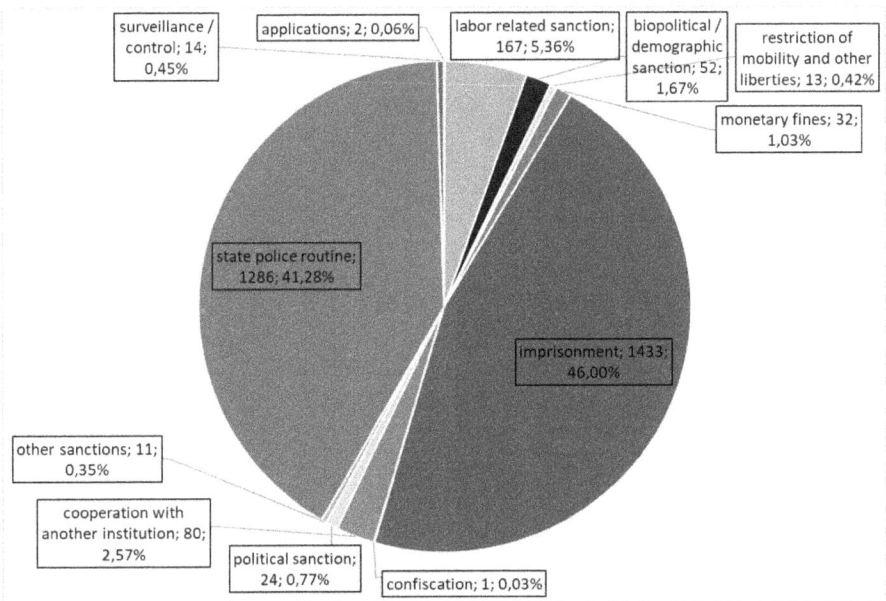

Figure 4.3: Sanction profile of the Sachverhalte related to labor offenses (n = 3,115). Graphic created by the author.

In both categories of *Sachverhalte* the proportion of state police routines is close to that of the general sanction profile. However, the quantity of other sanctions differs fundamentally and thus defines the respective sanction profiles. Even if, on first glance, the *Sachverhalte* were thematically close to each other, the two examples show that distinct patterns in the sanctions existed. Due to the large number of cases, this gives reason to assume that the punishments meted out by the Gestapo were not arbitrary but followed certain underlying regularities.

When it came to battling political opponents, the Gestapo used state police routines with a slightly above-average frequency and incarceration with a slightly below-average frequency. These deviations from the general sanction profile are not significant. What is significant, is that for most of the Nazis' rule, the Gestapo monitored these suspects closely. This is expressed in the fact that the number of sanctions involving surveillance and the scrutiny of mail against political opponents was roughly 8% and thus more than twice as high as in the general population. In addition, the political department restricted mobility and other freedoms six times more frequently for this group, particularly by imposing a requirement on social democrats whom it had already interrogated to check-in regularly at Gestapo offices. This was also the case with Willi Ortmann:

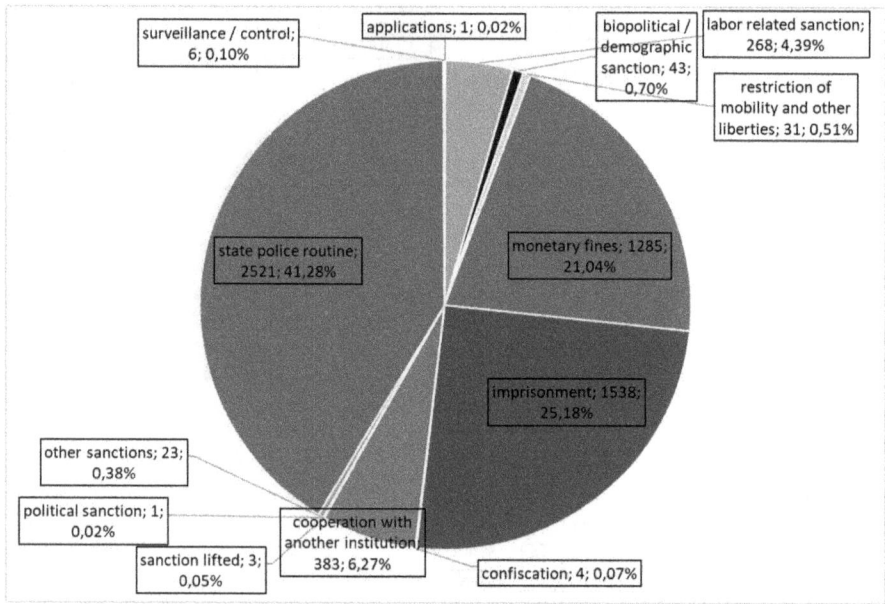

Figure 4.4: Sanction profile of the Sachverhalte related to forced labor (n = 6,107). Graphic created by the author.

Only one month after the so-called *Prussian coup*, on July 20, 1932, the Political Police department issued an index card for him. In the first *Sachverhalt*, it noted his function as first chairman of the Reichsbanner in Osnabrück. Despite his functionary position in this political organization, which opposed the Nazi party, he was not deported to one of the early concentration camps during the first wave of arrests. Instead, the Gestapo detained him on June 24, 1933, but released him the same day, on the condition that, from that day on, he was required to report to the office of the Political Police every day to confirm that he was still in town.[76]

In cases in which a *Sachverhalt* reported an infringement, the proportion of state police routines was significantly lower than the average. The Gestapo imposed fines particularly frequently in cases of *Nährwirtschaftsvergehen* (offenses against food regulations), forbidden collections of money, violations of the *Bezugsscheinordnung* (ration coupon regulations), but also, for example, in cases of burglary and embezzlement or *Rundfunkvergehen* (broadcasting offenses).

---

[76] See NLA OS Rep 439 No. 30439.

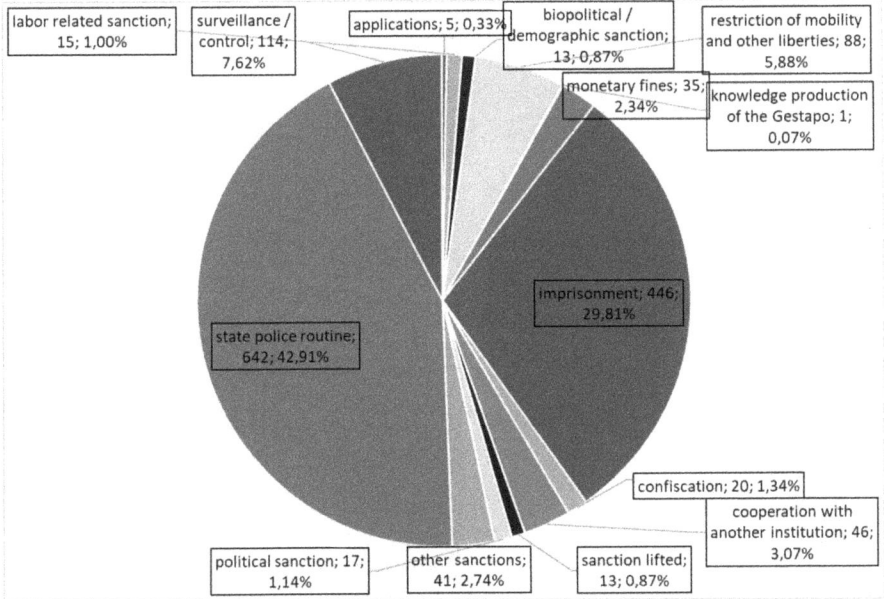

Figure 4.5: Sanction profile of the Sachverhalte related to political opponents (n = 1,496). Graphic created by the author.

Nearly 20 % of the sanctions mention a sum of money that was often imposed in addition to a prison sentence.

In contrast, actions or statements that the Gestapo felt would endanger the state were countered with state police routines much more often than average. In just under 55 % of such *Sachverhalte* this sanction was noted. The number of imprisonment and fines were about five percentage points below the general population. We have already seen an example of this category. The case of Heinrich Weustink, described in the introduction, showed that *Sachverhalte* reporting behavior that was perceived as a threat to the state often involved a process in which information that had been passed on to the Gestapo was first checked in an interrogation. In case of doubt, this merciless procedure alone ensured that a person and their communicative environment would have been more willing to disciplining themselves in the future.

Sachverhalte which had a more direct connection to the so-called *Volksgemeinschaft* contained information about prison sentences far more often. At 37 %, they were imposed one-sixth times more frequently than average. Furthermore, it is remarkable that in these cases fines only accounted for about 3 % of the sanctions, which is only about a quarter of the general sanction profile. In

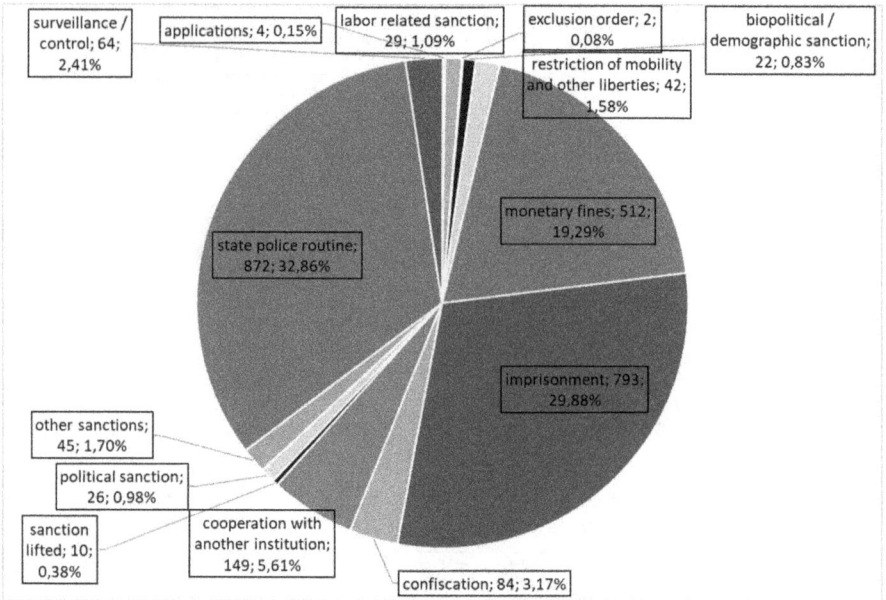

Figure 4.6: Sanction profile of the Sachverhalte related to infringements (n = 2,654). Graphic created by the author.

return, in cases where the Gestapo saw a connection to the *Volksgemeinschaft*, biopolitical sanctions such as forced sterilizations or even *Sonderbehandlung* were taken with an above-average frequency of about 5%. "*Rassenschande*"[77] (racial defilement), "*widernatürliche Unzucht*"[78] (unnatural sodomy), and other behaviors the Gestapo considered a moral offense, but also alcoholism, prowling, or begging were often punished severely by violating the physical integrity of the suspects. This finding reflects how serious the Gestapo considered *Sachverhalte* that concerned the *Volksgemeinschaft* to be.

The six different penal practices make visible which sanctions the Gestapo considered appropriate for different categories of *Sachverhalte*. Although deviant behavior was often initially countered with the same state police routine, depending on the category of deviant behavior, the persons who were punished beyond that were then treated quite differently. However, analysis also shows that the basic repertoire of secret police sanctions was quite limited. Rather, the Gestapo mostly used the same six sanctions and then had the additional option of

---

[77] For an example see NLA OS Rep 439 No. 10637.
[78] For an example see NLA OS Rep 439 No. 8358.

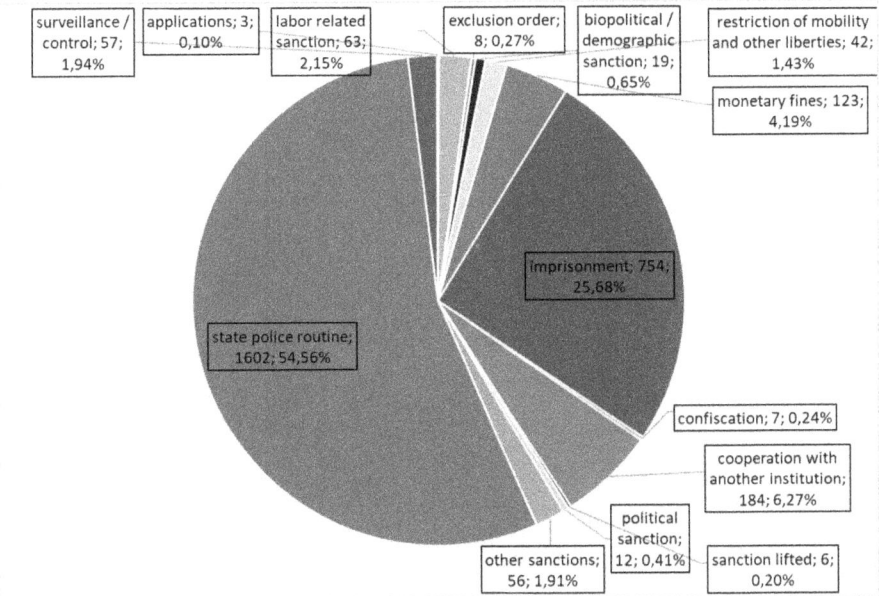

Figure 4.7: Sanction profile of the Sachverhalte related to endangerment of the state (n = 2,936). Graphic created by the author.

adjusting the degree of penalty—that is, the length of imprisonment or the size of fine. The combination of the few, rather simple elements available to the Nazi secret police ultimately resulted in multidimensional profiles of sanctions for different categories of *Sachverhalte*.

3.2.3 Fringe Cases

As fruitful as these systematic analyses of the Gestapo's sanction profiles are, other relevant characteristics of the Gestapo's ruling practices cannot be identified by such an approach. Rather, they have to be examined by diving deeper into the data of the digital replica using database queries, keyword-searches, or simply by browsing through the datasets. They are, however, no less important and therefore are the subject of the final step of the analysis undertaken in this chapter.

In the *Sachverhalte* of the Osnabrück Gestapo card index a total of 181 deaths are recorded. About half of them were the result of a sanction imposed by the Gestapo. In most cases, stories of victims of the Gestapo followed a similar pattern to that of the Russian forced laborer Iwan K. He had fled his workplace in

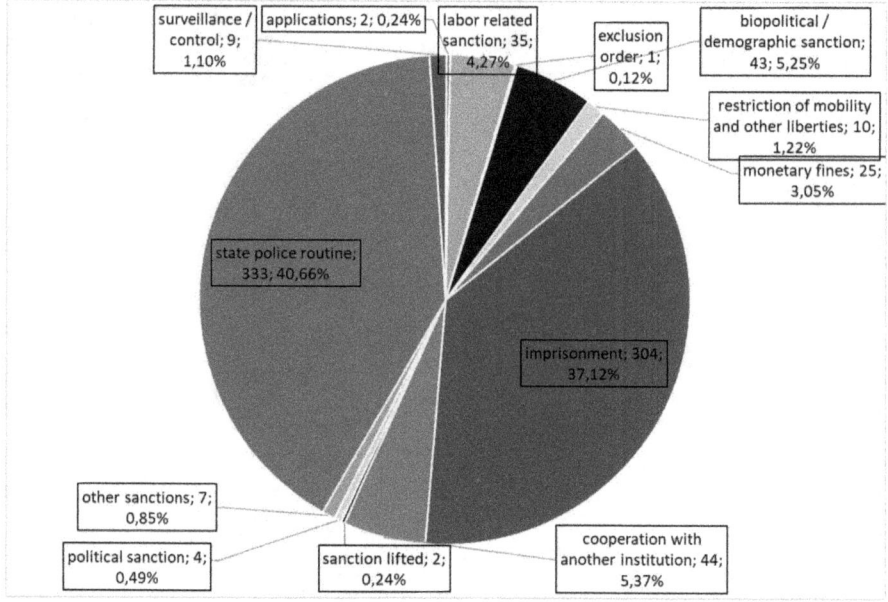

Figure 4.8: Sanction profile of the Sachverhalte related to Volksgemeinschaft (n = 819). Graphic created by the author.

July 1942 and was subsequently arrested and deported to Neuengamme concentration camp. There he died in December of the same year.[79] The Gestapo noted these incidents in a cold, administrative manner and thereby hid the evil nature of these killings behind what seemed to be linguistic banalities, allowing the Gestapo to distance itself from its own involvement and liability.

In other cases, the Gestapo was more directly responsible for the death of a person, and the biopolitical calculus behind the National Socialist *Volksgemeinschaft* becomes evident: On July 10, 1942, the Polish forced laborer Boleslaw W. was "auf Befehl des Reichsführers-SS in einem Waldstück in Andervenne erhängt"[80] (hanged by order of the Reichsführer-SS in the woods in Andervenne). According to the Gestapo, he had previously impregnated a German woman and had been examined to see whether he met the "Anforderungen für eine Eindeut-

---

[79] See NLA OS Rep 439 No. 20431 The index card for Kobjak is also interesting with regard to the Gestapo's knowledge production. The Gestapo did not create it until November 15, 1943—i.e., barely a year after the death of the person to whom it referred. The reason for this extraordinary phenomenon remains unclear.

[80] NLA OS Rep 439 No. 46234.

schung"[81] (requirements for Germanization). The *positive* result of this examination did not protect him from *Sonderbehandlung*—that is, his execution on the edge of a small village in eastern Emsland. For the expectant mother of the child, however, the result meant that she now had no choice but to carry the child and raise it without a father. After a shortened sentence, the RSHA ordered that, because of her circumstances, no further state police actions should be taken against her.[82] Here the Gestapo used its power to intervene violently in life plans in the name of an imagined *Volksgemeinschaft* and to decide who should die and who should live.

Another relevant finding concerns the standard period of imprisonment in an AEL imposed by the Gestapo. In late January 1944, the Gestapo apparently considered it necessary to tighten this punishment and extended the duration by one-third. While the Gestapo had previously punished forced laborers who dared to resist the system with six weeks of AEL imprisonment, the new norm was to impose a prison term of eight weeks.

In addition, for the period between February 1943 and May 1944, thirty-two *Sachverhalte* can be identified that report more severe treatments after an AEL detention. They describe that, following an AEL sentence, a person was transferred to a concentration camp. The index card of the Dutchman Pieter de Haas makes one of these incidents transparent: The Gestapo arrested him in September 1943 and interned him for six weeks in AEL Essen-Mühlheim. From there he managed to escape for a day before he was picked up again. As punishment for this, the Gestapo deported him to the Mauthausen concentration camp,[83] which was set up "für schwer belastete, insbesondere auch gleichzeitig kriminell vorbestrafte und asoziale, d.h. kaum noch erziehbare Schutzhäftlinge"[84] (for heavily incriminated and especially also previously convicted people and antisocials—that is, those who were deemed hardly responsive to Nazi re-education).

Whether de Haas is a typical case is unclear. On the other index cards the processes are not equally transparent. Twenty-three of the thirty-two *Sachverhalte* merely refer to an unspecified decree of the Head of Security Police and the Security Service from December 17, 1942 to justify the additional sanction.[85]

---

81 NLA OS Rep 439 No. 46234.
82 See NLA OS Rep 439 No. 41881.
83 NLA OS Rep 439 No. 13407.
84 Letter from head of the security police and the SD, Reinhard Heydrich, on the classification of concentration camps (January 2, 1941): http://germanhistorydocs.ghi-dc.org/docpage.cfm?docpage_id=2366 (accessed September 1, 2020).
85 For an example see NLA OS Rep 439 No. 25479.

These cases have in common that they all involved Dutch nationals who were deported to Buchenwald concentration camp after their AEL detention. This concentration camp of level II had been set up for *Schutzhäftlinge* who were "schwerer belastet, jedoch noch erziehungs- und besserungsfähig"[86] (more severely incriminated, but still educable and capable of improvement) and was thus intended for prisoners who were regarded less problematic than the prisoners in Mauthausen concentration camp. These twenty-three persons form only a small group, given the several hundred Dutch men and women whose presence as forced laborers in the district of Osnabrück can be verified by analyzing the card index of the Gestapo's Osnabrück Office. It remains unclear why only these few fell victim to more brutal penal practices of the Nazi disciplinary system.

Nevertheless, in all this—once again—the Gestapo's character as a *Weltanschauungsexekutive*[87] (ideological executive) becomes clear. The Gestapo used every sanction at its disposal to further implement the *Volksgemeinschaft* and to achieve the goals it considered necessary to it. At times, however, this ideological orientation also had the effect of mitigating punishment. Occasionally, the index cards contain *Sachverhalte* in which processes relevant to the state police were handled without mobilizing the disciplinary system. As a Catholic, Josef Möller from the town of Glane, for example, was bothered by the actions the Gestapo took in 1939 when it dissolved Catholic youth associations. He especially criticized the ban on singing church songs. While others were interrogated and warned by the Gestapo for religious statements of this kind, only a party court trial was initiated against Möller, who was a member of the National Socialist German Workers' Party (NSDAP). But even that trial was dismissed after Möller had formally apologized to his local NSDAP group leader.[88]

In other cases, the Gestapo forced gestures of ideological approval with what it called *voluntary donations* to the Nationalsozialistische Volkswohlfahrt (NSV) (National Socialist People's Welfare) and other party organizations, using them as an alternative to fines as a disciplinary tool. Hermann Evers, for example, who came from the southern district of Osnabrück, was forced by the Gestapo to make such a payment in order to dispel any remaining suspicion that might have remained after his contact with them. In the spring of 1940, he was accused of "sich einem Mieter seines Hauses gegenüber, in abfälliger Weise über die

---

[86] Letter from head of the security police and the SD, Reinhard Heydrich, on the classification of concentration camps (January 2, 1941): http://germanhistorydocs.ghi-dc.org/sub_document.cfm?document_id=1510 (accessed September 1, 2020).
[87] Mallmann and Paul, "Die Gestapo."
[88] See NLA OS Rep 439 No. 27964.

deutsche Luftwaffe und die wirtschaftlichen Verhältnisse Deutschlands geäussert zu haben"[89] (making derogatory remarks about the German Air Force and the economic situation in Germany to a tenant of his house). Although the Gestapo was not able to prove that Evers had committed a punishable offense, he nevertheless agreed to make a *voluntary donation* of 100 RM to the NSV after he endured a "verant.[wortlichen] Vernehmung und ernstliche Warnung"[90] (interrogation, in which he was held accountable, and a serious warning) and before he was released from Gestapo custody.[91]

In view of the sanctions described in the last two examples, however, it would be wrong to declare the ruling of the National Socialists arbitrary. Each time the underlying ideological motive was the same. The basis of every decision was the National Socialist *Volksgemeinschaft*.[92] With reference to this concept, the Gestapo judged deviant behavior, determined the level of appropriate punishment, and developed practices that followed certain rules. In this context Michael Wildt, in his interpretation of Ernst Fraenkel's theory of the National Socialist *dual state*, already pointed out that those who were thought of as members of the *Volksgemeinschaft* were systematically given privileged treatment by the Gestapo.[93] Often this privilege simply consisted of *only* being treated routinely by the state police and being spared a confrontation with the full force of the disciplinary system.

4 Conclusion—The Gestapo's Ruling Practices

Digital analysis of the card index of the Gestapo's Osnabrück Office has allowed us to identify some of the central ruling practices of the Nazi secret police. A prerequisite for the application of methods of Knowledge Discovery in Databases to the Gestapo's card index was its comprehensive digitization, in the course of which the entire records were transferred into a machine-readable form and stored in a relational research database. The availability of AI and other algorithms for reliable text extraction, increasing computing power, and the now relatively low hurdles in learning to use adequate analysis software make it possible even for historians who are not trained in computer sciences to apply such methods to large quantities of historical data.

---

89 NLA OS Rep 439 No. 9266.
90 NLA OS Rep 439 No. 9266.
91 See NLA OS Rep 439 No. 9266.
92 See Bondzio, "Doing 'Volksgemeinschaft.'"
93 See Wildt, *Die Ambivalenz des Volkes*, 276–78.

If, on top of that, historians also apply the historical-critical perspective to such stocks of historical data, they can develop elaborated and reflected access to the information in digitized collections of serial sources. The resulting knowledge regarding the institutional authorship of the Gestapo's card index then becomes the baseline and shapes the interpretation of the findings.

The awareness that arises from analyzing an official knowledge repository first lays bare the production of knowledge as a central ruling practice of the Nazi secret police itself, which became increasingly crucial. The comprehensive generation of knowledge repositories as a condition of the state's ability to use violence and thus as a prerequisite for the existence of the Nazi regime must be taken seriously. During the 12 years of Nazi rule, the political department of the Osnabrück Gestapo recorded *Sachverhalte* on personal index cards. In them it included the sanctions and the penalties it imposed. The analysis of these tens of thousands of records with the aim of identifying ruling practices was the main subject of this article.

In the approximately 33,000 *Sachverhalte* noted by the political department in Osnabrück, almost 20,000 sanctions were recorded. Overall, nearly half of the Political Police's index cards contain one or more sanctions. Compared with the Gestapo's predecessor, the Political Police of the Weimar State Security, which primarily recorded activities and observations on the index cards, but rarely took action itself,[94] this proportion was extremely high. Through the sanctions and especially through the *staatspolizeiliche Routinen* (routines of the state police), the Gestapo considerably boosted its presence in the Osnabrück administrative district and, throughout the entire Third Reich, was able to project its power into all parts of society.

These routine sanctions were always based on a presumption of guilt, where suspects were treated as if their accountability was already proven. This made the Gestapo, equipped with its extensive power, a terrible and above all unpredictable institution for its victims. In the face of an overwhelming state power, that claimed to know everything on the basis of a secret and inscrutable information technology—that is, the card index system—people were aware of their own deviant thoughts and could easily lose confidence in the accuracy of their own statements. Unsettled in this manner, people under suspicion had to justify themselves in the Gestapo's interrogations.

In the victims' individual contact with the Gestapo, the patterns and regularities that existed in the actions of the Nazi secret police remained hidden from sight. It is only today, when we are able to take a digitally supported look into

---

94 See Bondzio and Rass, "Data Driven History," 227–28.

a largely complete stock of Gestapo process-generated sources handed down to us, that we can highlight these ruling practices *ex post* and improve our understanding of the mechanisms of National Socialism by examining this mass source provided by the Gestapo. Analyzing the card index reveals that the treatment by the Gestapo, which was experienced by individuals as arbitrary and often as traumatic, on the side of the Secret State Police was subject to certain regularities and was driven by the fanatical motivation of a totalitarian ideological formation of society.

In order to implement the core element of the National Socialist ideology, the *Volksgemeinschaft*, as a *Weltanschauungsexekutive*, the Gestapo did not work alone. It operated its own investigative network and, at least until 1944, was also closely connected to other National Socialist institutions in a disciplinary system. The Nazi regime had created this system to discipline both the members of the *Volksgemeinschaft* and those who were thought of as excluded, but whose labor was needed. The support of this disciplinary system enabled the Nazi secret police to concentrate efficiently on a limited range of tasks and, beyond that, to rely on its cooperation with other institutions. The institutions of the National Socialist disciplinary society were massively expanded between 1933 and 1945, and at the same time new practices were created. The insight into this *division of labor of Nazi terror* as a ruling practice calls for a more network-like thinking regarding the Nazi state system and its institutions for a better understanding of its functioning.

This is also supported by the findings of the temporal differentiation of the sanctions and the analysis of the secret police's sanctions' profiles. Taken together, the findings from both steps of the investigation emphasize the dynamics of the Nazis' practices of punishment and rule. Depending on the imagined relation of a *Sachverhalt* to the *Volksgemeinschaft*, the Gestapo sanctioned differently and imposed various sanctions with varying degrees of frequency in certain phases of the Nazi rule.

Ultimately the analysis reveals that, through its own repository of knowledge, the Gestapo presents itself as a secret police force that was very aware of the frightening and intimidating effect of its actions. People disappeared for several hours, days, weeks, and sometimes forever without trial and without constitutional control in a nontransparent system of institutions. Neither the victims themselves nor their relatives knew what would happen to them. Slavoj Žižek recently stated about the practices of the current Chinese government: "This protracted period of silence delivers the key message: power is exerted in an impenetrable way where nothing has to be proven. Legal reasoning comes in distant second when this basic message is delivered."[95] With this, he—unintentionally but aptly—described one of the core functions of the sanctions imposed by the National Socialists: The ripple effect of communication about the Gestapo's actions and the disciplinary system confirmed the Gestapo's public image created by Nazi propaganda. This effect was part of the Gestapo's reckoning of power and was able to discipline far more people than the Gestapo could get in touch with directly. This way, one could say, the Gestapo's terror did not reign, its terror paralyzed.

Bibliography

Bade, Claudia. *"Die Mitarbeit der gesamten Bevölkerung ist erforderlich!": Denunziation und Instanzen sozialer Kontrolle am Beispiel des Regierungsbezirks Osnabrück 1933 bis 1949.* Osnabrücker Geschichtsquellen und Forschungen 50. Osnabrück: self-published, 2009.

Bade, Claudia. "Die Osnabrücker Gestapo-Kartei." *Historical Social Research / Historische Sozialforschung* 26, no. 2/3 (96/97) (2001): 235–38.

Bondzio, Sebastian. "Doing 'Volksgemeinschaft': Wissensproduktion und Ordnungshandeln der Gestapo." In Geschichte und Gesellschaft (forthcoming in 2021).

Bondzio, Sebastian. *Soldatentod und Durchhaltebereitschaft: Eine Stadtgesellschaft im Ersten Weltkrieg.* Krieg in der Geschichte 113. Leiden: Brill, 2020.

Bondzio, Sebastian, and Christoph Rass. "Allmächtig, allwissend, allgegenwärtig: Die Osnabrücker Gestapo Kartei als Massendatenspeicher und Weltmodell." *Osnabrücker Mitteiluneng* 124 (2019): 223–60.

Bondzio, Sebastian, and Christoph Rass. "Data Driven History: Methodische Überlegungen zur Osnabrücker Gestapo-Kartei als Quelle zur Erforschung datenbasierter Herrschaft." *Archiv-Nachrichten Niedersachsen* 22 (2018): 124–38.

Dams, Carsten, and Michael Stolle. *Die Gestapo: Herrschaft und Terror im Dritten Reich.* Munich: Beck, 2012.

Deleuze, Gilles, Félix Guattari, and Dagmar Berger. *Rhizom.* Internationale marxistische Diskussion 67. Berlin: Merve-Verl., 1977.

Dohmen, Herbert. *Denunziert: Jeder tut mit; Jeder denkt nach; Jeder meldet.* Vienna: Czernin, 2003.

Dördelmann, Katrin. *Die Macht der Worte: Denunziationen im nationalsozialistischen Köln.* Schriften des NS-Dokumentationszentrums der Stadt Köln 4. Cologne: Emons, 1997.

Eichler, Volker. "Die Frankfurter Gestapo-Kartei: Entstehung, Struktur, Funktion, Überlieferungsgeschichte und Quellenwert." In *Die Gestapo: Mythos und Realität.* Edited by Gerhard Paul and Klaus-Michael Mallmann, 178–99. Darmstadt: Primus, 2003.

Fayyad, Usama. "Data Mining and Knowledge Discovery in Databases: Implications for Scientific Databases." In *9th International Conference on Scientific and Statistical Database Management: Proceedings August 11–13, 1997, Olympia, Washington.* Edited by Yannis Ioannidis and David Hansen, 2–11. Piscataway, NJ: IEEE, 2000.

---

95 Slavoj Žižek, *Pandemic! Covid-19 Shakes the World* (New York: Polity Press, 2020), 8.

Foucault, Michel. *Die Ordnung der Dinge*. Frankfurt am Main: Suhrkamp, 2003.
Gellately, Robert. "Allwissend und Allgegenwärtig? Entstehung, Funktion und Wandel des Gestapo-Mythos." In *Die Gestapo: Mythos und Realität*. Edited by Gerhard Paul and Klaus-Michael Mallmann, 47–72. Darmstadt: Primus, 2003.
Giddens, Anthony. *Die Konstitution der Gesellschaft: Grundzüge einer Theorie der Strukturierung*. Frankfurt am Main: Campus, 1984.
Good, Irving John. "The Philosophy of Exploratory Data Analysis." *Philosophy of Science* 50, no. 2 (1983): 283–95.
Goschler, Constantin, Christopher Krichberg, and Jens Wegener. "Sicherheit, Demokratie und Transparenz. Elektronische Verbundsyseme in der Bundesrepublik und den USA in den 1970er und 1980er Jahren." In *Wege in die digitale Gesellschaft. Computernutzung in der Bundesrepublik*, edited by Frank Bösch, 64–85. Göttingen: Wallstein, 2018.
Grotum, Thomas, ed. *Die Gestapo Trier: Beiträge zur Geschichte einer regionalen Verfolgungsbehörde*. Cologne: Böhlau Verlag, 2018.
Gruchmann, Lothar. *Justiz im Dritten Reich 1933–1940: Anpassung und Unterwerfung in der Ära Gürtner*. Oldenbourg Geschichte 6–2010. Munich: Oldenbourg Wissenschaftsverlag, 2009.
Haase, Lena. "Die Gestapo in der Gesellschaft: Quellenlage und Forschungsfelder zur Geschichte Der Staatspolizeistelle Trier." In *Die Gestapo Trier: Beiträge zur Geschichte einer regionalen Verfolgungsbehörde*. Edited by Thomas Grotum, 23–61. Cologne: Böhlau Verlag, 2018.
Hall, Claire M. "An Army of Spies? The Gestapo Spy Network 1933–1945." *Journal of Contemporary History* 44, no. 2 (2009): 247–65.
Herbert, Ulrich, Karin Orth, and Christoph Dieckmann. "Die Nationalsozialistischen Konzentrationslager: Geschichte, Erinnerung, Forschung." In *Die Nationalsozialistischen Konzentrationslager: Entwicklung und Struktur*. Edited by Ulrich Herbert, Karin Orth, and Christoph Dieckmann, 17–41. Göttingen: Wallstein, 1995.
Hesse, Klaus, and Andrej Angrick, eds. *Topographie des Terrors: Gestapo, SS und Reichssicherheitshauptamt in der Wilhelm- und Prinz-Albrecht-Straße; eine Dokumentation; Katalogband zur gleichnamigen Präsentation*. 3rd ed. Berlin: Stiftung Topographie des Terrors, 2010.
Hoffschild, Rainer. *Die Verfolgung der Homosexuellen in der NS-Zeit: Zahlen und Schicksale aus Norddeutschland*. Berlin: Verlag Rosa Winkel, 1999.
Jochmann, Justus. "Abwehr: Die nachrichtendienstliche Tätigkeit der Abteilung III der Staatspolizeistelle Trier am Beispiel Luxemburgs." In *Die Gestapo Trier: Beiträge zur Geschichte einer regionalen Verfolgungsbehörde*. Edited by Thomas Grotum, 203–24. Cologne: Böhlau Verlag, 2018.
Kirchberg, Christopher. "'… Die Elektronisch erzeugte Schuldvermutung?' Die Auseinandersetzung um das 'Nachrichtendienstliche Informationssystem' Des Bundesamtes für Verfassungsschutz." In *Welche "Wirklichkeit" und Wessen "Wahrheit"? Das Geheimdienstarchiv als Quelle und Medium der Wissensproduktion*. Edited by Thomas Großbölting and Sabine Kittel, 125–48. Göttingen: Vandenhoeck & Ruprecht, 2019.
Kitchin, Rob. "Big Data, New Epistemologies and Paradigm Shifts." *Big Data & Society* 1, no. 1 (2014): 1–12.

Klormann, Felix. "'Eindeutschungs-Polen' im SS-Sonderlager/Konzentrationslager Hinzert: Zur Praxis des 'Wiedereindeutschungsverfahrens.'" In *Die Gestapo Trier: Beiträge zur Geschichte einer regionalen Verfolgungsbehörde*. Edited by Thomas Grotum, 115–28. Cologne: Böhlau Verlag, 2018.

Konitzer, Werner, ed. *Moralisierung des Rechts: Kontinuitäten und Diskontinuitäten Nationalsozialistischer Normativität*. Frankfurt: Campus, 2014.

Lässig, Simone. "The History of Knowledge and the Expansion of the Historical Research Agenda." *Bulletin of the German Historical Institute* 59 (2016): 29–58.

Löw, Andrea. *Die Verfolgung und Ermordung der europäischen Juden durch das nationalsozialistische Deutschland 1933–1945*. Vol. 3, *Deutsches Reich und Protektorat September 1939–September 1941*. Munich: Oldenbourg Wissenschaftsverlag, 2012.

Mallmann, Klaus-Michael, and Gerhard Paul. "Die Gestapo: Weltanschauungsexekutive mit gesellschaftlichem Rückhalt." In *Die Gestapo im Zweiten Weltkrieg: 'Heimatfront' und besetztes Europa*. Edited by Gerhard Paul and Klaus-Michael Mallmann, 599–650. Darmstadt: Primus, 2000.

Marx, Henry. *Die Verwaltung des Ausnahmezustands: Wissensgenerierung und Arbeitskräftelenkung im Nationalsozialismus*. Göttingen: Wallstein, 2019.

Pauer-Studer, Herlinde, and Julian Fink, eds. *Rechtfertigungen des Unrechts: Das Rechtsdenken im Nationalsozialismus in Originaltexten*. Berlin: Suhrkamp, 2014.

Paul, Gerhard, and Klaus-Michael Mallmann, eds. *Die Gestapo: Mythos und Realität*. Darmstadt: Primus, 2003.

Rass, Christoph. *'Menschenmaterial': Deutsche Soldaten an der Ostfront. Innenansichten einer Infanteriedivision 1939–1945*. Paderborn: Ferdinand Schöningh, 2003.

Reeken, Dietmar von, and Malte Thießen, eds. *'Volksgemeinschaft' als Soziale Praxis: Neue Forschungen zur NS-Gesellschaft vor Ort*. Paderborn: Ferdinand Schöningh, 2013.

Reeken, Dietmar von, and Malte Thießen. "'Volksgemeinschaft' als Soziale Praxis? Perspektiven und Potenziale neuer Forschungen vor Ort." In Dietmar von Reeken and Malte Thießen, eds. *'Volksgemeinschaft' als Soziale Praxis: Neue Forschungen zur NS-Gesellschaft vor Ort*, 9–33. Paderborn: Ferdinand Schöningh, 2013.

Reichardt, Sven. "Einführung: Überwachungsgeschichte(n): Facetten Eines Forschungsfeldes." *Geschichte und Gesellschaft* 42, no. 1 (2016): 5–33.

Reiter, Raimond. "'Heimtücke' und 'Volksschädlinge': Osnabrücker vor dem Sondergericht Hannover in der NS-Zeit." *Osnabrücker Mitteilungen* 103 (1998): 267–77.

Reuband, Karl-Heinz. "Denunziation im Dritten Reich: Die Bedeutung von Systemunterstützung und Gelegenheitsstrukturen." *Historical Social Research* 26, no. 2 (2001): 219–34.

Rockenmaier, Dieter W. *Denunzianten: 47 Fallgeschichten aus den Akten der Gestapo im NS-Gau Mainfranken*. Würzburg: Richter, 1998.

Roth, Thomas. "Die Gestapo Köln: Ansätze weiterer Forschung. Überlegungen zu einem Projekt des NS-Dokumentationszentrums der Stadt Köln." *Geschichte in Köln* 63, no. 1 (2016): 245–57.

Vogel, Jakob. "Von der Wissenschafts- zur Wissensgeschichte: Für eine Historisierung der 'Wissensgesellschaft.'" *Geschichte und Gesellschaft* 30, no. 4 (2004): 639–60.

Wagner, Herbert. *Die Gestapo war nicht allein: Politische Sozialkontrolle und Staatsterror im Deutsch-Niederländischen Grenzgebiet 1929–1945*. Anpassung – Selbstbehauptung – Widerstand 22. Münster: LIT, 2004.

Weitkamp, Sebastian. "Die Kartei der Politischen Polizei / Gestapo-Stelle Osnabrück 1929–1945." *Niedersächsisches Jahrbuch für Landesgeschichte* 89 (2017): 107–28.
Welskopp, Thomas. "Die Dualität von Struktur und Handeln: Anthony Giddens Strukturierungstheorie als 'Praxeologischer' Ansatz in der Geschichtswissenschaft." In *Struktur und Ereignis*. Edited by Andreas Suter and Manfred Hetting, 99–119. Geschichte und Gesellschaft Sonderheft 19. Göttingen: Vandenhoeck & Ruprecht, 2001.
Wildt, Michael. *Die Ambivalenz des Volkes: Der Nationalsozialismus Als Gesellschaftsgeschichte*. Berlin: Suhrkamp, 2019.
Wildt, Michael. "'Volksgemeinschaft' – Eine Zwischenbilanz." In Dietmar von Reeken and Malte Thießen, eds. *'Volksgemeinschaft' als Soziale Praxis: Neue Forschungen zur NS-Gesellschaft vor Ort*, 355–69. Paderborn: Ferdinand Schöningh, 2013.
Žižek, Slavoj. *Pandemic! Covid-19 Shakes the World*. New York: Polity Press, 2020.

Mark Dang-Anh and Stefan Scholl
Chapter 5
Digital Discourse Analysis of Language Use under National Socialism: Methodological Reflections and Applications

German Summary: Dieses Kapitel lotet Möglichkeiten und Methoden aus, digitale Diskursanalysen nationalsozialistischer Quellentexte durchzuführen. Digitale Technologie wird dabei als heuristisches Werkzeug betrachtet, mit dem der Sprachgebrauch während des Nationalsozialismus im Rahmen größerer Quellenkorpora untersucht werden kann. In einem theoretischen Abschnitt wird grundsätzlich dafür plädiert, während des Analyseprozesses hermeneutisches Sinnverstehen mit breitflächigen korpusbasierten Abfragen zu kombinieren. Verdeutlicht wird diese Herangehensweise an zwei empirischen Beispielen: Anhand eines Korpus von Hitler- und Goebbels-Reden wird dem Auftauchen und der diskursiven Ausgestaltung des nationalsozialistischen Konzepts „Lebensraum" nachgespürt. Schritt für Schritt wird offengelegt, welche Analysewege durch das Abfragen von Schlüsseltexten, Keywords, Konkordanzen und Kollokationen verfolgt werden können. Das zweite Beispiel zeigt anhand von Eingaben, die aus der Bevölkerung an Staats- und Parteiinstanzen gerichtet wurden, wie solche Quellen mithilfe eines digitalen Tools manuell annotiert werden können, um sie danach auf Musterhaftigkeiten im Sprachgebrauch hin auswerten zu können.

1 Introduction

Researchers who investigate the way in which people under National Socialism used language, both spoken and written, to communicate in different situations are confronted with a vast and heterogenous mass of sources and data. Of course, management and evaluation of corpora have always been key requirements of the research process both in historiography and in linguistics. However, with new digital research tools and applications novel possibilities and challenges have arisen.[1] This is especially true for a thematic field that has been given

---

[1] See Andreas Fickers, "Update für die Hermeneutik. Geschichtswissenschaft auf dem Weg zur digitalen Forensik?," *Zeithistorische Forschungen/Studies in Contemporary History* 17, no. 1 (2020), accessed July 6, 2020, doi: https://doi.org/10.14765/zzf.dok-1765.

OpenAccess. © 2022 Mark Dang-Anh and Stefan Scholl, published by De Gruyter. This work is licensed under the Creative Commons Attribution 4.0 International License.
https://doi.org/10.1515/9783110714692-007

attention since the early post-war years: from Victor Klemperer's *LTI*,[2] to Dolf Sternberger, Gerhard Storz and Wilhelm Süskind's *Wörterbuch des Unmenschen*,[3] Cornelia Schmitz-Berning's *Vokabular des Nationalsozialismus*,[4] and more recent research.[5] While all these studies contributed to a deeper understanding of the lexicographic and rhetorical characteristics of National Socialist discourses, they seldomly were able to grasp the pragmatics of language use in different communicative situations by different actors during National Socialism. Moreover, for the most part they did not dispose over the technological means of digitally treating and analyzing larger text-corpora.

In the following article, we would like to present methods and strategies of analysis developed within the framework of the research project *Sprachliche Sozialgeschichte 1933 bis 1945* (Linguistic Social History 1933 to 1945), situated at the Leibniz Institute for the German Language, Mannheim. Broadly outlined, the aim of this project is to examine linguistic practices and patterns of language use of various actors during the Third Reich.[6] Thus, it is taken into account that the German society of the years between 1933 and 1945 consisted of heterogeneous communities of practice, speaking, and writing under the specific discourse conditions of National Socialism.[7] Also, it is argued that the specificities and characteristics of different media, texts types, and communicative situations

---

[2] Victor Klemperer, *LTI. Notizbuch eines Philologen* [1947] (Stuttgart: Reclam, 2018).

[3] Dolf Sternberger, Gerhard Storz, and Wilhelm E. Süskind, *Aus dem Wörterbuch des Unmenschen* (Hamburg: Claassen, 1957).

[4] Cornelia Schmitz-Berning, *Vokabular des Nationalsozialismus* (Berlin: De Gruyter, 1998).

[5] See for example Utz Maas, "Als der Geist der Gemeinschaft eine Sprache fand". *Sprache im Nationalsozialismus, Versuch einer historischen Argumentationsanalyse* (Opladen: Westdeutscher Verlag, 1984); Gerhard Bauer, *Sprache und Sprachlosigkeit im "Dritten Reich"* (Cologne: Bund-Verlag, 1990); Christian A. Braun, *Nationalsozialistischer Sprachstil. Theoretischer Zugang und praktische Analysen auf der Grundlage einer pragmatisch-textlinguistisch orientierten Stilistik* (Heidelberg: Winter, 2007); Horst Dieter Schlosser, *Sprache unterm Hakenkreuz. Eine andere Geschichte des Nationalsozialismus* (Cologne: Böhlau, 2013). For an enlarged overview over the research field, see Stefan Scholl, "Für eine Sprach- und Kommunikationsgeschichte des Nationalsozialismus. Ein programmatischer Forschungsüberblick," *Archiv für Sozialgeschichte* 59 (2019): 409–44.

[6] See Heidrun Kämper, "Sprachliche Sozialgeschichte 1933 bis 1945 – ein Projektkonzept," in *Sprachliche Sozialgeschichte des Nationalsozialismus*, ed. Heidrun Kämper and Britt-Marie Schuster (Bremen: Hempen Verlag, 2018), 9–25. We thank the German Research Foundation (DFG) for funding the project.

[7] See Geraldine Horan, "'Er zog sich die "neue Sprache" des "Dritten Reiches" über wie ein Kleidungsstück': Communities of Practice and Performativity in National Socialist Discourse," *Linguistik Online* 30, no. 1 (2007): 57–80, accessed June 13, 2020, doi: https://doi.org/10.13092/lo.30.549.

have to be analytically considered. A linguistic practice is conceived as both evidence and constituent of a social practice if it is in some way repeatable and recognizable by both the participants at the time of its processing and the analysts at a later stage. Therefore, it is not only necessary to hermeneutically reconstruct meanings in various media, for example different kinds of letters, diaries, and protocols, but also to identify possible overarching patterns of language use with the help of digital corpus technology. As we will argue, corpus technology can serve as a tool for *heuristic explorations of corpora* within the framework of digital discourse analysis. The aim here, to be clear, is not to treat digital possibilities and means of analysis as ends in themselves, but to look for ways to fit these possibilities and means into analytical processes according to the research question and the data at hand.

In the following sections, we will illustrate two methodological approaches paving the way through the digitally guided and/or assisted research process. The first case can be classified as a top-down approach and will show how corpus linguistics can be used for heuristic explorations within a digital discourse analysis based on a large number of texts (section 3). The second case takes rather the form of a bottom-up approach and highlights one specific way manual digital annotation can be applied to historical sources (section 4). Initially, though, we would like to briefly introduce the theoretical and methodological background of our approach (section 2).

2 Analysis of Historical Language Use in Its Societal and Political Context—Digital Discourse Analysis and Hermeneutics

In his introduction to discourse analysis within the field of history, Achim Landwehr summarizes the criticism brought against structuralist linguistics as follows: "Above all, Saussure's preference for the *langue* over the *parole* as the object of linguistics led to a de-historicization, de-socialization and de-politicization of the study of language."[8] Even if he falls for the "Cours myth" which does

---

8 Achim Landwehr, *Historische Diskursanalyse*, 2nd impr. (Frankfurt am Main: Campus, 2009): 47 [all translations from German to English done by the authors]. Saussure is usually received in such a way that *langue* refers to structural aspects of language, while *parole* refers to the actual use of language. As a result of a reading of Saussure's work, which Landwehr also reproduces here, a structuralist view of the *langue* dominated in linguistics (but see footnote 5), while linguistic currents towards the *parole* formed with the pragmatic turn from the 1960s onwards. If

not do justice to the authentic lectures of de Saussure,[9] Landwehr justifiably suggests the need to examine historicity, sociality, and politicality with respect to their linguistic construction. A similar proposition has already been made by Dietrich Busse in his version of Historical Semantics that we loosely follow here.[10]

Historical Semantics according to Busse goes beyond a history of concepts and aims at a history of discourse which examines communicatively constructed realities by their linguistic means of constitution and unveils them by detailed discourse analysis.[11] Our approach is thus anchored in the premise that language and, more specifically, language use are constitutive for historical, political, and social realities. Such a language-focused view on history is primarily interested in the linguistic production of meaning and conceives "history of meaning as the history of communicatively constructed meaning."[12] As such, Historical Seman-

---

one is inclined to conceive of the described, very roughly, as two sides, the research presented here is positioned on the pragmatic side of linguistics.

9 Ferdinand de Saussure's main work, the *Cours de linguistique générale*—often conceived as the founding work of modern linguistics—was composed by Bally and Sechehaye who did not attend the original lectures, see Ludwig Jäger, "Mythos Cours. Saussures Sprachidee und die Gründungslegende des Strukturalismus," in *Strukturalismus, heute: Brüche, Spuren, Kontinuitäten: Abhandlungen zur Literaturwissenschaft*, ed. Martin Endres and Leonhard Herrmann (Stuttgart: J.B. Metzler, 2018), 11–28; on the criticism of de Saussure see Wolfgang Teubert, "Corpus Linguistics: An Alternative," *semen* 27 (2009): 1–25, accessed July 3, 2020, doi: 10.4000/semen.8912.
10 See Dietrich Busse, *Historische Semantik. Analyse eines Programms* (Stuttgart: Klett-Cotta, 1987); Dietrich Busse and Wolfgang Teubert, "Ist Diskurs ein sprachwissenschaftliches Objekt? Zur Methodenfrage der historischen Semantik," in *Begriffsgeschichte und Diskursgeschichte. Methodenfragen und Forschungsergebnisse der historischen Semantik*, ed. Dietrich Busse, Fritz Hermanns, and Wolfgang Teubert (Opladen: Westdeutscher Verlag, 1994), 10–28. We limit this discussion to Busse's notion of Historical Semantics and Hermanns's understanding of Linguistic Hermeneutics as starting points. However, the use of corpus linguistics as a heuristic tool for discourse analysis as applied in this work is practiced under various labels, such as Corpus Pragmatics (see Karin Aijmer and Christoph Rühlemann *Corpus Pragmatics: A Handbook* [Cambridge: Cambridge University Press, 2015]; Ekkehard Felder, Marcus Müller, and Friedemann Vogel, *Korpuspragmatik: Thematische Korpora als Basis diskurslinguistischer Analysen* [Berlin: De Gruyter, 2012]) or Corpus Assisted Discourse Studies (CADS, see Alan Partington, Alison Duguid, and Charlotte Taylor, *Patterns and Meanings in Discourse: Theory and Practice in Corpus-Assisted Discourse Studies (CADS)* [Amsterdam: John Benjamins, 2013]). For a recent summary see the articles in Charlotte Taylor and Anna Marchi, *Corpus Approaches to Discourse: A Critical Review* (London: Routledge, 2018).
11 See Dietrich Busse, "Begriffsgeschichte oder Diskursgeschichte? Zu theoretischen Grundlagen und Methodenfragen einer historisch-semantischen Epistemologie," in *Herausforderungen der Begriffsgeschichte*, ed. Carsten Dutt (Heidelberg: Winter, 2003), 17–38.
12 Busse, *Historische Semantik*, 105.

tics as the study of the changing meaning of words, concepts, and phrases through time has always been an empirical undertaking based on predefined corpora.[13] The pragmatic approach of Historical Semantics[14] we tend to follow here combines such an empiricism with analytical processes of hermeneutical understanding.

Quite commonly, hermeneutics is conceived as the "art of understanding."[15] Fritz Hermanns extends this notion by considering hermeneutics as a technique and method of linguistic analysis.[16] He claims that language use is always a linguistic interplay—a language game in the Wittgensteinian sense[17]—of "giving something to understand" and "understanding."[18] Thus, meaning is at the heart of any interactive and communicative situation. As a consequence, this definition also directly affects the hermeneutical analysis of the constitution of meaning, since understanding is crucial not only for the first level of language use at the time of its processing, but also for investigations of the second level in which linguistic manifestations of meaning become textual data in the framework of

---

13 See Busse and Teubert, "Ist Diskurs"; Wolfgang Teubert, "Korpuslinguistik, Hermeneutik und die soziale Konstruktion der Wirklichkeit," *Linguistik online* 28, no. 3 (2006), accessed July 3, 2020, doi: https://doi.org/10.13092/lo.28.610; Gerd Fritz, "Historische Semantik – einige Schlaglichter," *Jahrbuch für Germanistische Sprachgeschichte* 2 (2011): 1–19, accessed July 3, 2020, doi: 10.1515/9783110236620.1.
14 Fritz distinguishes two types of semantic theories that are advocated in Historical Semantics: cognitive and pragmatic semantics, see Fritz, "Historische Semantik," 2 ff.
15 See Fritz Hermanns, "Linguistische Hermeneutik. Überlegungen zur überfälligen Einrichtung eines in der Linguistik bislang fehlenden Teilfachs," in *Der Sitz der Sprache im Leben: Beiträge zu einer kulturanalytischen Linguistik*, ed. Heidrun Kämper, Angelika Linke, and Martin Wengeler (Berlin: De Gruyter, 2012), 71.
16 See Hermanns, "Linguistische Hermeneutik," 71 ff.
17 See Ludwig Wittgenstein, *Philosophische Untersuchungen* (Frankfurt am Main: Suhrkamp, 1971 [1953]). In his *Philosophische Untersuchungen* (PU, "Philosophical Investigations"), Wittgenstein develops a theory of the use of language. He can be read as a pioneer of a praxeologically oriented linguistics based on pragmatics, which regards language as action and as always interwoven with certain activities (see PU 7). Accordingly, language games are to be understood as linguistic practices which on the one hand follow rules, but on the other hand alter them by linguistic regularity. Accordingly, linguistic practices are characterized by conventionality and comprehensibility as well as by flexibility and creativity.
18 See Hermanns, "Linguistische Hermeneutik," 68. It is hard to translate the compound phrase "*Zu-verstehen-Geben.*" In everyday language it means that someone indicates or insinuates something. Here, however, Hermanns points out the more fundamental meaning that what is spoken or written must always be understood and therefore be rendered intelligible.

linguistic analysis.[19] Even on this second level, understanding entails semiotic, social, and processual aspects which must be methodologically reflected upon. As a general premise, understanding must always be conceived as preliminary. For Hermanns, therefore, hermeneutics means the "searching and groping, rehearsing and revision-ready effort of understanding, always willing to let itself be corrected."[20] While understanding is a cognitive process that is not directly accessible to us, explaining understanding is a communicative practice in itself and, following Hermanns, can be called interpreting. In discourse analysis, analytically relevant interpreting is thus a methodically guided and intersubjectively negotiated understanding. We argue that interpretation plays a crucial role at every stage of the research process and that the outcome of a digital discourse analysis is always determined by an interpretive, hermeneutic reflection of individual (micro)decisions on the path of analysis. In the following, we will illustrate these basic assumptions by focusing on two different ways to approach a digitally conducted discourse analysis. While the first part examines the concept of 'Lebensraum' in a corpus of National Socialist speeches, the second part will focus on letters of complaint and the potential which goes along with their digital annotation.

3 The Concept of *'Lebensraum'* in National Socialist Speeches

Our initial research question is: How was the concept of *'Lebensraum'* linguistically constructed under National Socialism by central spokespersons of the Nazi regime?[21] We assume that National Socialist key concepts were explicitly constituted particularly in political speeches. Therefore, we choose these sources as an entry-point for the investigation of the linguistic construction of the concept of *'Lebensraum.'* Again, this is a result of hermeneutic reflection. Referring back

---

19 See Alfred Schütz, "Concept and Theory Formation in the Social Sciences," *The Journal of Philosophy* 51, no. 9 (1954): 257–73, who differentiates between construction of the first and second degree.
20 Fritz Hermanns, "Diskurshermeneutik," in *Diskurslinguistik nach Foucault. Theorie und Gegenstände*, ed. Ingo Warnke (Berlin: De Gruyter, 2007), 188.
21 The concept of 'living space' is only used here as an example. We therefore refrain from a deeper examination of the manifold historical-scientific literature on this topic, but see Karl Lange, "Der Terminus 'Lebensraum' in Hitlers 'Mein Kampf,'" *Vierteljahrshefte für Zeitgeschichte* 13, no. 4 (1965): 426–37; Ulrike Jureit, *Das Ordnen von Räumen. Territorium und Lebensraum im 19. und 20. Jahrhundert* (Hamburg: Hamburger Edition, 2012).

to our preliminary remarks, we have to keep in mind that understanding and interpreting are fundamental principles in selecting data and building corpora:

> Discursive relationships can only be ascertained once a criterion for corpus building has been established. Whatever this criterion may be, it presupposes knowledge of the content of the texts in question. From this point of view, corpus building alone presupposes an understanding of the texts. Corpus building, i.e. the constitution of a discursive unit as a prospective object of investigation in linguistics, is therefore based on acts of interpretation.[22]

Concepts are established through conceptualization practices. By conceptualization we understand the context-dependent, discursive constitution of meaning in conversations and texts through lexical discourse elements.[23] We therefore hold that the lexical discourse elements of a concept must necessarily be analyzed in their discursive context, an assumption that will become methodologically important. As Nina Kalwa suggests, we have to zoom in and out of corpora and texts and oscillate between distant and close reading to comprehend the meaning of concepts and their linguistic constitution at different levels of granularity.[24] The adequate consideration of the binding of the lexical constitution of conceptual meaning to the co(n)texts of use is ensured in the presented analysis by a sequential combination of methods, which proceeds through the steps of keyword analysis, analysis of lexical dispersion, collocation analysis, to concordance analysis. Our corpus of speeches consists of about one thousand speeches from Adolf Hitler and Joseph Goebbels held between 1925 and 1945 and contains about 1.6 million tokens.[25]

---

[22] Busse and Teubert, "Ist Diskurs," 16.
[23] See Heidrun Kämper, *Aspekte des Demokratiediskurses der späten 1960er Jahre: Konstellationen, Kontexte, Konzepte* (Berlin: De Gruyter, 2012); Nina Kalwa, "Die Konstitution von Konzepten in Diskursen: Zoom als Methode der diskurslinguistischen Bedeutungsanalyse," in *Sprach(kritik)kompetenz als Mittel demokratischer Willensbildung. Sprachliche In- und Exklusionsstrategien als gesellschaftliche Herausforderung*, ed. Jürgen Schiewe, Thomas Niehr, and Sandro M. Moraldo (Bremen: Hempen Verlag, 2019).
[24] Kalwa, "Die Konstitution." Also see Silke Schwandt, "Digitale Methoden für die Historische Semantik. Auf den Spuren von Begriffen in digitalen Korpora," *Geschichte und Gesellschaft* 44 (2018): 107–34.
[25] A *token* is the smallest unit of a corpus—e.g., words, numbers, abbreviations, or punctuation—depending on the tokenization method. Tokenization—i.e., identifying units of analysis—is thus part of the pre-processing of texts for corpus linguistic analyses. The speeches are taken from De Gruyter, *Nationalsozialismus, Holocaust, Widerstand und Exil 1933–1945. Deutsche Geschichte im 20. Jahrhundert Online*. Online-Datenbank, accessed July 3, 2020, https://www.degruyter.com/view/db/dghfo.

3.1 Keywords

We start with a general view on the corpus in comparison to a reference corpus.[26] A statistical method from corpus linguistics to compare one corpus with another is the computing of *keywords:* "Keywords are words that are considerably more frequent in one corpus than in another corpus; we can therefore say that keywords are words that are typical of the corpus of interest compared to another corpus."[27] Keywords are determined by calculating their *keyness*.[28] We use keyword analysis for an initial access to the lexical level of the corpus in order to explore its characteristics. This results in the following ten top-ranked keywords in Hitler's and Goebbels's speeches: *volk, muß, bewegung, deutsch, nation, heute, kampf, kraft, reich, führer.*

Unsurprisingly, in the speeches of the leading National Socialists Hitler and Goebbels, nouns such as '*Volk*' (people), '*Nation*,' '*Kampf*' (fight), '*Kraft*' (strength), '*Führer*,' or '*Reich*' are used predominantly. These words can be regarded as National Socialist banner words (*Fahnenwörter*). Banner words are words that express political attitudes, positions, values, or goals in a positive deontic way—that is, depicting them as desirable. The opposite of banner words are stigma words with negative deontic connotations.[29] The use of '*heute*' (today) can be traced back to indexical references to time, which have a higher significance in a speech compared to texts that are less situationally bound. The frequent use of the verb '*müssen*' (must) indicates that National Socialist speeches were primarily characterized by pressing appeals to act—that is, by deontological objectives.

The initial exploration provides us with important information for the further procedure. While the top ten list of keywords prevalent in the speeches already contains references to spatial vocabulary ('*deutsch*,' '*Reich*'), it does not yet

---

26 We use the corpus "deu_news_2015" from the project "Deutscher Wortschatz"; see Thomas Eckart and Uwe Quasthoff, "Statistical Corpus and Language Comparison on Comparable Corpora," in *Building and Using Comparable Corpora*, ed. Serge Sharoff et al. (Berlin: Springer, 2013).
27 Vaclav Brezina, *Statistics in Corpus Linguistics: A Practical Guide* (Cambridge: Cambridge University Press, 2018), 79 f.
28 For an overview, see Adam Kilgarriff, "Comparing Corpora," *International Journal of Corpus Linguistics* 6, no. 1 (2001): 97–133.
29 See Fritz Hermanns, "Brisante Wörter. Zur lexikographischen Behandlung parteisprachlicher Wörter und Wendungen in Wörterbüchern der deutschen Gegenwartssprache," in *Studien zur neuhochdeutschen Lexikographie II*, ed. Herbert Ernst Wiegand (Hildesheim: Olms, 1982), 87–108. In the Third Reich, for example, '*Nationalsozialismus*' (National Socialism) was a banner word while '*Bolschewismus*' (Bolshevism) was a stigma word.

seem very specific for the concept of 'Lebensraum' (which itself is not one of the top ten keywords). As a compound, 'Lebensraum' is determined by its head '-raum.' Based on grammatical-morphological expertise, we consider '-raum-' as potentially productive for other compounds. Therefore, in a next step, we filter the keyword list for compounds with '-raum-' as partial component: *lebensraum* (frequency: 138), *raumnot* (19), *raummenge* (13), *raumerweiterung* (8), *raummäßig* (7), *raumfläche* (6). The filtering results in only a few compounds with '-raum-.' Especially 'Lebensraum' is often used as a term in speeches.

In the next step, we have to resolve the problem of unequal distribution. It can be assumed that speeches are thematically focused, which may lead to the fact that high word frequencies in quantitative analysis are caused by high occurrences in single texts, whereas in other texts words that occur with high frequency overall occur only rarely or not at all. The problem of unequal distribution of occurrences in corpora is addressed by dispersion measures.[30] We apply the measure DP_{norm},[31] which relates word frequency to the corpus parts in which the words occur and thus indicates lexical dispersion, to our corpus. The measurement is normalized, which means that DP_{norm} takes a value between 0 and 1. The closer the value tends to 1, the more unequally distributed the expression is. If the value tends towards zero, the corresponding token is distributed more evenly (see Table 5.1).

Table 5.1: Lexical dispersion of token with '-raum-' in Hitler's and Goebbels's speeches.[32]

Lexical dispersion: speeches		
lemma_POS	freq	DP_{norm}
raum_NN	258	0.700467
lebensraum_NN	138	0.827317
~~traum_NN~~	~~27~~	~~0.913512~~

---

30 See Brezina, *Statistics*; Stefan Th. Gries, "Dispersions and Adjusted Frequencies in Corpora," *International Journal of Corpus Linguistics* 13, no. 4 (2008), accessed July 3, 2020, doi: 10.1075/ijcl.13.4.02gri.
31 See Gries, "Dispersions."
32 The tags shown represent the following classifications according to the Stuttgart Tübinger Tagset (STTS): ADJA—attributive adjective; ADJD—adjective used adverbially or predicate adjective; NN—Nouns; VVFIN—finite full verb; VVPP—past participle of full verb. See Anne Schiller, Simone Teufel, Christine Stöckert, and Christine Thielen, *Guidelines für das Tagging deutscher Textcorpora mit STTS (Kleines und großes Tagset)* (Stuttgart and Tübingen: Universität Stuttgart and Universität Tübingen, 1999). Since Table 5.1 lists lemmata—i.e., uninflected basic forms of the words found—the entries of e. g. '*räumen_VVFIN*' and '*räumen_VVPP*' differ only with regard

Table 5.1: Lexical dispersion of token with '-raum-' in Hitler's and Goebbels's speeches. *(Continued)*

Lexical dispersion: speeches		
zeitraum_NN	23	0.934898
~~träumen_VVFIN~~	~~28~~	~~0.937085~~
raummäßig_ADJD	6	0.956652
räumen_VVPP	7	0.958887
räumen_VVFIN	10	0.962282
räumlich_ADJD	7	0.965333
raumnot_NN	19	0.969091
räumen_VVINF	10	0.976266
aufräumen_VVPP	6	0.977371
aufräumen_VVINF	7	0.978836
raumfläche_NN	6	0.980187
räumlich_ADJA	6	0.980239
raummenge_NN	13	0.980922
raumerweiterung_NN	7	0.985525

We have added words with the umlaut diphthong (-*räum-*) to our search terms in order to cover further grammatical inflection forms. Words with the word stem '-*traum-/-träum-*' (dream) do also appear in the results but are crossed out here. In addition, the tokens were annotated according to word class with part-of-speech tags, which are indicated by capital letters in Table 5.1. By doing so, we would just like to mention that in addition to a lexical and morphological orientated approach, grammatical classification could also serve as an analytical criterion. However, we continue to focus on the previously selected compounds and find that '*Lebensraum*' is more evenly distributed than the words '*Raumnot*,' '*Raummenge*,' and '*Raumerweiterung*.' The result of the lexical dispersion analysis indicates that the latter words occur only in some specific texts and not across the whole corpus like '*Lebensraum*.' Accordingly, we zoom further into the corpus and search for relevant key texts.

The section of a concordance plot[33] shown in Figure 5.1 visualizes the occurrence of search terms in individual texts. It shows that the search term occurs remarkably often in one specific text. This text could thus be identified as a key text for our research focus. It is a speech by Hitler held at an assembly of

---

to the POS tags. Lemmatization is a method of corpus-linguistic preprocessing in order to summarize inflected word forms such as '*räumt*,' '*räumten*,' or '*geräumt*.'

[33] The concordance plot was created with the software AntConc (http://www.laurenceanthony.net/software.html).

Chapter 5 Digital Discourse Analysis of Language Use under National Socialism — 109

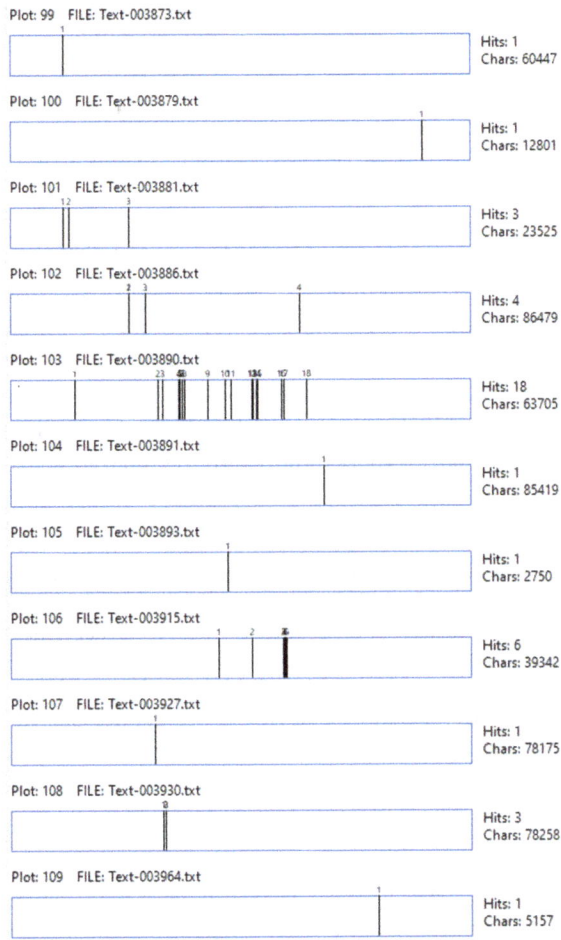

Figure 5.1: Concordance plot for words containing '-raum-/-räum-'. Graphic created by the authors.

the National Socialist German Workers' Party (NSDAP) in Nuremberg on December 3, 1928. Let us take a short look at a key passage of this speech:

> The German *Volk* is the typical *Raumvolk*, the Jewish *Volk* is the typical *spaceless Volk*. While the German *Volk* only knows one means of production *to gain soil*, the others are only the *bridge which submits to the process of making the production*. While the German *Volk* is composed of peasants and soldiers, the Jewish *Volk* is composed of merchants. Germans and Jews are two *Völker* who differ in their basic nature, one *Volk* of universal ability, the other always dependent on a second, or better third, who first lays the *ground* for the existence of this *Volkes*. Opposite to the German *Volk* as a *Volk full of space* is the Jewish

Volk as a *Volk* without space, opposite to the German *Volk* as a *Volk* of soldiers is the Jewish *Volk* as a *Volk* of traders. Our *Volk* can create culture out of primeval forests and deserts, but the other *Volk* can only go where there is already culture. Our *Volk* can therefore build culture itself, imaginative culture, the other more mechanical culture, our *Volk* do more philosophy, the other more mathematics. Our *Volk* is more state political, the other more economic. In short, we see how two *Völker* stand juxtaposed here, two *Völker* that are infinitely different.[34]

Hitler's use of the concept '*Lebensraum*' here is inextricably linked with linguistic practices of inclusion and exclusion.[35] The Germans are represented by their semantic role[36] *agent* as an active, acting people while the 'others'—by means of an explicit othering—are depersonalized and reified as *patients*.[37] The '*Lebensraum*' concept is linked to another central concept of National Socialism, the concept of the '*Volk*.' Hitler used this connection for the up- or downgrading juxtaposition of Germans and Jews, which, by the way, is a dichotomizing opposition of de-

---

34 Our emphasis, translated from: "Das deutsche Volk ist das typische Raumvolk, das jüdische Volk ist das typische raumlose Volk. Während das deutsche Volk nur eine Produktionsmöglichkeit kennt, Boden zu gewinnen, bilden die anderen nur die Brücke, die den Prozeß der Herstellung der Produktion über sich ergehen lassen. Während das deutsche Volk sich aus dem Bauern- und Soldatentum zusammensetzt, setzt sich das jüdische Volk aus Händlern zusammen. Deutsche und Juden sind zwei Völker, die in ihrem Grundwesen auseinander gehen, das eine Volk von universaler Fähigkeit, das andere stets abhängig von einem zweiten oder besser dritten, der erst den Boden für die Existenzen dieses Volkes abgibt. Dem deutschen Volk als raumvollem Volk steht das jüdische Volk als raumloses, dem deutschen Volk als Soldatenvolk, steht das jüdische als Händlervolk gegenüber. Unser Volk kann aus Urwald und Wüsteneien Kultur schaffen, das andere Volk hingegen kann nur hingehen, wo sich bereits Kultur befindet. Unser Volk kann deshalb selbst Kultur aufbauen, phantasievolle, das andere mehr mechanische, unser Volk treibt mehr Philosophie, das andere mehr Mathematik. Unser Volk ist mehr staatspolitisch, das andere mehr wirtschaftspolitisch. Kurz und gut, wir sehen, wie hier zwei Völker nebeneinander stehen, die unendlich verschieden sind." (Hitler at an assembly of the NSDAP in Nuremberg on December 3, 1928 in: De Gruyter, *Nationalsozialismus*, Dokument-ID: HRSA-0536, accessed July 3, 2020, http://db.saur.de/DGO/basicFullCitationView.jsf?documentId=HRSA-0536.
35 See Detlef Schmiechen-Ackermann et al., eds., *Der Ort der "Volksgemeinschaft" in der deutschen Gesellschaftsgeschichte* (Paderborn: Ferdinand Schöningh, 2018); Michael Wildt, "Volksgemeinschaft: A Modern Perspective on National Socialist Society," in *Visions of Community in Nazi Germany*, ed. Martina Steber and Bernhard Gotto (Oxford: Oxford University Press, 2014).
36 Peter von Polenz, *Deutsche Satzsemantik: Grundbegriffe des Zwischen-den-Zeilen-Lesens* (Berlin: De Gruyter, 1985).
37 For a detailed analysis of such linguistic practices of exclusion in field post letters during the World War II, see Mark Dang-Anh, "Excluding Agency: Infrastructural and Interactional Practices of Exclusion in the National Socialist Dispositif of Field Post," *M/C Journal* 23 no. 6 (2020), accessed August 5, 2021, https://doi.org/10.5204/mcj.2725.

nomination in itself. The linguistic observation leading to this interpretation is that the term '-*raum*-' acquires conceptual meaning not only as a partial element of compounds, but also as a collocate of other words which we will discuss in more detail below.

3.2 Collocation

While the identification of keywords is one possible step towards zooming into texts and thus deepening the analysis, we are now taking a different approach and focus on collocations whose importance for corpus analyses was first recognized by John R. Firth.[38] Vaclav Brezina refers to collocations as "combinations of words that habitually co-occur in texts and corpora."[39] The words that co-occur with a specific word, which is called a node in the context of collocation, are collocates.[40] Noah Bubenhofer emphasizes the statistical aspect of collocations, claiming that these associations of words can be measured and expressed as statistical significance.[41] The distance or span around the node—that is, the number of tokens taken into account before or after the node, delimited by sentence boundaries—is defined by the analyst, which means that according to this definition, collocates do not have to be in close proximity, such as in narrower concepts which argue phraseologically or grammatically.[42]

For our illustrative purposes, we will concentrate in the following on a specific collocate of the word stem '-*raum*-/-*räum*-' (see Figure 5.2).

---

38 John R. Firth, *Papers in Linguistics, 1934–51* (Oxford: Oxford University Press, 1957).
39 Brezina, *Statistics*, 67.
40 John Sinclair, *Corpus, Concordance, Collocation*, 3rd impr. (Oxford: Oxford University Press 1995), 115.
41 Noah Bubenhofer, "Kollokationen, n-Gramme, Mehrworteinheiten," in *Handbuch Sprache in Politik und Gesellschaft*, ed. Kersten Sven Roth, Martin Wengeler, and Alexander Ziem (Berlin: De Gruyter, 2017), 69; Brezina, *Statistics*, 67. The discussion about collocation measures cannot be elaborated here, see Stefan Evert, "Corpora and Collocations," in *Corpus Linguistics: An International Handbook*, ed. Anke Lüdeling and Merja Kytö (Berlin: Mouton de Gruyter, 2008), 1212–48.
42 See Bubenhofer, *Kollokationen*, 70.

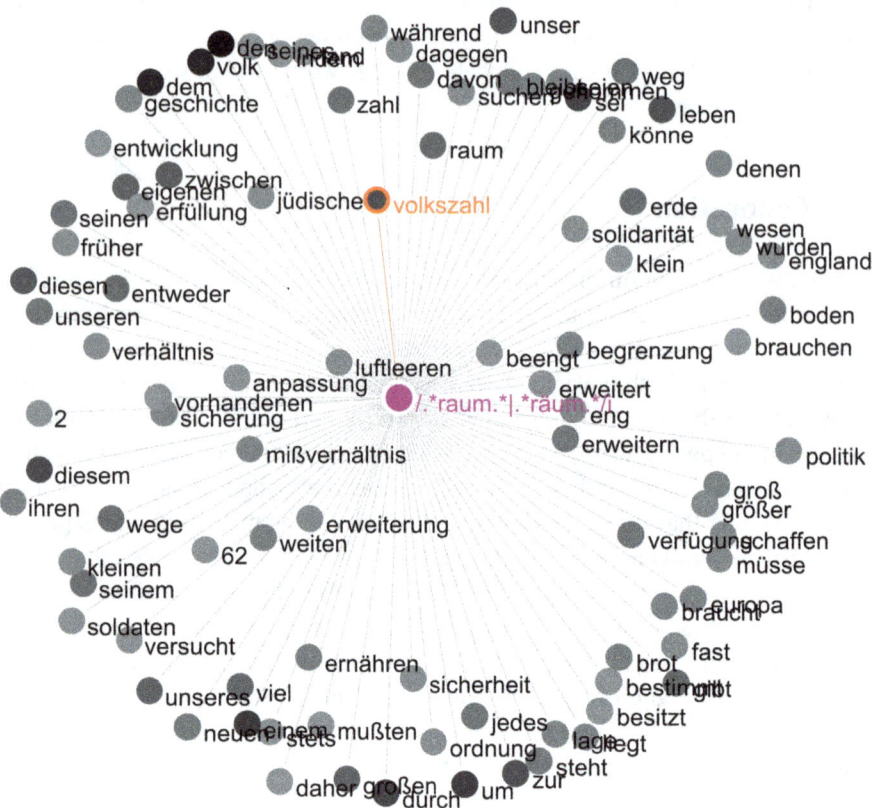

Figure 5.2: Collocates of '-raum-/-räum-'; CPN: 3a-MI(4), L5-R5, C5[43]. Created with LancsBox by the authors.

With the node in the center, the graph visualizes three aspects of the relation between node and collocate. The distance between the node and the collocate indicates the strength of the collocation as determined by the association measure. The color of the dots displays the frequency of the words: The darker the gray the more collocations were counted. The position left or right of the node

---

[43] We apply the collocation parameters notification (CPN) as proposed by Vaclav Brezina, Tony McEnery, and Stephen Wattam, "Collocations in Context: A New Perspective on Collocation Networks," *International Journal of Corpus Linguistics* 20, no. 2 (2015): 139–73, accessed July 3, 2020, doi: 10.1075/ijcl.20.2.01bre. The collocates graph was computed and created with LancsBox 4.5. We used the association measure Mutual Information ("MI") with the ID "3a" with the cut-off value 4, a span of five words before and after the node, and a minimum collocate frequency of 5.

specifies whether a collocation occurs predominantly to the left or right of the node or, if it is in the middle position, whether this relation is balanced. In several analysis cycles with different collocation measures, the collocation of '*-raum-*/*-räum-*' with '*Volkszahl*' (population) proved to be conspicuously associative.

3.3 Concordance

Therefore, in a further step, we now zoom from the level of multi-word units or collocations into a more detailed analysis on the basis of collocation co-texts. Co-texts of search terms or, in this case, collocates can be explored in concordances. Concordances are "collection[s] of the occurrences of a word-form, each in its own textual environment. In its simplest form it is an index. Each word-form is indexed and a reference is given to the place of occurrence in a text."[44] The quasi-standard for representing and examining concordances in corpus linguistics are keyword-in-context-lists (KWIC) in which the co-texts around the nodes are shown.[45]

Figure 5.3 displays an excerpt from a KWIC-list for the node '*-raum-*' co-occurring with the collocate '*Volkszahl.*'

At this point, it would be useful to annotate the individual lines of the KWIC-list systematically and thereby identify relevant evidence for the concept '*Lebensraum*' in a qualitative analysis. However, for illustration purposes, at this point of the path we want to take another turn and obtain more insight into the usage of the collocates '*-raum-*' and '*Volkszahl*' by computing shared collocates. Shared collocates, which are marked by orange dots in Figure 5.4, allow a statement about the manner in which two words are used together.

Here, we concentrate on the shared collocate '*Mißverhältnis*' (imbalance) as an example. Describing 'living space' ('*Lebensraum*') and population ('*Volks-*

---

[44] Sinclair, *Corpus*, 32.
[45] The notion of 'keywords in context' is potentially subject to misconception. It is therefore important to point out two terminological details. On the one hand, keywords here refer to search terms—i.e., nodes, and not words determined by keyness analyses. On the other hand, the displayed words are co-texts in a narrower sense—i.e., the words that appear to the right and left of the nodes in texts, and not contexts in a broader sense. It should also be underlined, especially against the background of a discourse-hermeneutic analysis, that KWIC representations are not the only possible concordance depictions, but that concordances can and should also be considered and analyzed in larger scales. See Christopher Tribble, "What Are Concordances and How Are They Used?," in *The Routledge Handbook of Corpus Linguistics*, ed. Anne O'Keeffe und Michael McCarthy (London: Routledge, 2010), 167–83.

Figure 5.3: KWIC-list of '-raum-' co-occurring with 'Volkszahl' in speeches, created with LancsBox by the authors.

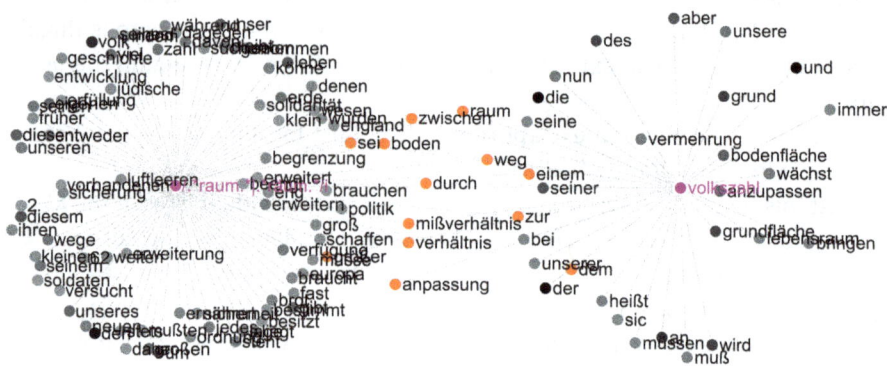

Figure 5.4: Shared collocates of '-raum-' and 'Volkszahl,' created with LancsBox by the authors.

zahl') as 'imbalanced' exemplifies a very condensed version of the National Socialist concept, which is linguistically established and repeatedly reproduced here. We are once again inclined to follow this lexical observation with a display of textual evidence to support this thesis through more detailed reading. For each node of the shared collocate we want to check joint occurrences.

One of the peculiarities of the second list is the repeated occurrence of '*Boden*' (soil) as a collocate to '*Volkszahl*.' In a sense, this brings us back to the observation made at the beginning that '*Boden*' is possibly in a paradigmatic relationship with '-*raum-*.' Moreover, '*Bodenfläche*' (land area) appears frequently in this context, which even more so than already through the use of '*Volkszahl*'

Chapter 5 Digital Discourse Analysis of Language Use under National Socialism — 115

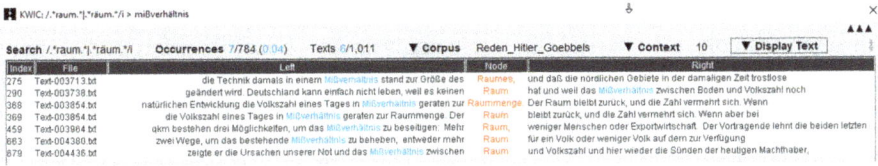

Figure 5.5: KWIC-list of node '-raum-/-räum-' with collocate 'Mißverhältnis,' created with LancsBox by the authors.

Figure 5.6: KWIC-list of node 'Volkszahl' with collocate 'Mißverhältnis,' created with LancsBox by the authors.

and '*Mißverhältnis*' suggests that the concept of 'living space' is deeply founded upon a geometric-arithmetic reasoning.

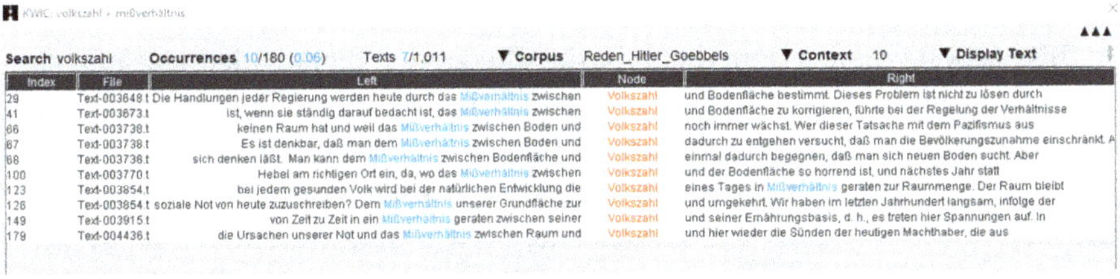

At this point, though, we have to stop the exemplary description of research strategies that applied methods from corpus linguistics and combined them with insights from discourse hermeneutics. We wanted to show the potential of a digitally driven access to a considerably large corpus of texts (in this case speeches of Hitler and Goebbels). At diacritical points, we have taken certain research directions which have led to further methodological decisions. As we have seen, analytical parameters such as keywords, lexical dispersion, collocates, and concordances have enabled us to identify entry-points from which a qualitative analysis would have to follow. For the purpose of this first part, however, we have refrained from entering too much into qualitative analysis, although we have also generated hypotheses that would certainly require a deeper hermeneutical analysis. For example, we have argued that the concept of '*Lebensraum*' was closely tied to other central concepts like '*Volk*' and that it was crucially constituted by practices of inclusion and exclusion. On this basis, a predominantly geometrical-mathematical argumentation was carried out in National Socialist discourse according to which the conquest of space as a positive deontic goal was both morally legitimized and seemed to have become a mere matter of calculation. The main point of our remarks was, however, that methods from corpus linguistics may help us to identify both concept-constituting patterns and relevant text passages for qualitative analysis when we hermeneutically navigate through the corpus in digital discourse analysis. By choosing different directions during the digitally driven research process, though, we as analysts are constantly responsible for taking adequate analytical decisions.

4 Analyzing Language in Letters of Complaint and Request

In this section we start from the opposite direction of digitally led research strategies that can be used to handle a large number of texts and thus examine language use during National Socialism. While the strategy described above consisted in zooming into and out of a corpus (and its single texts and passages) with the help of defined analytical parameters, we will now present a strategy which goes from text to text, makes use of a digital markup tool, and at the end produces a corpus which can then be analyzed according to self-defined annotations.

The thematic framework of this second part is a research project which examines letters of complaint and request that 'ordinary people' sent to public authorities and party officials during the pre-war years of the Third Reich.[46] In the scarce literature that exists on this phenomenon, especially compared to the period after 1945,[47] we are provided with interesting insights which serve as entrypoints to our study. Thus, a local examination of letters sent to the *Kreisleitung* of the NSDAP in Eisenach has underlined the social implications of the ubiqui-

---

[46] We do not have the space here to elaborate too much on the research project, but for a first programmatic sketch and more literature on the subject see Stefan Scholl, "Für eine Sprach- und Kommunikationsgeschichte des Nationalsozialismus"; Stefan Scholl, "Beschwerde- und Bittschreiben von Mannheimer Bürgern während des Nationalsozialismus: Eine Analyse alltagssprachlicher Kollusion anhand von ausgewählten Beispielen," *Sprachreport* 35, no. 4 (2019): 6–15, accessed July 6, 2020, https://pub.ids-mannheim.de/laufend/sprachreport/pdf/sr19-4.pdf.
[47] For the GDR and the FRG see Michaela Fenske, *Demokratie erschreiben. Bürgerbriefe und Petitionen als Medien politischer Kultur 1950–1974* (Frankfurt am Main: Campus, 2013); Sabine Manke, *Brandt anfeuern. Das Misstrauensvotum 1972 in Bürgerbriefen an den Bundeskanzler. Ein kulturwissenschaftlicher Beitrag zu modernen Resonanz- und Korrespondenzphänomenen* (Marburg: Tectum, 2008); Harm Peer Zimmermann, "Lebenswelt und Politik. Bürgerbriefe an Helmut Schmidt," in *Humane Orientierungswissenschaft. Was leisten Wissenschaftskulturen für das Verständnis menschlicher Lebenswelt*, ed. Peter Janich (Würzburg: Königshausen und Neumann, 2008), 203–26; Ina Merkel, ed., *"Wir sind doch nicht die Meckerecke der Nation". Briefe an das DDR-Fernsehen* (Cologne: Böhlau, 1998); Felix Mühlberg, *Bürger, Bitten und Behörden. Geschichte der Eingabe in der DDR* (Berlin: Karl Dietz, 2004).

tous use of the rhetoric of the *Volksgemeinschaft*.[48] In a similar vein, other contributors have recently pointed to the fact that quite a few people addressed the authorities rather self-confidently, creatively appropriating elements of National Socialist discourses in order to legitimate their claims.[49] However, the full scope and significance of this phenomenon within the structures of the National Socialist communicative space have still to be analyzed in depth. In our research project, the analytical focus is specifically laid on linguistic practices such as complaining, pleading, revolting, and appealing, as well as depictions of the self and of others that went along with these practices. Also, temporal dimensions of self-depictions (and depictions of others) as well as temporal aspects of relevant linguistic practices are taken into account. As we will see in the example below, very often, these different analytical layers overlapped in the letters.

Besides the bottom-up perspective that starts with a close reading and digital marking of single texts, in this case letters, the approach differs in two important points from the one described in the first section. On the one hand, we have to deal for the most part with non-digitized archival sources. Therefore, digitization, and for our purpose of analyzing language use it has to be an optical character recognition (OCR) digitization, is an integral element of the research process.[50] On the other hand, the analytical focus defined above goes beyond keywords or even concordances but aims at potentially more complex linguistic elements such as phrases, figures of speech, or whole lines of argumentation. Thus, digital tools which operate on the level of word units will not suffice, but we need a possibility to mark passages digitally in the first

---

48 John Connelly, "The Uses of the Volksgemeinschaft: Letters to the NSDAP Kreisleitung Eisenach, 1939–1940," *The Journal of Modern History* 68 (1996): 899–930.
49 See for example Anette Blaschke, *Zwischen "Dorfgemeinschaft" und "Volksgemeinschaft". Landbevölkerung und ländliche Lebenswelten im Nationalsozialismus* (Paderborn: Schöningh, 2018); Moritz Föllmer, "Wie kollektivistisch war der Nationalsozialismus? Zur Geschichte der Individualität zwischen Weimarer Republik und Nachkriegszeit," in *Kontinuitäten und Diskontinuitäten. Der Nationalsozialismus in der Geschichte des 20. Jahrhunderts*, ed. Birthe Kundrus and Sybille Steinbacher (Göttingen: Wallstein, 2013), 34f.; Florian Wimmer, *Die völkische Ordnung der Armut. Kommunale Sozialpolitik im nationalsozialistischen München* (Göttingen, Wallstein, 2014), 213–22. More specifically for the wartime period see Nicole Kramer, *Volksgenossinnen an der Heimatfront. Mobilisierung, Verhalten, Erinnerung* (Göttingen: Wallstein, 2011); Birthe Kundrus, *Kriegerfrauen. Familienpolitik und Geschlechterverhältnisse im Ersten und Zweiten Weltkrieg* (Hamburg: Wallstein, 1995).
50 As those who are familiar with the digitization of archival sources know, this is not a trivial point. Quite often, the documents are not easy (if at all) to scan with OCR. Also, a lot of the letters are written in *Sütterlin* which poses further problems for digital text recognition, even if the new program Transkribus (https://transkribus.eu/Transkribus/) is now available.

place, for example instances where letter-writers complain about the behavior of someone else, in order to make them digitally searchable in higher quantity at a later moment. Inversely to the strategy presented in the first part, thus, we have to first zoom deeply into single texts to then be able to zoom out of them and recognize patterns of language use.

An adequate tool for such an approach is CATMA.[51] The main advantage of this program is that the user can build her or his own "tagset"—that is, a set of colored mark-ups that will be attributed to parts of a text, according to the research interest and the guiding criteria of analysis. Also, the tagset can be adjusted during the process of analysis, for example if it has to be enlarged or specified. In our case of linguistic practices of complaining, the following tagset has been established. As we will see, the different tags are rather vague, allowing for the fact that, for example the description of oneself as being an ideologically convinced National Socialist can be linguistically performed in different ways. Of course, the establishment of the tagset has already been an outcome of heuristic reflection and of presuppositions based on extensive study of sources as well as research interest. Concretely, we are looking for:

I. Constructions of Self and Others
I.1. Self-Descriptions
– National Socialist (party member, 'old fighter')
– Ideologically convinced
– Victim of others
– Has made sacrifices
– Former opponent, now converted
– Belonging to the community
I.2. Descriptions of Others
– Not truly believers
– Late-comers
– Opponents
– Enemies (Communists, Jews, Christians)

II. Temporal Dimensions
– World War I
– Early '*Kampfzeit*'
– Late '*Kampfzeit*'
– '*Systemzeit*' / Weimar Republic
– Before the '*Machtergreifung*'

---

51 See https://catma.de/. The online based tool is free of charge after registration. On the homepage you will find a manual with further information. See also Jan Christoph Meister, "From TACT to CATMA or A Mindful Approach to Text Annotation and Analysis," accessed July 6, 2020, http://jcmeister.de/downloads/texts/Meister_2020-TACT-to-CATMA.pdf.

Chapter 5 Digital Discourse Analysis of Language Use under National Socialism — 119

- After the '*Machtergreifung*'
- Now / in the National Socialist era
- In the future

III. Linguistic Practices
- Speaking one's mind
- Moaning about injustice
- Expressing lack of understanding
- Expressing indignation
- Asking provocative questions
- Making demands
- Referring to the '*Führer*'
- Referring to promises made
- Pointing to negative consequences
- Expressing loyalty or trust

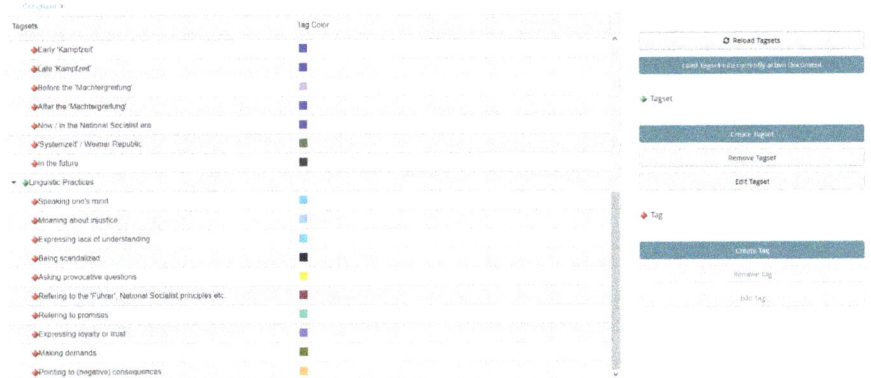

Figure 5.7: Screenshot of the tagset.

As can be seen in the screenshot (Figure 5.7), a different color, which can be chosen by the researcher, is assigned to each tag. The next step consists in tagging the digitized texts, which can be uploaded into the tool one by one.

For illustrative purposes, we have chosen one letter of complaint out of our corpus of texts in order to demonstrate the tagging process. In April 1937, Hertha B., a woman from Karlsruhe, wrote to Rudolf Heß, the deputy party leader ("*Stellvertreter des Führers*"):

> Nach 6 Jahren langem hartem Existenzkampf von vielen Enttäuschungen niedergeschlagen, muss ich mich heute aus Not gedrungen an Sie wenden und Ihnen (ohne Wissen meines Mannes) das Schicksal eines alten Kämpfers schildern.

Mein Mann Mitgl. Nr. 128147 wurde im Jahre 1930 wegen seiner Parteizugehörigkeit von der Stadt Wiesbaden entlassen, und war volle 4 Jahre danach arbeitslos. Nach der Machtübernahme machte er [...] sein Anrecht auf seine alte Stellung als Leiter des städtischen Fuhrparks geltend, wurde aber von den Herren Parteigenossen (jüngerer Zugehörigkeit) abgelehnt. [...]

Im Jahre 1930 war mein Mann bei der Ausschreibung betreffend Ersetzung der Betriebsamtsmannstelle in Bremen unter den zahlreichen Bewerbern bereits gewählt, jedoch wurde nachträglich bei der Stadt Wiesbaden betrf. seiner politischen Gesinnung nachgefragt und ihm daraufhin mitgeteilt: ‚man hat bei der Wahl des Kandidaten politische Gesichtspunkte nicht außer Betracht gelassen und ist also die Wahl auf einen anderen Bewerber gefallen.' Man könnte unmöglich einen nationalsozialistischen Betriebsleiter über eine rote Arbeiterschaft setzen.

Nachdem mein Mann auch nach der Machtübernahme überall abgewiesen wurde, kehrten wir in meine Heimatstadt Karlsruhe zurück und bauten uns da aus eigenen Kräften eine Sachverständigen-Praxis auf. Es sollten 2 Juden als Sachverständige für das Kraftfahrwesen ausscheiden, jedoch nachdem einer davon Deutschland verlassen hat, wühlt der andere Jude gegen meinen Mann. Dieser Vollblutjude behauptet (Kriegsteilnehmer) vollste Unterstützung seitens des Reiches zu haben (ich vermute aber nur seitens der örtlichen Regierung) und warnt, irgendetwas gegen ihn zu unternehmen. [...] Es ist nur sehr sonderbar, dass der Jude vollste Unterstützung bekommt und heute noch die beste Praxis hat, kein Wunder, wenn sogar die Adler-Vertretung ihn ausschließlich beschäftigt. [...]

Das größte Unrecht aber, das geschieht, ist, dass das Gericht bis vor kurzem ausschließlich einen pensionierten Beamten des Dampfkessel-Überwachungs-Vereins beschäftigte. Dieser Herr war seiner Zeit wegen seiner politischen Unzuverlässigkeit aus obigem Verein entlassen worden. Solche Volksgenossen werden unterstützt und finden gleich wieder Arbeit und ein alter Kämpfer wird vernichtet. [...] Ja, so geht es eben, wenn man nicht mit dem Gau-Obmann der DAF befreundet ist und keinerlei Beziehungen hat. [...] Es ist absolut kein Wunder, wenn man verbittert wird, aber nur zu gut zu verstehen, wenn man solche Enttäuschungen erleben muss. [...]

Unsere mit vieler Mühe ohne jegliche Hilfe aufgebaute Existenz wird durch gemeine Intrige wieder vernichtet. Aber einem alten Kämpfer kann man dies Alles ja bieten, er soll nur ruhig weiter kämpfen um sein Dasein, wenn es nur den Volksgenossen die seiner Zeit dem Kampf sehr fern standen, gut geht. Nur der Glaube an unseren Führer hielt uns aufrecht, da es aber immer noch keinen Lichtblick für uns gegeben hat, wende ich mich heute an Sie und bitte um Hilfe, d. h. um Untersuchung der hier herrschenden ungerechten Zustände. Ich hoffe, dass ein alter Kämpfer auch einmal das Recht hat auf Unterstützung und Gerechtigkeit.

Nach unserem Umzug von Frankfurt nach Karlsruhe sandte mein Mann auf Anforderung seinen NSK Ausweis nach Frankfurt, da die Papiere erneuert werden sollten. Jedoch bekam er dabei eine andere Nummer. Er hatte die Nummer 2886 und erhielt die Nummer 10172 (beim Eintritt im Jahre 1932?). Das geht doch nicht in Ordnung! Wer hat sich diese Nummer angeeignet? [...] Wozu gibt es denn Ortsgruppen, wenn sie sich nicht um die Angelegenheiten ihrer Mitglieder kümmern? [...]

Ich möchte absolut nicht als Nörglerin oder als Denunziantin angesehen werden, aber was zu viel ist, ist zu viel. 6 Jahre haben wir nun ohne jegliche Hilfe uns durchgerungen, uns endlich ein wenig emporgebracht und werden nun von Intrigen wieder niedergeschlagen.

Wir können uns nicht dauernd unterdrücken lassen, wir fordern Gerechtigkeit und hoffen, dass bald die Wahrheit siegen möge.[52]

Despondent after 6 years of hard existential struggle full of disappointments, I today, from a position of great need have to reach out to you to tell you (without the knowledge of my husband) of the fight of an *alter Kämpfer* [lit., "old fighter," term used for early Nazi supporters.] My husband, membership Nr. 128147, was dismissed in the year 1930 by the city of Wiesbaden due to his party membership, and was subsequently unemployed for 4 full years. After *Machtübernahme* [lit. "Seizure of power," term used by Nazis to describe the moment when Hitler was appointed German Reich Chancellor in 1933], he asserted that he should regain his old position as director of the municipal vehicle fleet, but was rejected by the party comrades (younger memberships.) [...]

In the year 1930, my husband had already been elected amongst several other candidates for replacing the position of a municipal company's representative [*Betriebsamtsmann*] in Bremen, but afterwards there was an inquiry at the city of Wiesbaden in regard to his political leanings and then he was told: "political aspects were not disregarded when choosing a candidate and thus another applicant was chosen." It would be impossible to put a National Socialist company leader above a red labor force.

After my husband was rejected everywhere after *Machtübernahme* as well, we returned to my home city of Karlsruhe and, on our own, established an office for technical expertise. Two Jews were expected to leave their positions as experts for motor vehicles, but after one of them had left Germany, the other Jew rallied against my husband. This Jew of full blood [*Vollblutjude*] claimed (war participant) to have fullest support from the Reich (but I suspect this was only from the local government) and warns, to take any action against him. [...] It is just very strange, that this Jew received full support and still today has the best office running, no surprise, if even the Adler dealership employed him exclusively. [...]

The largest injustice, however, that is occurring, is that the court until recently exclusively employed a retired civil servant from the steam boiler inspection association. This gentleman had been in the past dismissed from the above-mentioned association due to political unreliability. Such people's comrades [*Volksgenossen*] receive support and immediately find jobs again and an *alter Kämpfer* is destroyed. [...] Well, this is how it goes if you are not friends with the *Gau* chairman of the German Labor Front and have no networks. [...] It is absolutely no wonder that one turns bitter, but it is easily understood if one has to live through such disappointments. [...]

Our existence, built up with much effort and without any help, is now being destroyed again by mean-spirited intrigues. But everything can be thrown at an *alter Kämpfer*, he should just continue to fight for his existence, as long as all the people's comrades, which in the past were distant from the fight, do well. It was only the belief in the Führer that held us up, but since there is still no ray of hope for us, I today turn to you and ask for help, i.e. for an investigation of the prevailing, unjust situation here. I hope that an *alter Kämpfer* once also has the right to receive support and justice. [...]

After we moved from Frankfurt to Karlsruhe, my husband sent his NSK passport to Frankfurt on request, as his papers were to be renewed. However, with this, he received

---

52 Hertha Bachmann (Karlsruhe) to Rudolf Heß, April 4, 1937, *Generallandesarchiv Karlsruhe*, 465c, 1022.

a different number. He used to have number 2886 and received the number 10172 (having entered in 1932?). That is not alright! Who appropriated this number? [...] What is the purpose of local party groups, if they don't take care of the matters of their members? [...]
I absolutely do not want to be considered a moaner or a denunciator, but what is too much is too much. We have now survived for 6 years without any help, have finally risen a little bit and now are beaten down again by intrigues. We cannot let ourselves to be continuously suppressed, we demand justice and hope, that the truth will soon win.

In her letter, she told the 'story' of her husband, an "old fighter" (*alter Kämpfer*), who had suffered from private and vocational discrimination during the Weimar Republic due to his political affiliation, but even after the Nazi seizure of power did not find an adequate job. After having founded a small expert office for steam boilers on their own, their business had been hampered by a "Jew," according to Hertha B. She claimed that the local administration supported this hampering, and that the local court gave job assignments exclusively to a person of dubious political reliability. In general, she criticized with quite a lot of sarcasm that 'old fighters' and long-time supporters of the 'movement' were disadvantaged vis-à-vis late-comers and people that had been hostile towards National Socialism before Hitler's coming to power. This, by the way, was a narrative quite widespread within the circles of 'old fighters.'[53] At the end of the letter, she claimed not to be a moaner (*Nörglerin*) or denouncer (*Denunziantin*), but that "enough is enough." She demanded "justice" and hoped for the victory of "truth."

While this short résumé of the letter may already be interesting, on the level of language use we want to go more into detail and analyze how Hertha B.'s complaint is linguistically structured, which discursive elements were used by her, and which linguistic practices were performed.[54] In order to do so, we have to manually annotate the text in several cycles with our previously constructed tagset (see Figures 5.8 and 5.9).

---

53 See Bernd Stöver, *Volksgemeinschaft im Dritten Reich. Die Konsensbereitschaft der Deutschen aus der Sicht sozialistischer Exilberichte* (Düsseldorf: Droste, 1993), 383–88; Christoph Schmidt, "Zu den Motiven 'alter Kämpfer' in der NSDAP," in *Die Reihen fast geschlossen. Beiträge zur Geschichte des Alltags unterm Nationalsozialismus*, ed. Detlev Peukert and Jürgen Reulecke (Wuppertal: Peter Hammer Verlag, 1981), 38–41.
54 It is important to note that the term 'use' does not necessarily imply a cognitive or strategic intention here. Rather, we focus on the simple fact that certain types of words, phrases, and arguments were employed by someone. If the person did this intentionally, habitually, or just accidentally is another question. However, in the context of letters that were sent to public authorities and party organizations during the Third Reich, we can at least assume that the writers tried to present their case in a form and style that they sought was beneficial to their cause.

Chapter 5 Digital Discourse Analysis of Language Use under National Socialism — 123

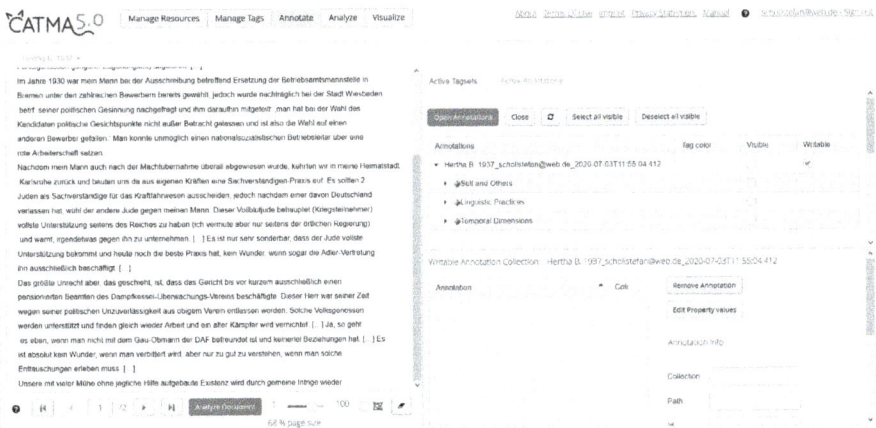

Figure 5.8: Screenshot of uploaded document (on the left) before annotation.

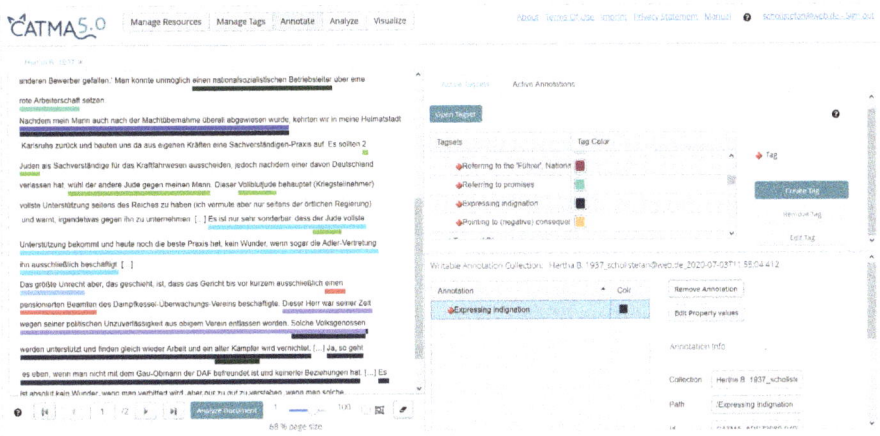

Figure 5.9: Screenshot of the annotation process.

As an outcome of the tagging process, we arrive at a document which is digitally annotated according to our analytical research criteria. As can be seen in Figure 5.9, different tags may overlap. For example, we have marked up the subclause "Nachdem mein Mann auch nach der Machtübernahme überall abgewiesen wurde" (After my husband got repelled everywhere even after the take-over of power) with a temporal tag (blue) as well with a tag that interprets this utterance as an expression of indignation (black). Similarly, in the sentence "Solche Volksgenossen werden unterstützt und finden gleich wieder Arbeit und ein alter Kämpfer wird vernichtet" (Such people's comrades are supported and immediately find work and an old fighter is getting destroyed), we have tagged it as a whole as an expression of indignation, while "Solche Volksgenossen" can be seen as a pejorative description of the other—here, specifically, someone who was deemed to be politically unreliable, which, again, is only clarified in connection to the sentence before—and "alter Kämpfer" of course refers to her husband.

While the detailed and careful tagging already leads to close readings of texts, the full potential of the method unfolds only after having annotated a larger number of texts (in our case letters to the authorities) with the same tagset. Now, it is possible to formulate qualified research queries and apply them to the annotated texts. For example, we are now able to generate a list of all instances where letter-writers expressed their indignation of not having found an appropriate job after the Nazi's seizure of power and combined this with a self-depiction as an 'old fighter' and a demarcation from people who were accused of not being true National Socialists. Complex patterns of language use can thus be detected much more easily than in 'traditional' serial reading. Or we can simply detect chronological peaks in the use of a certain linguistic practice that is not necessarily connected to single words, like 'expressing indignation' for example. In any case, this method allows for an accurate fitting of analytical criteria of language use defined in the tagset, the annotation of these criteria in single texts, and the possibility to recognize patterns of language use in a large corpus.

Since our research project is currently in the process of tagging letters one by one, we are not able yet to give a clear-cut overview of the results. However, we can already identify some outlines, some of which can also be found in our exemplary letter of Hertha B.: First, most of the letter-writers positioned themselves as ardent supporters of the National Socialist movement and its heterogenous ideological offerings. At the same time, they often demarcated themselves from others that were characterized as not being true and convinced National Socialists. The temporal dimension—that is, for how long someone claimed to have been a National Socialist—played a major role. Also, it becomes apparent that many of those who complained about something did this by referring to National Socialist promises and 'principles.' A central trait of the linguistic interaction between 'ordinary Germans' and official authorities was the performance of belonging and adherence to National Socialism by appropriating specific patterns of National Socialist discourses—and thus co-constructed theses discourses. More qualified and differentiated results will eventually be gained by using the method of digitized annotation.

To be sure, the procedure that we have presented in this second section is time-consuming and is best suited to texts of short or medium length. While speeches, books, or journal articles may be too long for a detailed serial manual annotation, different kinds of letters, administrative records (for example of the

Gestapo), or short reports may be better qualified for such a research method of analysis.

5 Conclusion

As should have become clear, by presenting our understanding of a digitally led study of language use during National Socialism we focused rather on the description of methodological decisions and research strategies than presenting a thoroughgoing analysis of specific concepts or linguistic practices. The empirical examples—the concept '*Lebensraum*' in speeches of Hitler and Goebbels and the linguistic practice of complaining in letters to the authorities—served as illustrations for our methodological reflections. In general, researchers who want to study patterns of language use are dependent on large corpora of texts. Digital tools and methods can help (and sometimes guide) us here, because they enable us to detect, recognize, arrange, and visualize patterns that we would probably not always see by close reading.

In the first section, we zoomed in and out of the corpus and texts to varying levels of granularity by employing analytical parameters such as keyword, collocation, and concordance, thus combining methods from corpus linguistics and discourse analysis. As we have underlined, these parameters are not to be considered separately from each other, but rather as steps on a research path. Brought together, the partial results of individual evaluations always give rise to new possible search directions that can be pursued further.

In the second part, we presented a way to digitally annotate a corpus of texts with a self-defined tagset, which potentially leads to enhanced research options. The advantage here is that it allows us to look beyond the level of the lexical surface of texts, since the annotations can encompass more complex and uneven linguistic constructions.

However, as we tended to stress in our preliminary remarks, the use of digital tools and methods does not discharge the discourse analyst from the basic procedures of critical historical and linguistic investigation. Hence, we must bear in mind that we as researchers, through the composition of corpora, criteria of analysis, interpretations, search queries, and so on, constantly influence the way digital corpus technology provides us with results. Thus, hermeneutical understanding and interpreting are crucial elements that accompany digital discourse analysis.

Bibliography

Aijmer, Karin, and Christoph Rühlemann. *Corpus Pragmatics: A Handbook*. Cambridge: Cambridge University Press, 2015.
Bauer, Gerhard. *Sprache und Sprachlosigkeit im "Dritten Reich."* Cologne: Bund-Verlag, 1990.
Blaschke, Anette. *Zwischen "Dorfgemeinschaft" und "Volksgemeinschaft". Landbevölkerung und ländliche Lebenswelten im Nationalsozialismus*. Paderborn: Schöningh, 2018.
Braun, Christian A. *Nationalsozialistischer Sprachstil. Theoretischer Zugang und praktische Analysen auf der Grundlage einer pragmatisch-textlinguistisch orientierten Stilistik*. Heidelberg: Winter, 2007.
Brezina, Vaclav. *Statistics in Corpus Linguistics: A Practical Guide*. Cambridge: Cambridge University Press, 2018.
Brezina, Vaclav, Tony McEnery, and Stephen Wattam. "Collocations in Context: A New Perspective on Collocation Networks." *International Journal of Corpus Linguistics* 20, no. 2 (2015): 139–73. Accessed July 3, 2020. doi: 10.1075/ijcl.20.2.01bre.
Bubenhofer, Noah. "Kollokationen, n-Gramme, Mehrworteinheiten." In *Handbuch Sprache in Politik und Gesellschaft*, edited by Kersten Sven Roth, Martin Wengeler, and Alexander Ziem, 69–93. Berlin: De Gruyter, 2017.
Busse, Dietrich. "Begriffsgeschichte oder Diskursgeschichte? Zu theoretischen Grundlagen und Methodenfragen einer historisch-semantischen Epistemologie." In *Herausforderungen der Begriffsgeschichte*, edited by Carsten Dutt, 17–38. Heidelberg: Winter, 2003.
Busse, Dietrich. *Historische Semantik. Analyse eines Programms*. Stuttgart: Klett-Cotta, 1987.
Busse, Dietrich, and Wolfgang Teubert. "Ist Diskurs ein sprachwissenschaftliches Objekt? Zur Methodenfrage der historischen Semantik." In *Begriffsgeschichte und Diskursgeschichte. Methodenfragen und Forschungsergebnisse der historischen Semantik*, edited by Dietrich Busse, Fritz Hermanns, and Wolfgang Teubert, 10–28. Opladen: Westdeutscher Verlag, 1994.
Connelly, John. "The Uses of the Volksgemeinschaft: Letters to the NSDAP Kreisleitung Eisenach, 1939–1940." *The Journal of Modern History* 68 (1996): 899–930.
Dang-Anh, Mark. "Excluding Agency: Infrastructural and Interactional Practices of Exclusion in the National Socialist Dispositif of Field Post." *M/C Journal* 23, no. 6 (2020). Accessed August 5, 2021. https://doi.org/10.5204/mcj.2725.
Eckart, Thomas, and Uwe Quasthoff. "Statistical Corpus and Language Comparison on Comparable Corpora." In *Building and Using Comparable Corpora*, edited by Serge Sharoff, Reinhard Rapp, Pierre Zweigenbaum, and Pascale Fung, 151–65. Berlin: Springer, 2013.
Evert, Stefan. "Corpora and Collocations." In *Corpus Linguistics: An International Handbook*, edited by Anke Lüdeling and Merja Kytö, 1212–48. Berlin: Mouton de Gruyter, 2008.
Felder, Ekkehard, Marcus Müller, and Friedemann Vogel. *Korpuspragmatik: Thematische Korpora als Basis diskurslinguistischer Analysen*. Berlin: De Gruyter, 2012.
Fenske, Michaela. *Demokratie erschreiben. Bürgerbriefe und Petitionen als Medien politischer Kultur 1950–1974*. Frankfurt am Main: Campus, 2013.
Fickers, Andreas. "Update für die Hermeneutik. Geschichtswissenschaft auf dem Weg zur digitalen Forensik?" *Zeithistorische Forschungen/Studies in Contemporary History* 17, no. 1 (2020). Accessed July 6, 2020. doi: https://doi.org/10.14765/zzf.dok-1765.

Firth, John Rupert. *Papers in Linguistics, 1934–51.* Oxford: Oxford University Press, 1957.
Föllmer, Moritz. "Wie kollektivistisch war der Nationalsozialismus? Zur Geschichte der Individualität zwischen Weimarer Republik und Nachkriegszeit." In *Kontinuitäten und Diskontinuitäten. Der Nationalsozialismus in der Geschichte des 20. Jahrhunderts*, edited by Birthe Kundrus and Sybille Steinbacher, 30–52. Göttingen: Wallstein, 2013.
Fritz, Gerd. "Historische Semantik – einige Schlaglichter." *Jahrbuch für Germanistische Sprachgeschichte* 2 (2011): 1–19. Accessed July 3, 2020. doi: 10.1515/9783110236620.1.
Gries, Stefan Th. "Dispersions and Adjusted Frequencies in Corpora." *International Journal of Corpus Linguistics* 13, no. 4 (2008): 403–37. Accessed July 3, 2020. doi: 10.1075/ijcl.13.4.02gri.
Hermanns, Fritz. "Brisante Wörter. Zur lexikographischen Behandlung parteisprachlicher Wörter und Wendungen in Wörterbüchern der deutschen Gegenwartssprache." In *Studien zur neuhochdeutschen Lexikographie II*, edited by Herbert Ernst Wiegand, 87–108. Hildesheim: Olms, 1982.
Hermanns, Fritz. "Diskurshermeneutik." In *Diskurslinguistik nach Foucault. Theorie und Gegenstände*, edited by Ingo Warnke, 187–210. Berlin: De Gruyter, 2007.
Hermanns, Fritz. "Linguistische Hermeneutik. Überlegungen zur überfälligen Einrichtung eines in der Linguistik bislang fehlenden Teilfachs." In *Der Sitz der Sprache im Leben: Beiträge zu einer kulturanalytischen Linguistik*, edited by Heidrun Kämper, Angelika Linke, and Martin Wengeler, 67–102. Berlin: De Gruyter, 2012.
Horan, Geraldine. "'Er zog sich die "neue Sprache" des "Dritten Reiches" über wie ein Kleidungsstück': Communities of Practice and Performativity in National Socialist Discourse." *Linguistik Online* 30, no. 1 (2007): 57–80. Accessed June 13, 2020. doi: https://doi.org/10.13092/lo.30.549.
Jäger, Ludwig. "Mythos Cours. Saussures Sprachidee und die Gründungslegende des Strukturalismus." In *Strukturalismus, heute: Brüche, Spuren, Kontinuitäten: Abhandlungen zur Literaturwissenschaft*, edited by Martin Endres and Leonhard Herrmann, 11–28. Stuttgart: J.B. Metzler, 2018.
Jureit, Ulrike. *Das Ordnen von Räumen. Territorium und Lebensraum im 19. und 20. Jahrhundert.* Hamburg: Hamburger Edition, 2012.
Kalwa, Nina. "Die Konstitution von Konzepten in Diskursen: Zoom als Methode der diskurslinguistischen Bedeutungsanalyse." In *Sprach(kritik)kompetenz als Mittel demokratischer Willensbildung. Sprachliche In- und Exklusionsstrategien als gesellschaftliche Herausforderung*, edited by Jürgen Schiewe, Thomas Niehr, and Sandro M. Moraldo, 11–25. Bremen: Hempen Verlag, 2019.
Kämper, Heidrun. *Aspekte des Demokratiediskurses der späten 1960er Jahre: Konstellationen, Kontexte, Konzepte.* Berlin: De Gruyter, 2012.
Kämper, Heidrun. "Sprachliche Sozialgeschichte 1933 bis 1945 – ein Projektkonzept." In *Sprachliche Sozialgeschichte des Nationalsozialismus*, edited by Heidrun Kämper and Britt-Marie Schuster, 9–25. Bremen: Hempen Verlag, 2018.
Kilgarriff, Adam. "Comparing Corpora." *International Journal of Corpus Linguistics* 6, no. 1 (2001): 97–133.
Klemperer, Victor. *LTI. Notizbuch eines Philologen* [1947]. Stuttgart: Reclam, 2018.
Kramer, Nicole. *Volksgenossinnen an der Heimatfront. Mobilisierung, Verhalten, Erinnerung.* Göttingen: Wallstein, 2011.

Kundrus, Birthe. *Kriegerfrauen. Familienpolitik und Geschlechterverhältnisse im Ersten und Zweiten Weltkrieg.* Hamburg: Wallstein, 1995.
Landwehr, Achim. *Historische Diskursanalyse.* 2nd impr. Frankfurt am Main: Campus, 2009.
Lange, Karl. "Der Terminus 'Lebensraum' in Hitlers 'Mein Kampf.'" *Vierteljahrshefte für Zeitgeschichte* 13, no. 4 (1965): 426–37.
Maas, Utz. *"Als der Geist der Gemeinschaft eine Sprache fand". Sprache im Nationalsozialismus, Versuch einer historischen Argumentationsanalyse.* Opladen: Westdeutscher Verlag, 1984.
Manke, Sabine. *Brandt anfeuern. Das Misstrauensvotum 1972 in Bürgerbriefen an den Bundeskanzler. Ein kulturwissenschaftlicher Beitrag zu modernen Resonanz- und Korrespondenzphänomenen.* Marburg: Tectum, 2008.
Meister, Jan Christoph. "From TACT to CATMA or A Mindful Approach to Text Annotation and Analysis." Accessed July 6, 2020. http://jcmeister.de/downloads/texts/Meister_2020-TACT-to-CATMA.pdf.
Merkel, Ina, ed. *"Wir sind doch nicht die Meckerecke der Nation". Briefe an das DDR-Fernsehen.* Cologne: Böhlau, 1998.
Mühlberg, Felix. *Bürger, Bitten und Behörden. Geschichte der Eingabe in der DDR.* Berlin: Karl Dietz, 2004.
Partington, Alan, Alison Duguid, and Charlotte Taylor. *Patterns and Meanings in Discourse: Theory and Practice in Corpus-Assisted Discourse Studies (CADS).* Amsterdam: John Benjamins, 2013.
Polenz, Peter von. *Deutsche Satzsemantik: Grundbegriffe des Zwischen-den-Zeilen-Lesens.* Berlin: De Gruyter, 1985.
Schiller, Anne, Simone Teufel, Christine Stöckert, and Christine Thielen. *Guidelines für das Tagging deutscher Textcorpora mit STTS (Kleines und großes Tagset).* Stuttgart and Tübingen: Universität Stuttgart and Universität Tübingen, 1999.
Schlosser, Horst Dieter. *Sprache unterm Hakenkreuz. Eine andere Geschichte des Nationalsozialismus.* Cologne: Böhlau, 2013.
Schmidt, Christoph. "Zu den Motiven 'alter Kämpfer' in der NSDAP." In *Die Reihen fast geschlossen. Beiträge zur Geschichte des Alltags unterm Nationalsozialismus*, edited by Detlev Peukert and Jürgen Reulecke, 21–44. Wuppertal: Peter Hammer Verlag, 1981.
Schmiechen-Ackermann, Detlef, Marlis Buchholz, Bianca Roitsch, and Christiane Schröder, eds. *Der Ort der "Volksgemeinschaft" in der deutschen Gesellschaftsgeschichte.* Paderborn: Ferdinand Schöningh, 2018.
Schmitz-Berning, Cornelia. *Vokabular des Nationalsozialismus.* Berlin: De Gruyter, 1998.
Scholl, Stefan. "Beschwerde- und Bittschreiben von Mannheimer Bürgern während des Nationalsozialismus: Eine Analyse alltagssprachlicher Kollusion anhand von ausgewählten Beispielen." *Sprachreport* 35, no. 4 (2019): 6–15. Accessed July 6, 2020. https://pub.ids-mannheim.de/laufend/sprachreport/pdf/sr19-4.pdf.
Scholl, Stefan. "Für eine Sprach- und Kommunikationsgeschichte des Nationalsozialismus. Ein programmatischer Forschungsüberblick." *Archiv für Sozialgeschichte* 59 (2019): 409–44.
Schütz, Alfred. "Concept and Theory Formation in the Social Sciences." *The Journal of Philosophy* 51, no. 9 (1954): 257–73.
Schwandt, Silke. "Digitale Methoden für die Historische Semantik. Auf den Spuren von Begriffen in digitalen Korpora." *Geschichte und Gesellschaft* 44 (2018): 107–34.

Sinclair, John. *Corpus, Concordance, Collocation*. 3rd impr. Oxford: Oxford University Press, 1995.
Sternberger, Dolf, Gerhard Storz, and Wilhelm E. Süskind. *Aus dem Wörterbuch des Unmenschen*. Hamburg: Claassen, 1957.
Stöver, Bernd. *Volksgemeinschaft im Dritten Reich. Die Konsensbereitschaft der Deutschen aus der Sicht sozialistischer Exilberichte*. Düsseldorf: Droste, 1993.
Taylor, Charlotte, and Anna Marchi. *Corpus Approaches to Discourse: A Critical Review*. London: Routledge, 2018.
Teubert, Wolfgang. "Corpus Linguistics: An Alternative." *semen* 27 (2009): 1–25. Accessed July 3, 2020. doi: 10.4000/semen.8912.
Teubert, Wolfgang. "Korpuslinguistik, Hermeneutik und die soziale Konstruktion der Wirklichkeit." *Linguistik online* 28, no. 3 (2006): 41–60. Accessed July 3, 2020. doi: https://doi.org/10.13092/lo.28.610.
Tribble, Christopher. "What Are Concordances and How Are They Used?" In *The Routledge Handbook of Corpus Linguistics*, edited by Anne O'Keeffe und Michael McCarthy, 167–83. London: Routledge, 2010.
Wildt, Michael. "Volksgemeinschaft: A Modern Perspective on National Socialist Society." In *Visions of Community in Nazi Germany*, edited by Martina Steber and Bernhard Gotto, 43–59. Oxford: Oxford University Press, 2014.
Wimmer, Florian. *Die völkische Ordnung der Armut. Kommunale Sozialpolitik im nationalsozialistischen München*. Göttingen, Wallstein, 2014.
Wittgenstein, Ludwig, *Philosophische Untersuchungen*. Frankfurt am Main: Suhrkamp, 1971 [1953].
Zimmermann, Harm Peer. "Lebenswelt und Politik. Bürgerbriefe an Helmut Schmidt." In *Humane Orientierungswissenschaft. Was leisten Wissenschaftskulturen für das Verständnis menschlicher Lebenswelt*, edited by Peter Janich, 203–26. Würzburg: Königshausen und Neumann, 2008.

Programs Used

AntConc. Accessed July 3, 2020. laurenceanthnony.net.
CATMA. Accessed July 3, 2020. https://catma.de/.
LancsBox. Brezina, V., M. Timperley, and T. McEnery. #LancsBox v. 4.5 [software]. 2018. Accessed July 3, 2020. http://corpora.lancs.ac.uk/lancsbox.

Part III **Digital Exhibitions and Digital Forms of Commemoration**

Andreas Birk, Frederike Buda, Heiko Bülow, Arturo Gomez Chavez, Christian A. Müller, and Julia Timpe

Chapter 6
Digitizing a Gigantic Nazi Construction: 3D-Mapping of Bunker Valentin in Bremen

German Summary: Dieses Kapitel präsentiert die (Zwischen-) Ergebnisse und Herausforderungen des durch das Bundesministerium für Bildung und Forschung geförderten Projektes „3D Erfassung der Gedenkstätte U-Boot Bunker Valentin durch Luft-, Boden- und Unterwasserroboter" (Valentin3D). Das Projekt, das 2018 startete, wird von einem interdisziplinären Team der Robotics und Geschichtswissenschaften an der Jacobs University Bremen durchgeführt. Ziel ist die Erstellung eines digitalen, dreidimensionalen Modells des während des Nationalsozialismus erbauten U-Boot Bunker Valentin.

Der Bunker wurde ab 1943 im äußersten Norden Bremens unter massivem Einsatz von Zwangsarbeit errichtet. In ihm sollten nach der Fertigstellung U-Boote für die deutsche Marine nach dem Fließband-Prinzip produziert werden, in der Hoffnung, so noch eine Wende im U-Boot-Krieg in der Nordsee herbeiführen zu können. Stattdessen wurden im März 1945 die Baustelle sowie der Bunker selbst bombardiert, die Bauarbeiten im April nach erneuter Bombardierung eingestellt. Durch die Bombenabwürfe wurden auch Teile der unfertigen Decke des Gebäudes durchschlagen. Für Besucher*innen der 2015 eröffneten Gedenkstätte „Denkort Bunker Valentin" bedeutet dies, dass für sie ein Großteil der geplanten Produktionshalle aufgrund der Gefahr von Steinschlag nicht zugängig ist. Zudem sind weitere Teile des Bunkers für Besucher*innen und auch für Forschende bislang gesperrt gewesen. Dazu gehört ein sich im östlichen Teil des Bauwerkes befindlicher gefluteter Keller, von dem die Leiter*innen des Denkortes ausgehen, dass es sich um einen ehemaligen Luftschutzkeller handelt.

Für die Erstellung des 3D Modells wurde aufgrund der Unwegsamkeit und Gefahren der weitgehend unzugänglichen Areale die Erforschung und Kartographierung mit Methoden und Werkzeugen der Robotics vorgenommen. Das Modell wird zukünftig open access verfügbar sein und damit Forscher*innen sowie Besucher*innen unabhängig von ihrem Standort Zugang zu dem Bunker gewähren. Zudem ist nun auch die Produktionshalle besser einseh- und erforschbar.

Durch die Erkundung des Kellers mithilfe eines Underwater Remote Operated Vehicles (ROV) konnten zudem neue Erkenntnisse über die (Bau-)Geschichte des Bunker Valentin gewonnen werden. Im Zusammenspiel mit zuvor nie ausgewerteten Bauplänen konnte die bisherige Annahme, dass es sich hierbei, zumindest teilweise, um einen Luftschutzkeller gehandelt hat, verifiziert werden.

1 Introduction

This chapter discusses the Valentin 3D project, a collaborative work by researchers at Jacobs University Bremen and the Denkort Bunker Valentin in Bremen. It has been running since 2018 and is funded by the German Ministry for Education and Research (Bundesministerium für Bildung und Forschung, BMBF).[1] The project's main goal is the 3D-digitization of Bunker Valentin, a huge submarine pen or bunker that represents one of the most massive remnants of German World War II armaments projects. The bunker is located on the river Weser and was intended to manufacture and launch advanced submarines, with access to the North Sea via the Weser. It was built using forced labor. The war ended before the facility was completed, but the incomplete hulk is nonetheless an immense physical reminder of the Nazi period. Yet, and despite its status today as a *Denkort*, much remains to be learned about Bunker Valentin, including details of its layout and physical construction. The goal of this project is to provide a detailed three-dimensional mapping and modeling of the bunker.

This digitization project combines the efforts and expertise of both historians and computer scientists from Jacobs University with support from the *Denkort*'s management. The Valentin Bunker is a vast structure with an area of 35,375 m², with a length of 419 m, width of 67–97 m, and a height of 20–33 m. Parts of it are poorly accessible, due to structural issues and to large sections being submerged underwater. To deal with this situation, the project employs a wide range of robotic tools—including a Laser Range Finder (LRF), a Micro Aerial Vehicle (MAV) or drone, and an underwater Remote Operated Vehicle (ROV)—to survey the bunker. In this respect, the project endeavors to uncover data that would not be available without the use of specialized computerized and digital equipment. As this data is gathered, digital tools are also used to produce and process the raw data as well as models generated to researchers and other interested parties. Therefore, from start to finish, the goals of this project are to use technical means to reveal information and to make it as widely available as possible. The use of robotic tools will allow access to data that would be otherwise inaccessible,

---

[1] The project is part of the BMBF's "eHeritage program," which aims to digitize objects of cultural significance apart from museum, library, or archive collections.

and the use of digital tools will democratize this information among researchers and the general public alike.

The focal point for this chapter is a discussion of the technical aspects of the project and its implication in the historical analysis of Bunker Valentin. This is based on our assumption that understanding the technology that produces the data is important to the historians' approach and use of this data.

The chapter's first section will introduce the bunker and its general history to give context to the project overall. In the second section, the common robotics tools used during historical explorations with the aim of digitizing cultural heritage sites will be briefly introduced; the goal is to point the reader towards literature which can be used when starting such an enterprise.

The third section will discuss the digitization processes in two different areas of the bunker and the implications of the data for historical research. Here, we first describe how the on-land ruined part was explored and digitized. The ruined part is one of the best-known parts of the bunker as it is visible to anyone who visits the site. Accessing it, however, is very difficult and in fact dangerous due to its structural instability. This inaccessibility means it has remained in its original state throughout the years, making it a very interesting area for researchers and visitors to the bunker alike. Responding to this interest, it became our main focus in the digitization. The process and equipment used for digitization of this ruined part will be detailed before discussing possible benefits of the digitization process for the *Denkort*. Subsequently, as the digitization of the ruined part is not coherent without a visualization, we will explain our approach towards the visual representation of our 3D-model. We will conclude this section with the exploration of the flooded basement under the bunker. This area has never been explored and its exact purpose is unknown. Neither were any structural details known prior to our first inspection. By analyzing the visual data gathered by the robots and comparing it to newly discovered and digitized blueprints, we can provide further evidence of the use of the bunker's basement as an air-raid shelter during its construction. Our chapter will also highlight that the digitization of the ruined part shows value especially for the *Denkort*'s educational work as the subsequent 3D-model will serve as an important tool in showing the entirety of the ruined part.

An important element of our project is its interdisciplinarity. Standing in the gigantic bunker, digitizing our surroundings, we quickly learned that we needed the expertise of both historians and roboticists to conduct our investigation fruitfully. The historians gained insights into technical possibilities and limitations of building a 3D-model. At the same time, the roboticists relied on the input of the historians while on site. We were in constant exchange about points of interest from the historical perspective and about the place's past, thus enriching each others knowledge and interests.

2 History of Bunker Valentin

Bunker Valentin is part of the National Socialist military infrastructure set up during World War II. Following Joseph Goebbels's call for "total war," Albert Speer, Germany's Minister for Armaments and Munitions, and Karl Dönitz, the navy's commander-in-chief, decided amongst other things to concentrate armaments production on submarines. Germany's naval forces had suffered heavy submarine losses in the North Sea since December 1942. In reaction to this, a new submarine had been designed, called Typ XXI. It was faster and capable of longer submersion periods than its predecessors. The production process of this new submarine needed to be protected from an increasing number of air raids by Allied Forces. Hence, in the summer of 1943, construction of Bunker Valentin started in Farge, a small village in Bremen's northernmost hinterlands.[2] The giant bunker was meant to be a safe site for the assembling of Typ XXI submarines.

A key reason for choosing Bremen as the location for the bunker was the city's existing shipbuilding industry. This meant that there was already a sufficient number of major shipyards along the Weser, which provided the necessary infrastructure to the manufacturing process. Shipyards further inland along the river, like A.G. Weser and Vulkan Werft, would build sections of the new submarines which would then be assembled at Bunker Valentin. The Ministry of Armaments and Munition decided to adopt the American assembly-line system to build the Typ XXI as it promised to reduce the construction time for a submarine from more than eleven to just two months.[3]

The building of the bunker in Farge started in May 1943. As a priority project in support of the "total war" aim, construction progressed quickly. This was aided by being provided with huge material resources as well as a giant labor force. Up to 8,000 forced laborers, from across Europe, worked uninterruptedly on the construction site seven days a week. These workers were interned in several camps located between 3 and 8 km east of the building site. These camps were not homogenous in shape, size, and internal organization. Among them

---

[2] Marc Buggeln, "Der U-Boot-Bunker Valentin in Bremen," in *Bunker. Kriegsort, Zuflucht, Erinnerungsraum*, ed. Inge Marszolek and Marc Buggeln (Frankfurt am Main: Campus, 2008), 104–7.
[3] Barbara Johr and Hartmut Roder, *Der Bunker. Ein Beispiel nationalsozialistischen Wahns, Bremen-Farge 1943–1945* (Bremen: Edition Temmen, 1989), 20.

was a satellite of the concentration camp Neuengamme in Hamburg and an *Arbeitserziehungslager* (Labor Education Camp, AEL).[4] For the forced laborers, the difference in the nature of the camps meant not only varying experiences of incarcerations but also different odds of survival; for example, the AEL was one of the deadliest of its kind in Germany.[5] Notwithstanding which camp they were interned at, the life of the forced laborers was divided between the camp, the construction site, and the journey[6] to and from the bunker, giving them little time for rest while, at times, getting minimal to no nutrition.[7]

Not all the camps were constructed exclusively for forced laborers working on the bunker. The AEL had been built in 1940 to support the armaments industry in Bremen with workers. In 1939, the Wirtschaftliche Forschungsgesellschaft mbH (Economic Research Ltd., abbreviated as Wifo[8]) contracted the Berlin-based construction company Gottlieb Tesch to build fuel depots with large tanks for the storage of various types of fuel east of Farge. Most of Tesch's workers were foreign laborers because even at the beginning of the war, Germany was already experiencing labor shortage. The laborers were forced to work for the Germans following the policy of *"Reichseinsatz."* This euphemistic National Socialist term described deployment practices during World War II, which obligated unemployed men in occupied countries to work in Germany if they failed to find work at home. Because of discriminations and rough work conditions, many

---

4 It is difficult to give an exact number of the camps since official records were partially destroyed and some camps were renamed or repurposed over time. Five camps can be identified with certainty; the existence of three other possible camps remains unsure. Besides the one mentioned above, more is known about Heidkamp I and II and the "Marinegemeinschaftslager" (Navy Community Camp). All three were established in connection with the construction of Valentin and not previously. Cf. further down in this section.
5 Gabriele Lotfi, *KZ der Gestapo. Arbeitserziehungslager im Dritten Reich* (Frankfurt am Main: Fischer, 2003), 193.
6 The duration of the journey would have differed between the camps. Buggeln estimates that the journey for concentration camp inmates took one hour for each route, while an inmate of the AEL remembered that his route to the construction site took around 30 minutes. It is also unclear whether camp inmates closer to the construction site would have walked, while there is evidence that concentration camp inmates were transported in open trolleys. In any case, whether 30 or 60 minutes, when working 12 hours a day, every minute not spent resting would have been an effort. Cf. Marc Buggeln, *Der U-Boot-Bunker "Valentin". Marinerüstung, Zwangsarbeit und Erinnerung* (Bremen: Edition Temmen, 2010), 78–79, 130–31.
7 Marcus Meyer and Christel Trouvé, "Denkort Bunker Valentin. Eine erste Bilanz zwei Jahre nach der Eröffnung," *Gedenkstättenrundbrief* 188 (2017): 4.
8 The name is intentionally misleading. It was a front company for the procurement, production, and storage of essential war resources, such as crude oil; Buggeln, *Der U-Boot-Bunker "Valentin,"* 12–19.

of these "foreign laborers" tried to evade work, either by performing slowly and carelessly or by absenteeism or flight. German police forces undertook various measures to fight against this so-called *Arbeitsbummelei*, amongst them the establishment of Labor Education Camps, which were supervised by the Geheime Staatspolizei (Secret State Police, the Gestapo).[9] In Bremen, the first AEL was probably built on the initiative of the Tesch company, which had complained constantly about high fluctuation and low work discipline among their Czech, Belgian, Dutch, French, and German laborers. Though primarily an instrument of repression by the Gestapo, it became a convenient means for Bremen companies to discipline their workers while still maintaining their workforce: In contrast to concentration camps, AELs were located in closer vicinity to shop floors and incarceration periods were supposed to be limited to 56 days.[10]

When construction at the bunker started in 1943, the AEL was relocated, no longer serving the Tesch company and Wifo, but now providing workers for the massive construction site. With this relocation, conditions in the AEL became extremely dire. Conditions had already been bad previously, with both beatings and the withholding of food being established actions to "discipline" and "educate" inmates; at the newly relocated camp working and living conditions became immeasurably worse, mostly due to the much harsher working conditions.[11]

In contrast to the AEL, the concentration camp in Farge was established with the purpose to provide workers to the bunker's construction site. As a satellite camp of the concentration camp Neuengamme in Hamburg, it was settled about 4 km east of the construction site in the vicinity of the village Rekum, a relatively deserted heathland. This was also the area where Tesch built some of the fuel tanks for the Wifo. Concentration camp inmates were now interned in one of the unused fuel tanks at the depot. This meant they were forced to sleep underground, hidden from view, in a circular "room" 50 m wide and 15 m high. By March 1945, one month before the Germans evacuated the camp, 2,029 inmates were living in this concentration camp. Even considering that some inmates slept in barracks above ground, this left about one square meter per person in the tank.[12] This limited sleeping space was just one of the hardships the inmates had to endure. They were also working 12-hour shifts on a diet consisting mostly of thin soup and small quantities of bread. Furthermore, inmates of the concentration camp were assigned the most dangerous and devastating work on the

---

9 Lotfi, *KZ der Gestapo*, 70–74.
10 Buggeln, "Der U-Boot-Bunker Valentin," 108–9.
11 Johr, *Der Bunker*, 37.
12 Buggeln, "Der U-Boot-Bunker Valentin," 111, and Johr, *Der Bunker*, 45.

construction site, for example carrying steel girders to the unsecured top of the building or 50-kilo cement bags to the concrete mixers.[13]

Further camps were established in connection with the Wifo project whose work forces were later redirected to the bunker's construction site. The Heidkamp I & II camps—established by the Organisation Todt (OT)[14]—housed Soviet prisoners of war (POWs). There were also two *Marinegemeinschaftslager* (Naval community camps), which provided housing for the guards, soldiers, and construction management who worked at the bunker.[15]

Despite the crucial role Bunker Valentin was meant to play in Germany's war effort and the number of resources poured into its construction since 1943, including the thousands of forced laborers who worked ceaselessly on the project, it was not completed by the end of the war in 1945. Although the bunker was designed to be bombproof eventually, it was inevitably more vulnerable during construction. On March 27, 1945, two British bombs punctured the bunker's roof at a spot that still lacked several layers of concrete armor. Then, three days later, American air raids destroyed most of the construction site around the bunker. However, even then, work on the bunker persisted.[16] It was only abandoned on April 7, 1945, and the camps were cleared. In fact, at this point the construction had progressed so far that the bunker was essentially complete. This is reflected in the giant structure of the building that can still be seen today. Indeed, interior construction and fitting had also been carried through, and machinery, cranes, cables, and facilities had all been largely installed; today, this is no longer apparent. However, despite its advanced stage of construction, the work had never reached the stage to see a submarine being assembled, let alone deployed, at Bunker Valentin.[17]

From 1946 to 1950, the bunker building was used as a bombing test site by the American Air Force. From 1967 on and after much debate about what to do with the massive building—options included demolition, conversion to use as a nuclear power plant, a nuclear missiles silo, and more—the Bundeswehr (German army) used it as a depot. For this, the Bundeswehr partially reconstructed

---

13 Johr, *Der Bunker*, 37, 45.
14 OT was responsible for the realization of construction projects concerning armaments and protective constructions, like the Siegfried Line. It was named after its leader Fritz Todt.
15 Buggeln, *Der U-Boot-Bunker "Valentin,"* 144–54.
16 In fact, one of the recently discovered blueprints shows a plan, drawn on April 1, 1945, to repair the damage in the roof, "Vorschlag für die Ausbesserung der Decke", 01.04.1945, Bl-Nr. 2150/60aArchiv Denkort Bunker Valentin (ADBV).
17 Johr, *Der Bunker*, 21; all interiors were stripped immediately after the war either by the construction companies or villagers.

the bunker. It also denied the general public and even researchers access to the bunker, and—in a very literal sense—wiped it from the map: Hidden as a military installation, it was no longer represented on publicly available maps.[18]

Subsequently, the bunker disappeared from the public. It was only during the late 1970s that an awareness of the grim and inhuman history of the bunker and its construction began to re-emerge. This was due to a general shift in Germany's remembrance culture and the initiative of a few interested individuals. Their activities culminated in a memorial being placed just outside the military perimeter in 1983, leading in turn to a growing public interest in the bunker. Perhaps as a consequence, the Bundeswehr allowed partial public access to the site in the 1990s.[19] In 2010, Bunker Valentin passed out of the Bundeswehr's possession and the process of transitioning the entire site into a memorial officially started in 2011. The Denkort Bunker Valentin was inaugurated in November 2015 as a public memorial site which offers exhibitions about the site's past, as well as guided tours that explore the physical and historical space of Bunker Valentin.[20]

It is important to emphasize that the memorial is focused on the bunker itself. Little remains of the work camps that surrounded the site during World War II, and they are distributed too far from the actual bunker to be included in the guided tours, even though they constitute a crucial part of its history. Additionally, and as mentioned above, much of the site belonging to the memorial cannot be accessed, as areas would be too dangerous to enter or are submerged underwater. This applies especially to the ruined part, where the bombings punctured the ceiling. Given that this area of the bunker has been rarely entered in the past 75 years,[21] the ruined part has more or less retained its original state, while the rest of the building has been renovated and repurposed by the Bundeswehr. This area was intended to have housed around two-thirds of the production's operations, with many technical aspects of the assembly line. Twelve workstations were planned as part of the assembly process. In order to maneuver the submarines between those workstations, remnants of turn wheels and transport-mechanisms are still visible inside the ruined part. Also, from this part of the bunker the submarines would have been deployed into the river. Therefore, it holds a

---

18 Buggeln, *Der U-Boot-Bunker "Valentin,"* 168–85.
19 Buggeln, *Der U-Boot-Bunker "Valentin,"* 188–95.
20 https://www.denkort-bunker-valentin.de/startseite.html, accessed July 15, 2020.
21 A notable exception are the performances of Karl Kraus's "Die letzten Tage der Menschheit" by the Theater Bremen in six seasons from 1999 to 2005. The performances are still well remembered by Bremen citizens and, when talking about Bunker Valentin, are often associated with it. Cf. Meyer and Trouvé, "Denkort Bunker Valentin," 9.

diving basin on the northern front as well as foundations for a sluice, capable of completely flooding the bunker's northern side. Thus, even though machines installed during its construction phase were immediately dismantled after the war, the functionality of the bunker remains visible in the ruined part.[22] This is the point of departure for our digitization project, which aims at capturing these inaccessible and submerged spaces with the goal to eventually provide virtual access. In the next section, we discuss the technical aspects of this digitization.

3 Robotics for Digitization of Cultural Heritage

3.1 Remote Sensing and Geo-Survey

In the past years, *Remote Sensing* and *Geo-Survey* tools have rapidly progressed and become state-of-the-art techniques in modeling (digitizing) cultural heritage sites. One of the main reasons for their rise is that they allow for digitization of large and complex historical structures, which then can be preserved, studied, and easily shared among experts for further discussion. Furthermore, they allow accessing dangerous sites and obtaining more structural details about them. In this context, Remote Sensing and Geo-Surveying can be defined as the area of methods and processes for acquiring 2D/3D information about objects (such as cultural sites) and their perceivable properties from a distance through a wide range of sensors. The observation distance can substantially vary from very remote using satellite and aircraft data to much closer sensing with locally deployed sensors and sensor-platforms including indoor surveying.

In a typical in situ scenario, professional surveyors, including those with historical, archaeological, and technical expertise, access the target site with the needed sensors—cameras, Laser Range Finders, teleoperated robots, etc.—to collect as much data as possible. This data is then processed to extract meaningful information and representations for experts to use—maps, 3D-models, annotated images or documents, to mention just a few examples. Finally, all this heterogeneous data must be organized, integrated, and maintained through systems capable of handling massive volumes of information, also known as Big Data.

---

22 Marcus Meyer, "Historische Räume und forensische Pädagogik: Die Konzeption des 'Denkortes Bunker Valentin' in Bremen," in *Gedächtnisräume. Geschichtsbilder und Erinnerungskulturen in Norddeutschland*, ed. Janina Fuge, Rainer Hering, and Harald Schmid (Göttingen: v&r unipress, 2014), 357–59; for a more detailed account of the planned assembly line see also: Buggeln: *Der U-Boot-Bunker "Valentin,"* 42–43.

From the point of view of an engineer, the methods for data acquisition, aggregation, and maintenance along with their accuracy and efficiency are an evolving field. Improvements of the methods can lead to an increase in human safety and decrease in time spent during field explorations, but they also lead to better accessibility to the generated models and information from the cultural sites and objects. Recent approaches take advantage of autonomous robots to make surveys of indoor/outdoor cultural heritage sites more time-efficient and safer (the latter being a particular concern as some sites may be difficult or dangerous to access). It is also important to mention that these robots can be engineered to operate in diverse environments (land, air, and water), which offers an advantage in exploring outdoor sites.[23]

3.2 Robots and Sensors for Mapping and Surveying

Most of the work related to the documentation of cultural heritage objects relies on either Laser Range Finders (LRF) or structured light 3D sensors,[24] or photogrammetry; such and other examples are: RGB and multispectral cameras,[25] Terrestrial Laser Scanners (TLS),[26] Ground Penetrating Radar (GPR),[27] and Raman

---

23 Literature on the topic is mentioned in the next section. The reader can inspect the short text and video provided in Robin Murphy, *A Decade of Rescue Robots*, abstract of a paper presented on the IEEE/RSJ International Conference on Intelligent Robots and Systems, Vilamoura, Algarve, Portugal, October 7–12, 2012, accessed August 15, 2020, https://ieeexplore.ieee.org/stamp/stamp.jsp?arnumber=6386301), for highlights of how robotic systems have contributed to exploratory missions in very challenging environments.
24 Asia Botto et al., "Applications of Laser-Induced Breakdown Spectroscopy to Cultural Heritage and Archaeology: A Critical Review," *Journal of Analytical Atomic Spectrometry* 1 (2019), accessed August 15, 2020, doi: 10.1039/C8JA00319 J.
25 G. Guidi et al., "Image-Based 3D Capture of Cultural Heritage Artifacts: An Experimental Study about 3D Data Quality," paper presented at the Digital Heritage International Congress 2, Granada, Spain, September 28–October 2, 2015, accessed August 18, 2020, doi: 10.1109/DigitalHeritage.2015.7419514; Susana Del Pozo et al., "Multispectral Radiometric Analysis of Façades to Detect Pathologies from Active and Passive Remote Sensing," *Remote Sensing* 80 (2016), accessed August 20, 2020, doi: 10.3390/rs8010080.
26 Dorrit Borrmann et al., "Robotic Mapping of Cultural Heritage Sites," *The International Archives of the Photogrammetry, Remote Sensing and Spatial Information Science*, suppl. W4, vol. 40, no. 5 (2015): 9–16.
27 Iván Puente et al., "NDT Documentation and Evaluation of the Roman Bridge of Lugo Using GPR and Mobile and Static LiDAR," *Journal of Performance of Constructed Facilities* 29 (2013), accessed September 5, 2020, doi: 10.1061/(ASCE)CF.1943–5509.0000531.

Spectroscopy.[28] Due to the above discussed need to find solutions for the issues related to human safety, accessibility, and time-efficiency during surveys, hybrid sensors such as Mobile LiDAR Systems (MLS, LiDAR—Laser Imaging Detection and Ranging[29]) have been rapidly developed in recent years. At first, MLS were commonly deployed in large vehicles or backpacks; recent progress allows for MLS to be boarded in compact autonomous robots that offer more flexibility in terms of accuracy, sample density, and access to indoor and hazardous areas.[30]

Without a doubt, the design and creation of such systems have enabled a more accurate documentation of cultural sites and reduction of time and resources dedicated to the data collection phase, which normally entails finding the best position for a scan, moving the equipment to the chosen position, and making the corresponding georeferenced annotation. However, as the plethora of devices to capture data increases, effective information management systems and software are needed. For example, it is necessary to aggregate data describing a particular object provided by different sensor modalities (RGB images, spectrography, etc.) and by different levels of detail. Likewise, some of the object's representations are formed by millions of 3D points per scan, namely point clouds, which need to be stored and aggregated to create 3D-models. To achieve this, efficient mathematical methods are crucial for their visualization and dissemination among surveyors and end-users.

Based on these remarks, in the next sections we explain the technologies and methods used to digitize Bunker Valentin and to provide the processed as well as the raw data to experts and the public. In brief, for the flooded parts of the bunker, underwater robots, namely Remotely Operated Vehicles (ROVs), are used. To map the outside of the bunker, image data from Micro Aerial Vehicles (MAVs) is used to generate 3D-maps based on photogrammetry. For the inside, light conditions, absence of GPS, etc., make the use of MAVs challenging.[31]

---

[28] Francesco Casadio, Céline Daher, Ludovic Bellot-Gurlet, "Raman Spectroscopy of Cultural Heritage Materials: Overview of Applications and New Frontiers in Instrumentation, Sampling Modalities, and Data Processing," *Topics in Current Chemistry* 62 (2016), accessed September 5, 2020, doi: 10.1007/s41061–016–0061-z.
[29] An explanation of the basic concept of LiDAR technologies is given in section 4.1.1.
[30] Daniele Calisi et al., "Digitizing Indoor and Underground Cultural Heritage Sites with Robots," *Science Research and Information Technology* 6, no. 1 (2016): 23–30.
[31] Heiko Bülow et al., "A Divide and Conquer Method for 3D Registration of Inhomogeneous, Partially Overlapping Scans with Fourier Mellin SOFT (FMS)," *2020 IEEE International Conference on Robotics and Automation (ICRA), Paris, France, May 31–August 31, 2020*, accessed October 7, 2020, doi: 10.1109/ICRA40945.2020.9197453.

Therefore, for this area, a 3D Laser Range Finder (LRF), concretely a FARO Focus 3D, is the canonical choice and the source of data.[32]

4 Digitization of Bunker Valentin

4.1 Digitization of the Bunker's Ruined Part

4.1.1 3D-Model Generation (Laser Range Finders—LRF)

As mentioned in the previous section (3), one of the main objectives of using robotic technologies for the digitization of cultural sites is the reduction of the quantity of resources and time used for this task, as well as the risk for human surveyors when exploring damaged or inaccessible structures. One option is to use MLS—that is, autonomous or teleoperated robots equipped with sensors. However, these systems need to be robust enough for the different types of terrain that can be encountered. In the case of Bunker Valentin, as explained previously, several areas are flooded or completely underwater (Figure 6.1) while other areas are covered in gravel from the collapsed ceiling, with some of these sections connected to underground tunnels (Figure 6.2).

This complexity in the environment demands a high level of flexibility and robustness from an MLS; for this reason and because of the poor lighting conditions and the absence of GPS, it was opted to use a LRF, specifically a FARO Focus 3D (Figure 6.3), placed manually in strategic points within the ruined part to obtain data that is processed into a 3D-model. The FARO LRF outputs a laser beam to measure the distance from the sensor to an object point by point. This distance is computed by measuring the time it takes for the laser beam to hit an object and bounce back to the sensor, namely time of flight. A rotating mirror directs the beam to scan the scene (walls, rocks, pipes) vertically in rows. The result is a text file with information about millions of points—that is, distance, vertical, and horizontal angle. A basic diagram of its functionality is shown in Figure 6.4.

Such high-end 3D LRFs provide 2.5D scans—that is, range information from the point of placement of the device, with quite accurate data over extended ranges. While it is an advantage to cover long ranges, it also creates challenges for *registration algorithms*—that is, methods used to find correspondences be-

---

[32] These explanations cover only the basic principles of the systems' and sensors' functionality since this article focuses on their usage and synergy with historical methodologies.

Figure 6.1: Flooded turn-wheel.

tween different 2.5D scans to merge them into a single 3D-model with more details, fewer occlusions, and spanning a larger area. Note that 2.5D range data only captures the first surface hit by the sensor beam; hence, it cannot look around an object and multiple scans are needed for registration and generating a proper 3D-model. Ideally, an area or section should be covered by as few scans as possible to minimize surveying time; nevertheless, this means that the overlap between scans is also reduced, as well as the number of correspondences, which makes registration harder. Moreover, the fact that long-range scans from LRFs perform a non-uniform sampling of the environment (acquired data is denser closer to the sensor) affects the number of scans needed and their location.[33] To overcome these challenges, we developed a 3D registration method based on a spectral representation of the data, named Fourier Mellin SOFT (FMS),[34]

---

33 Figure 6.6 demonstrates this performance issue. It can be seen that the density of collected 3D points is less towards the edges of the scan.
34 Heiko Bülow and Andreas Birk, "Scale-Free Registrations in 3d: 7 Degrees of Freedom with Fourier-Mellin-Soft Transforms," *International Journal of Computer Vision* (IJCV) 126, no 7 (2018): 731–50.

Figure 6.2: Underground tunnel with gravel from collapsed ceiling.

and a divide-and-conquer method that checks for the best registration between several partitions of two scans.[35]

To illustrate the mentioned challenges for registration algorithms, Figure 6.5 shows a diagram with the locations of all the LRF scans made in the ruined part of the bunker. It is important to mention that more scans than necessary were taken for redundancy purposes and to further compare different registration methods, which are out of the scope of this article. The diagram shows some of the annotations used by technicians, such as the coordinate system used during the time of recording and their approximate relative position inside the bunker (the latter being approximate only as no GPS is available inside the building). The point clouds for different scan-pairs shown in Figure 6.6, in combination with Figure 6.5, show this exemplarily: If scans 35 and 37 are chosen to be registered or merged, most state-of-the-art methods would fail due to the small overlap between the scans. Scans 31 and 34 have too much overlap, which means scan 34 adds almost no new information about the environment and the time

---

35 H. Bülow et al., "A Divide and Conquer Method."

Figure 6.3: FARO Focus 3D Laser Range Finder (LRF).

invested in this recording could have been saved. The registration of scans 28 and 34 is a good example of recordings with enough overlap to have a successful registration and cover a larger area.

In the depicted scans, the millions of 3D points recorded and the aforementioned non-uniform sampling can also be appreciated. The amount of data and sampling artifacts poses significant challenges for state-of-the-art registration methods, but the Jacobs Robotics research group has developed a method based on the spectral representation of the data, Fourier Mellin SOFT, which effectively deals with these challenges. As an outcome, a 3D visualization of the ruined part of the bunker can be offered to visitors and researchers for a more detailed inspection through an interactive website.[36] Figure 6.7 shows the perspective view from the visitor's area of the ruins (access beyond this point is forbidden), and Figure 6.8 shows a snapshot of the interactive 3D-model and level

---

[36] An official website for these visualizations has not been made yet; however, these 3D-models can be accessed through the Jacobs Robotics website: http://robotics.jacobs-university.de/projects/Valentin3D-DE, accessed July 25, 2020.

Figure 6.4: LRF scanning process diagram. Graphic by the authors.

of detail offered—that is, the far end of the hallway seen on Figure 6.7. More details about the implementation and the exploitation of the visualization for historical purposes are discussed in section 4.2.

4.1.2 Historical Dimensions

An important outcome of the bunker's digitization is the possibility it affords for the work of the *Denkort*. As previously explained, the ruined part is not accessible, but at the same time it is a big attraction to visitors, especially since it has remained in its original state. It is not feasible to renovate the ruined part and make it accessible to visitors and it is currently only visible through an opening

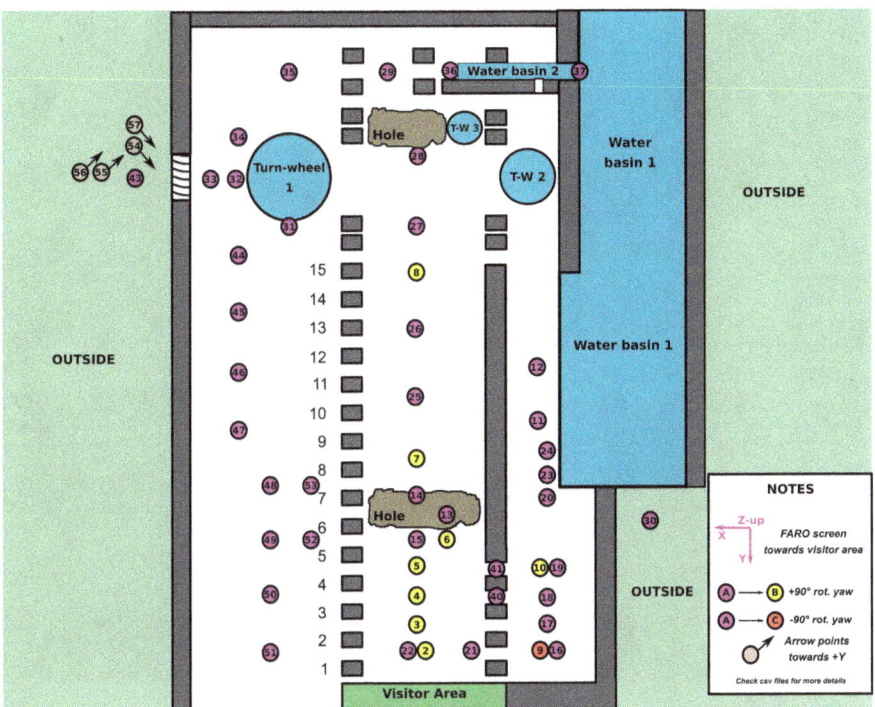

Figure 6.5: Diagram of the location and coordinate system of the LRF scans recorded in the Bunker's ruined part. Graphic by the authors.

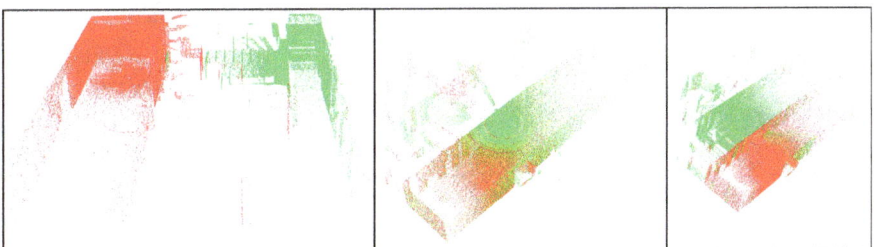

Figure 6.6: Scan-pairs point clouds: (left) Scans 35 and 37; (middle) Scans 31 and 34; (right) Scans 28 and 34.

at its far end. Hence, the *Denkort* currently has to rely on textual, explanatory notices or information provided via guided tours to describe the significance and meaning of this part of the bunker. Visitors can never fully see it, which is why myths are sometimes created. It invites rumors about hidden paths, rooms and nooks, and, more generally, secrets left by the Nazis. Or as Marcus

Figure 6.7: Ruined part as seen from visitor's area.

Figure 6.8: Snapshot of the ruined part of the bunker in the generated 3D-model.

Meyer, historian and one of the two directors of the *Denkort* describes it: "A hall stretches out in front of the visitors, lying in semi-darkness ... the end of which is barely visible from the gate and which actually has an auratic effect, i. e. characterized by individual projections and expectations."[37]

The digitization currently taking place in our project helps to deal with this issue of inaccessibility and supports the *Denkort*'s educational work, by providing it with a 3D-model with which visitors can virtually access the ruined part and better understand its history.

4.2 Interactive 3D Visualization for Research and the Public

4.2.1 Rendering 3D-Models in Web Browsers

As explained in section 4.1.1. Laser Range Finder scans produce enormous amounts of data—that is, millions to billions of points—to model 3D structures. Each of these points is represented by 3D coordinates, color values, laser energy intensity, and beam angles, etc., which means a large digital storage is needed to record them, in the order of gigabytes (GB) for each scan. This is not practical for easy visualization or sharing of the 3D-models among interested parties by (partial) download. For example, the United States Geological Survey (USGS) aims to perform through its "3D Elevation Program Initiative"[38] a nation-wide scan of the country and estimates 27 trillion points needed for its representation; this equates approximately 540 terabytes in uncompressed storage or roughly 540 laptops of average capacity available in 2020. Surveyors, archaeologists, historians, and other researchers want to access and share these data sets without copying or downloading these huge digital files. Likewise, easier access to the data will result in greater audiences; not all users will opt to upgrade their hardware or invest a lot of time to obtain and inspect the information. Taking this into consideration, one of the objectives of our project is to reach a bigger audience by making the 3D-model accessible through a web browser.

---

37 Meyer, "Historische Räume," 359, translated by the authors. The original German reads: "Statt dessen erstreckt sich vor den Besucherinnen und Besuchern eine im Halbdunkel liegende ... Halle, deren Ende vom Tor aus kaum sichtbar ist und die tatsächlich eine auratische, also von individuellen Projektionen und Erwartungen geprägte Wirkung besitzt."
38 Larry J. Sugarbaker et al., "The 3D Elevation Program Initiative: A Call for Action," *United States Geological Survey (USGS) Circular* 1399 (2014), accessed October 6, 2020, doi:10.3133/cir1399.

With the introduction of Web Graphics Library (WebGL),[39] the distribution of 3D content over web browsers has become easier since it is natively supported by all mainstream browsers and mobile and desktop devices. However, in most cases the shared content is relatively small—that is, all data fits into memory and is rendered in real time. Terrain mapping and 3D-models of large structures, like cultural sites, usually do not fall into this category. To solve this, Potree,[40] an open-source WebGL point cloud renderer developed by the Institute of Computer Graphics and Algorithms at the Technical University Vienna, is used for our project. This software library makes use of efficient data structures and sampling techniques to select the appropriate level of detail to show to the user, depending on the 3D perspective and scale chosen to view the 3D-model. Potree is optimized to work on web browsers considering their lower data transfer rates, compared to loading data from disk, and enables several tools for inspection: area of interest clipping (clip boxes), 3D measurements, elevation profiles, and interactive annotations. Figures 6.9 and 6.10 show examples of these tools for elevation profiling and box clipping with annotations respectively.

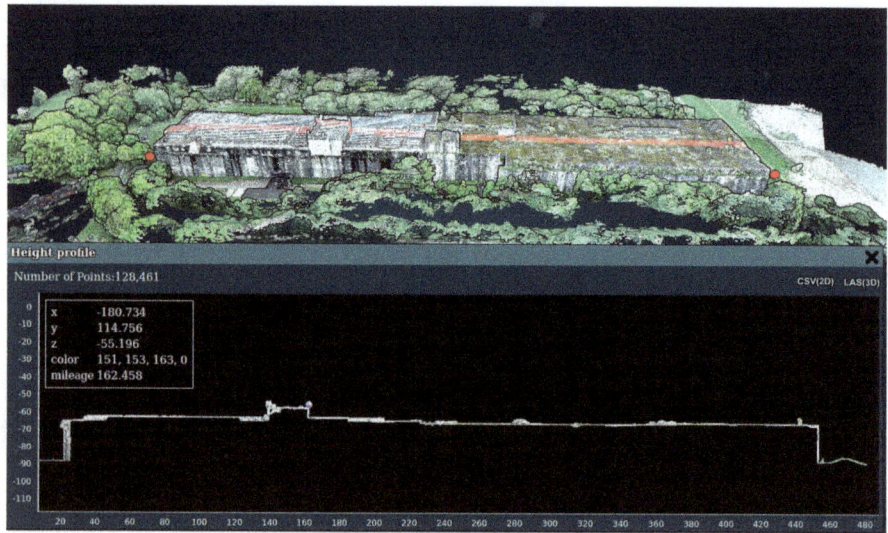

Figure 6.9: Elevation profile of the bunker.

---

39 https://www.khronos.org/webgl/, accessed October 6, 2020.
40 Markus Schütz, "Potree: Rendering Large Point Clouds in Web Browsers" (Diploma Thesis, Vienna University of Technology, 2016).

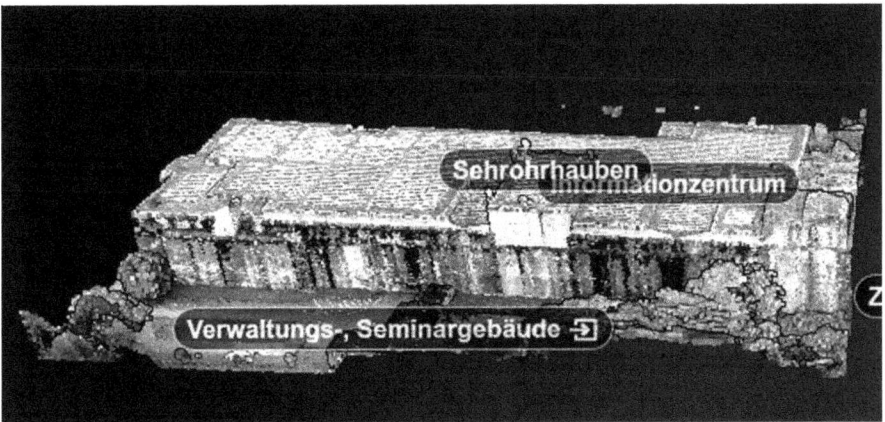

Figure 6.10: Potree visualization—interactive clipping of the 3D-model to focus on certain sections.

4.2.2 Holistic Bunker View—Exterior and Interior Models

In order to offer a more comprehensive and immersive visualization of Bunker Valentin, it was decided to also create a 3D-model of the outside and merge it with the one from the ruined part. This way, users can visualize specific sections of the bunker and inspect them, while still being able to switch to the complete view of the model for context and spatial reference. In this case, GPS can be used given that recordings can be taken outdoors. Georeferenced positions greatly simplify the registration task, as scans can be merged by simply positioning them in the 3D-model with their GPS coordinates and considering some uncertainty in these coordinates, rather than having to find visual correspondences, as is the case with the FMS method.

Even with the GPS advantage for this outdoor scenario, however, many LRF scans and significant time investment are required given that the complete perimeter of the bunker is approximately 2 km. For this reason, a MAV was used, specifically the DJI Phantom 4 Pro v2.0 shown in Figure 6.11. This MAV can be programmed to autonomously fly around the bunker and record RGB images. Most MAVs, such as the one used, do not have a laser scanner integrated. This is because it is desirable to keep their electronics and weight to a minimum. Instead, they only have a camera sensor. To generate a 3D-model from these images, which are known as photogrammetry, there are many open-source and proprietary programs available. They only require basic technical knowledge.

Figure 6.11: Micro Aerial Vehicle (MAV)—DJI Phantom 4 Pro v2.0—used to record the bunker outdoors.

For this project, Agisoft Metashape was used.[41] This and most photogrammetry software use variations of an algorithm called Structure from Motion (SfM),[42] which finds correspondences between consecutive camera images—that is, pixels from different sequential images representing the same object/scene, and computing depth information from them. In basic terms, this follows the same principle as human stereoscopic vision: when the observer moves, the observed objects move different amounts depending on their distance to the observer—for example, closer objects move more than those further away. Based on this depth and GPS position, a 3D representation of the scene can be constructed.

In Figure 6.12, the SfM 3D generated model of the bunker's exterior is shown. This model was created using approximately 900 images augmented with GPS information; the trajectory the MAV followed around the bunker is shown in blue along with some of the images taken from different locations and perspectives. These exterior and interior (Figure 6.13) 3D-models were merged using the spectral method described in section 4.1.1. Subsequently, historical annotations and images were added to finally produce the publicly available web browser Potree version.[43]

Potree presents different options for annotations that are especially useful and interesting for historians. Besides allowing simple text annotations, differ-

---

41 https://www.agisoft.com/buy/licensing-options/, accessed October 8, 2020.
42 Jonathan L. Carrivick, Mark W. Smith, and Duncan J. Quincey, *Structure from Motion in the Geosciences* (Chichester, UK: Wiley-Blackwell, 2016).
43 See for the exterior: http://robotics.jacobs-university.de/datasets/Valentin3D/3Dmodels/birdeye-exterior/visualization.html, and the interior: http://robotics.jacobs-university.de/datasets/Valentin3D/3Dmodels/ruins-interior/visualization.html, both accessed October 12, 2020.

ent media can be inserted, ranging from weblinks to photographs and videos. These annotations thus make historical contextualization possible. For example, a structure currently existing could be compared against previous versions and different states at a given point in time. For our project this means that the functionalities of each bunker section, especially the ruined part, can be conveyed—something that is not possible in the analog world, as discussed above. An annotated model can thus help to demystify water filled hollows and dark nooks or corners and their planned purpose can be shown. What is more, the bunker's violent past can be made visible by inserting pictures from forced laborers during the construction phase. In the model, these can be linked to the corresponding parts of the bunker on which they worked. When implemented into the *Denkort*, with these methods the public will be able to look holistically at and into the bunker not just in its current state but also at the violence that was the basis of its construction.

Figure 6.12: (Top) Structure from Motion (SfM) 3D-model generated with (below) camera images taken with the Micro Aerial Vehicle (MAV) while flying around the bunker, its trajectory is shown in blue.

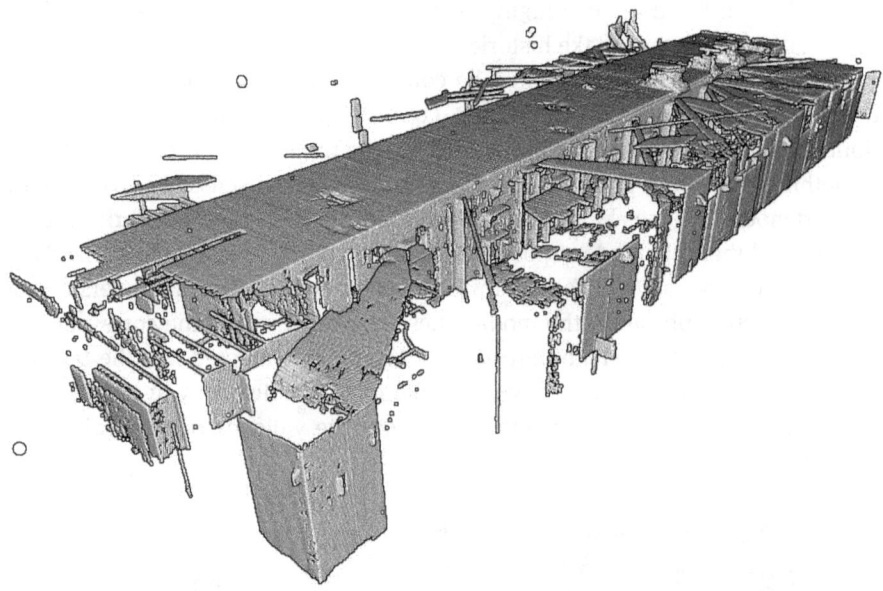

Figure 6.13: 3D-model of the indoor ruined part of the bunker (grayscale version) generated with the Fourier Mellin SOFT (FMS) registration method.

4.3 Bunker Basement

4.3.1 Historical Dimensions

In addition to the ruined part, the most eastern section of the bunker is also inaccessible to the public. The reason for this, however, is different than for the western side. This eastern part of Bunker Valentin is not part of today's exhibition offered by the *Denkort*, as it is still used by the owner of the building, the Bundesanstalt für Immobilienaufgaben (Institute for Federal Real Estate, BImA). In the historical layout planned for the bunker during World War II, this eastern area would have been divided into at least two floors and would have mostly held manufacturing workshops. Recently discovered blueprints, now kept in the *Denkort* and partially digitized as part of our project, show how diverse these workshops would have been. For example, it was planned that on the ground floor a shipbuilder would have been housed, as well as a machine workshop and a toolmaker with a forge. A paramedic's office would have been found here as well.⁴⁴ On the second floor, a pipe maker, carpenter, and locksmith were supposed to settle. However, this floor was also meant to hold the offices of two electrical companies, Afa and AEG. It can be assumed that these two companies would have been responsible for manufacturing and installing the submarines' vital lead acid batteries.⁴⁵

The floor plans show the diversity and complexity of the work involved in completing the submarines. The fact that these workshops would also have created new jobs could have been an argument of the National Socialist government to make the massive construction more acceptable to local residents.⁴⁶

Overall, in the most eastern section of the bunker, our project focused most on its basement. Due to its constant flooding, it has been barely explored in the past. There is only one discernible entrance to the basement, a staircase close to the eastern outside wall of the bunker. It is narrow and badly illuminated, as can be seen in Figure 6.14. There has been no assessment about the structural integrity of this part of the bunker. For these reasons, human (diving) explorations have been impossible.

Based on witness reports, the executives of the *Denkort* believe it to be an airraid basement, used during World War II by nearby residents of the village of Farge and managing staff from the construction site.⁴⁷ The only other source of information about this bunker's section is recently discovered blueprints. This makes a precise structural and historical description of the basement difficult. Our project, for the first time in probably decades, made a closer exploration of the basement possible, with the goal to answer the question of its purpose.

For the exploration of the basement, a different approach was adopted than that used for the ruined part. Instead of using robotics tools to augment and merge already existing data about this site—from sensors and construction plans—semi-autonomous robots performed exploratory missions supervised by the project's historian. The goal was to pinpoint possible objects or areas of interest from the video footage. This exploration in conjunction with consulting the blueprints supported the assumption that the basement was used as an air-raid

---

44 "Bauvorhaben-Valentin. Einrichtungsplan Erdgeschoß," 9.02.1944, Bl.-Nr. 80a, ADBV.
45 "Bauvorhaben-Valentin. Einrichtungslager – Obergeschoß," 09.02–13.03.1944, Bl-Nr. 81a, ADBV.
46 On the relationship of local residents of Farge, the bunker, and the forced laborers see Buggeln, *Der U-Boot-Bunker "Valentin,"* 155–59 and especially Silke Betscher, "Der Bunker und das Dorf," in Marszolek and Buggeln, *Bunker,* 121–36.
47 Forced laborers would most likely have been denied entrance to the bomb shelter.

shelter during World War II. In the following, we will first discuss the technical aspects of this exploration and afterwards detail the resulting historical findings.

Figure 6.14: Only known entrance to the basement in the eastern section of the bunker. Images show the poor illumination conditions, narrow access, and level of flooding in the basement, as well as the Remote Operating Vehicle (ROV) used for exploration.

4.3.2 Underwater Remote Operated Vehicles for Historical Surveys

The Remote Operated Vehicle (ROV) used for this task is a VideoRay Pro 4.[48] This ROV is a 37.5 × 28.9 × 22.3 cm and 6.1 kg underwater robot that can be submerged to approximately 300 m; it is attached to a control box with a 40 m tether. The tether not only allows command over the direction and speed of the ROV via joystick, but also the reception of video footage from the integrated camera (640 × 480 pixels) in real time. In this way, the technical operators and historians can cooperate during survey missions to investigate points of interest, which are described later in the text. However, we first discuss some of the challenges that are commonly encountered while performing underwater surveys.

---

[48] https://www.videoray.com/rovs/videoray-pro-4.html#!_SRC1370_sm, last accessed October 10, 2020.

An underwater scenario poses in general a more difficult task than its counterpart on land, as a GPS signal cannot travel underwater and the human operator may not always have a direct view of the robot used for exploration. There are several methods for obtaining an approximate underwater localization; one of the most common is to have another vehicle or station on the surface, which communicates acoustically with the ROV to know its relative position, then the station on the surface can access GPS data and provide a global position for the ROV. Another way is to deploy an infrastructure of sensors underwater on fixed and known locations beforehand with which, again, the position of the ROV can be calculated based on the acoustic transmissions between all these sensors as shown in Figure 6.15.

However, in our project, the narrow and already submerged entrance to the basement does not allow for the fixing of a surface station. Additionally, as diving is so dangerous as to be effectively impossible, no acoustic infrastructure can be deployed in advance. Furthermore, confined spaces with concrete walls make acoustic underwater localization almost impossible due to echoes and the related multipath and interference effects. Thus, a very rough localization is made heuristically by the operator based on landmarks and compass measurements from the ROV, and no accurate 3D mapping is possible under these conditions.

Likewise, the layout of the basement presents a scenario with more physical obstacles (including rubble, walls, pipes, etc.) than the typical open-sea or lake environment where the ROVs are usually used. Hence, the operator needs to be careful not to tangle the tether in such a way that it can be broken, leaving the ROV irretrievable. This makes the survey missions time consuming since the ROV needs to be maneuvered carefully and thus slowly in these surroundings. The final important challenge is underwater visibility. Visibility was highly variable because of the sediment particles floating in the water as shown in Figure 6.16. The number of particles obscuring vision was mostly dependent on the ROV's distance to the particle-covered surfaces and the thrust of its propellers. These particles reflect the light used by the ROV causing what is known as light backscatter, diffusing the light, making the images blurry and attenuating colors. As mentioned, to surmount this challenge, very slow speeds were used when controlling the ROV and manual annotations about landmarks were made to gain a very rough 3D estimate based on knowledge of the blueprints.

After a couple of rehearsal missions to acquire experience operating through the basement while keeping the equipment safe and adjusting the lights and camera for better visibility, several surveys were made and objects of interest were annotated. These will be discussed in the following sections.

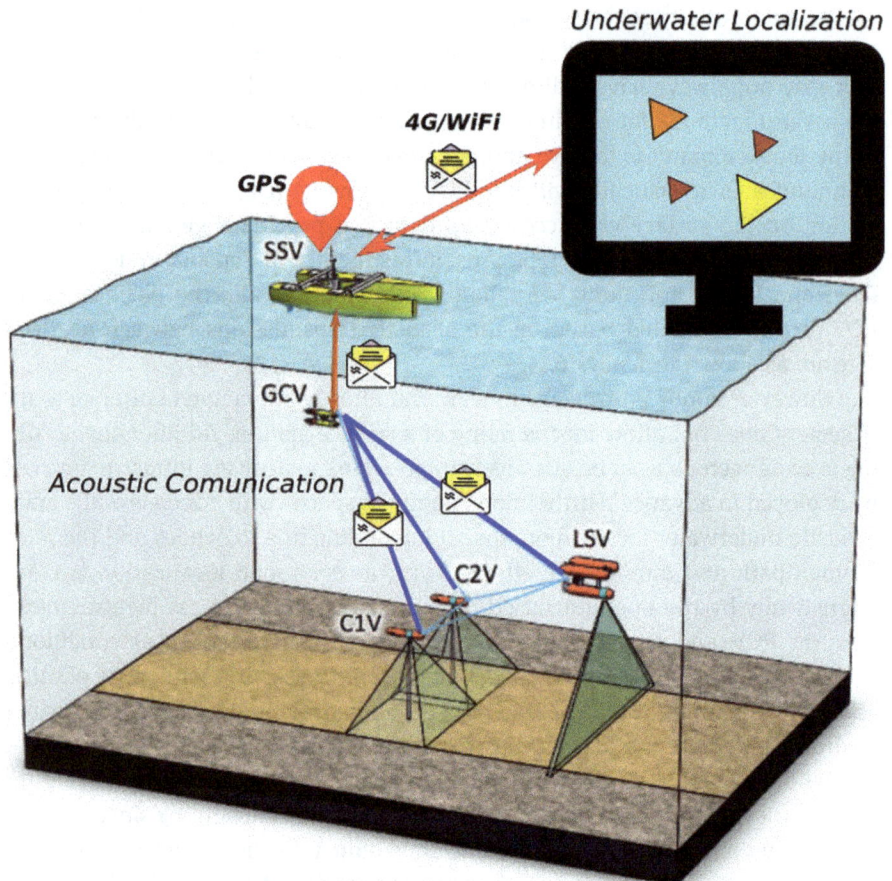

Figure 6.15: Common sensor/robotic setup to achieve accurate localization underwater. A surface vehicle has access to GPS or wireless localization, which is propagated to the underwater vehicles through acoustics. Graphic by the authors.

4.3.3 Survey and Historical Findings

The exploration of this space revealed a sizable room whose floor is in large parts scattered with rubble. The rubble is difficult to further identify because of a constant layer of algae or some other form of particles in the water; it seems to consist mostly of unidentifiable stony objects and some bricks. Furthermore, we discovered a brick wall. This was surprising, since all other wall structures are made of concrete. Given this context, this wall seems to be out of place. The most unexpected finding, however, was a circular construction with a rim

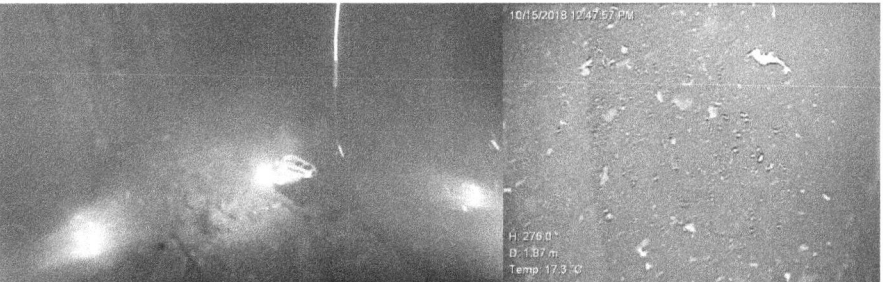

Figure 6.16: (Left) view of the Remote Operating Vehicle exploring a water basin with clear water; (right) example of sediment particles hindering camera vision through light backscatter.

rising from the floor located close by this brick wall. The outside of the rim looks like it is made from stone. A pipe seems to come from the ceiling and hover over the middle of the well. In Figure 6.17 these parts of the basement are depicted.

Comparing the ROV's images with the blueprints allowed us to identify this structure as a well (the German word *Brunnen* is used on the blueprint). As can be seen in blueprint 2440/2d, which shows a lateral cut through the base plate, this well leads from the basement to the ground floor. It is also visible in a floor plan that shows parts of the workshop section.[49] The floor plan further reveals that recesses would have led from the well through parts of the workshop, partially ending in a rectangular deepening. Consultation of the facility's blueprints of the workshop's ground floor show that sanitary facilities were planned on the spot of the deepening.[50] Based on this, it can be discerned that the well would have been part of a sewage system.

During the initial exploration of the basement, and without consulting the blueprints, we assumed the well must be connected to the flooding of the cellar and should in some ways have ensured avoidance of the influence of groundwater. The close proximity to the river Weser in combination with its significant tide[51] makes it likely that groundwater being pushed from the river's tide into the building would be a serious issue not only during construction but also later. This could explain the current flooding of the basement. In accordance with this theory, the blueprints show that several pump stations were planned, especially in the eastern part of the bunker. For example, blueprint 2440/41a

---

49 "Sohlplatte. Schalplan über LU-Keller Nord," 31.5.–14.7.1944, Bl. 2440/2d, ADBV.
50 "Einrichtungsplan Erdgeschoß," 9.2.1944, ADBV.
51 In Farge the river drops and rises more than 3.5 meters per tide: http://www.pegelonline.wsv.de/gast/stammdaten?pegelnr=4950020, accessed October 25, 2020.

Figure 6.17: (Top left) rubble with layer of algae; (top right) clear path with rubble on the side, suspected of being human-made before flooding; (bottom left) brick wall apparently not in the blueprints; (bottom right) well with stone rim which apparently was connected to the floor above through a pipe.

shows a sump basin (*Pumpensumpf*) with a drainage pipe close to the northeastern gate. This construction plan also refers to another blueprint for details; 2240/38 shows a staircase leading into an air-raid basement ("Lutzkeller Süd," abbreviation for the German term for air-raid basement, *Luftschutzkeller*). Adjacent to the staircase, a room was planned in which the floor slopes around 1% towards the staircase.[52] At the end of the slope, again, a sump basin can be found in the blueprints. Sump basins can also be seen on the construction plans for the turn wheels in the western part of the bunker.[53] All this suggests the bunker has a larger issue with water, most likely ground water. It could explain today's flooding of the basement as well as that of the southern turn-wheel

---

52 "Schalplan für Sohlplatten SI bis SV," 10.8.1944–17.8.1944, 2440/38b, ADBV and "Sohlplatte SVI bis IX. Schalungsplan," 21.8.1944–28.8.1944, 2440/41a, ADBV.
53 "Schalplan für die Sohlplatte S XV," 13.12.1944–3.1.1945, 2440/112a, ADBV and "unbekannt" [Schalplan für Sohlplatte Drehscheibe bei VI/1], n.d., ADBV.

in the ruined part, as depicted in Figure 6.1. It can be assumed that the phenomenon of rising water also needed to be managed during construction of Bunker Valentin and for the planned assembly of submarines.

As briefly mentioned, blueprint 2240/38 shows the entrance towards "Lutzkeller Süd." This is complemented by another construction plan, describing parts of another air-raid basement referred to as "Lu-Keller-Nord" (abbr. for *Luftschutzkeller-Nord*, as in "air-raid basement north").[54] As both plans show entries of the air-raid-basement towards the same part of the bunker, it is safe to assume that the shelter had two entrances, although they would have been at the beginning of the workshop section rather than its end, where there is a staircase into the basement today. Furthermore, the blueprints indicate that access to the air-raid shelter would not have been permanent. They include a note that advises to close at least the northern entry later in the construction process. This would make sense, insofar as further bomb shelters inside the bunker would have been superfluous once construction was completed, because as a whole it should have been impenetrable to bombs.

Thus, in sum, by evaluating all digital material from the ROV in combination with the blueprints we can verify the assumption that at least some parts of the basement were used as air-raid shelters. In fact, our research shows it was indeed planned exactly for that purpose.

Further inquiry is needed to determine just how exactly the rubble on the floor of the basement got there. It would not have been feasible for an air-raid shelter to have items on the floor, as these would have been hurdles or obstacles where a free path is strictly necessary to ensure accessibility, especially for people in panic. The most likely scenario is that the basement was used as a dumping ground during renovations by the Bundeswehr after the war. However, it remains an open question why the basement, and not a more accessible area was chosen for this purpose. In any case, the rubble must have been put in the basement while it was not flooded, since the rocks are evenly distributed and "pathways," clear of any rubble, are distinctly discernible.[55]

Further investigations into the basement itself are also necessary. More field explorations need to be done to conclusively confirm that the basement explored so far is accurately displayed on the blueprints showing the north and south air-raid shelters. Our project's explorations came to a halt due to the Covid-19 pandemic, and are now only slowly progressing.

---

54 "Sohlplatte. Schalplan über LU-Keller Nord," 31.5.1944–14.7.1944, 2440/2d, ADBV.
55 As can be seen in Figure 6.17, top right.

The blueprints themselves also need to be further examined, which should at least be partially done in cooperation with an architect to ensure architectural specifics in the plans are understood. There are several reasons, though, why further examination will prove complicated. The quality of the sources in combination with their size make it difficult, if not impossible, to move them without damaging them further. As is usual with construction plans, the paper is very thin and fragile, and the biggest blueprint comes to a size of approximately 200 × 100 cm. Handling and storage of the plans so far has already left marks to such an extent that some blueprints are barely usable anymore. To minimize further handling and damages, the sources are being digitized. Until now, we have reviewed, photographed, and cataloged half of the blueprints (around 230). It is important to mention that the photographs are very rudimentary[56] and most likely will not serve as a substitute for professional digitization, such as scans, at least for the most important and interesting blueprints. We are currently looking into effective digitization strategies that consider both the size and fragility of the sources.

5 Conclusion and Outlook

The three-dimensional mapping of Bunker Valentin is a challenging endeavor from which the historical research community will benefit. Digitization and the mapping resulting from our project mean that the bunker and in particular its inaccessible ruined part can soon be visited and researched remotely from every point of the globe. Especially for spatial and architectural research, our 3D-model offers features that simplify analyses. For example, measurements can be easily and accurately performed within the 3D-model. In real life, this would be extremely complex and time consuming because of the bunker's large dimensions and accessibility constraints. Simple visualization and access to the 3D-model was not initially a priority of the project. However, the research team quickly realized the importance of organizing the massive amount of data obtained, and of providing an easy way to interact and share the data with the public and researchers. The visualization is still work in-progress and it will be improved with feedback from the community. Furthermore, since the raw data will be partially available through open access upon request, it can be manipulated to serve and assist historical research. Researchers can organize and analyze the source data depending on their needs and methodologies.

---

56 Which is also why we refrained from printing them in this chapter.

Our current 3D-model will be augmented with historical annotations, images, and digitized blueprints—that is, with traditional sources. This will be done to provide a coherent source for historical research. When the integration of 3D scans and other material is complete, the achieved results will help to further clarify the history of the ruined part. Furthermore, our project will contribute to make the bunker's functionality more visible and understandable. It will therefore also serve as an aid to the *Denkort*'s aim to convey the history of the bunker as holistically as possible.

After extensive inspection and cataloging of the blueprints in combination with the visual references, several parts of the bunker were analyzed. This allowed us to confirm that the basement was at least in part planned and used as an air-raid shelter.

In this chapter we have shown that historical research benefits from the synergy between traditional historical sources and state-of-the-art robotics tools. The exploration of the basement shows how historical research can be supported by Remotely Operated Vehicles. In our project, it led to this bunker section being explored for the first time in decades. However, without the original blueprints as sources and points of reference, our findings could not have been reached. In other words, while the exploration would not have been possible without technical aid, the historical research question could only be examined fruitfully by connecting digital exploration with the reading of "traditional" material.

But it is important to emphasize that more is needed than a synergy between information sources or tools. Additionally, a collaboration between different scientific communities—history and engineering—is required to advance the exploration and understanding of cultural sites. This is not trivial: Often historians cannot keep track with the fast-paced technological advancements used for surveying, while engineers do not know how to best portray the obtained information so that it can be of use for other disciplines.

From the technical perspective, it became clear that structures such as Bunker Valentin can be very complex to survey as they consist of several different environments: almost inaccessible sections, underwater parts, highly variable illumination, etc. It is not enough to have one precise tool for exploration but a collection of them is needed, so that anyone can easily adapt to these different scenarios and crosscheck the acquired information. Ideally the next step would be to assemble multi-robot teams performing surveys in parallel in the different parts of the bunker while reporting back to a central system. This could make these exploration endeavors highly efficient and reduce the efforts in aggregating the information from all these different sources. Nonetheless, as explained previously, such enterprises must have the supervision and guidance of historians, who point to relevant places, so as not to blindly collect massive amounts of data that could be cumbersome to filter and would not be required for answering historical research questions.

In the future, such synergies should be used to work on the less explored areas of the bunker's past. More precisely, further interdisciplinary projects should target the area which housed the camps where forced laborers working on the bunker were detained. Even though this area constitutes a key component of the bunker's history, some camps have been researched only rudimentarily. Since the locations of the former camps, starting 3 km east of the bunker extend over an area of 5 km, it is difficult for the *Denkort* to integrate this area into their guided tours. Furthermore, access is difficult as parts of the terrain are used today as a military exercising site by the Bundeswehr and also cross the federal borders between Bremen and Lower Saxony. All these aspects were also why the digitization of the former camps was not within the scope of our project. However, this limitation should be overcome in a future project. A digitization of this area, concentrating on the former camps, would create a virtual access opportunity benefiting both researchers and visitors to the *Denkort* interested in the history of Bunker Valentin and the Nazi period in Bremen.

Bibliography

Agisoft. "Metashape." Accessed October 8, 2020. https://www.agisoft.com/buy/licensing-options/.
Betscher, Silke. "Der Bunker und das Dorf." In *Bunker Kriegsorte, Zuflucht, Erinnerungsraum*, edited by Inge Marszolek and Marc Buggeln, 121–36. Frankfurt am Main: Campus, 2018.
Borrmann, Dorit, Robin Heß, HamidReza Houshiar, Daniel Eck, Klaus Schilling, and Andreas Nüchter. "Robotic Mapping of Cultural Heritage Sites." *The International Archives of the Photogrammetry, Remote Sensing and Spatial Information Sciences*, suppl. W4, vol. 40, no. 5 (2015): 9–16.
Botto, Asia, Beatrice Campanella, Stefano Legnaioli, Marco Lezzerini, G. Lorenzetti, Stefano Pagnotta, Francesco Poggialini, and Vincenzo Palleschi. "Applications of Laser-Induced Breakdown Spectroscopy to Cultural Heritage and Archaeology: A Critical Review." *Journal of Analytical Atomic Spectrometry* 1 (2019). Accessed August 15, 2020. doi: 10.1039/C8JA00319 J.
Buggeln, Marc. "Der U-Boot-Bunker Valentin in Bremen." In *Bunker. Kriegsort, Zuflucht, Erinnerungsraum*, edited by Inge Marszolek and Marc Buggeln, 102–19. Frankfurt am Main: Campus, 2008.
Buggeln, Marc. *Der U-Boot-Bunker "Valentin". Marinerüstung, Zwangsarbeit und Erinnerung.* Bremen: Edition Temmen, 2010.
Bülow, Heiko, and Andreas Birk. "Scale-Free Registrations in 3d: 7 Degrees of Freedom with Fourier-Mellin-Soft Transforms." *International Journal of Computer Vision* (IJCV) 126, no. 7 (2018): 731–50.

Bülow, Heiko, Christian A. Mueller, Arturo Gomez Chavez, Frederike Buda, and Andreas Birk, "A Divide and Conquer Method for 3D Registration of Inhomogeneous, Partially Overlapping Scans with Fourier Mellin SOFT (FMS)," *2020 IEEE International Conference on Robotics and Automation (ICRA), Paris, France, May 31–August 31, 2020:* 8594–601. Accessed October 7, 2020. doi: 10.1109/ICRA40945.2020.9197453.

Calisi, Daniele, Francesca Giannone, Claudia Ventura, Paolo Salonia, Fabio Cottefoglie, and Vittorio Amos Ziparo. "Digitizing Indoor and Underground Cultural Heritage Sites with Robots." *Science Research and Information Technology* 6, no. 1 (2016): 23–30.

Carrivick, Jonathan, Mark W. Smith, and Duncan J. Quincey. *Structure from Motion in the Geosciences.* Chichester, UK: Wiley Blackwell, 2016.

Casadio, Francesco, Céline Daher, and Ludovic Bellot-Gurlet. "Raman Spectroscopy of Cultural Heritage Materials: Overview of Applications and New Frontiers in Instrumentation, Sampling Modalities, and Data Processing." *Topics in Current Chemistry* 62 (2016): 1–51. Accessed September 5, 2020. doi: 10.1007/s41061-016-0061-z.

Del Pozo, Susana, Jesús Herrero-Pascual, Beatriz Felipe-García, David Hernández-López, Pablo Rodríguez-Gonzálvez, and Diego González-Aguilera. "Multispectral Radiometric Analysis of Façades to Detect Pathologies from Active and Passive Remote Sensing." *Remote Sensing* 80 (2016). Accessed August 20, 2020. doi: 10.3390/rs8010080.

Denkort Bunker Valentin. "Startseite." Accessed July 15, 2020. https://www.denkort-bunker-valentin.de/startseite.html.

Guidi, G., L.L. Micoli, S. Gonizzi, M. Brennan, and B. Frischer. "Image-Based 3D Capture of Cultural Heritage Artifacts: An Experimental Study about 3D Data Quality." Paper presented at the Digital Heritage International Congress 2, Granada, Spain, September 28–October 2, 2015. Accessed August 18, 2020. doi: 10.1109/DigitalHeritage.2015.7419514.

Jacobs Robotics. "Valentin 3D". Accessed July 25, 2020. http://robotics.jacobs-university.de/projects/Valentin3D-DE.

Johr, Barbara, and Hartmut Roder. *Der Bunker. Ein Beispiel nationalsozialistischen Wahns, Bremen-Farge 1943–1945.* Bremen: Edition Temmen, 1989.

Khronos. "Open GL ES for the Web." Accessed October 6, 2020. https://www.khronos.org/webgl/.

Lotfi, Gabriele. *KZ der Gestapo. Arbeitserziehungslager im Dritten Reich.* Frankfurt am Main: Fischer, 2003.

Meyer, Marcus. "Historische Räume und forensische Pädagogik: Die Konzeption des 'Denkortes Bunker Valentin' in Bremen." In *Gedächtnisräume. Geschichtsbilder und Erinnerungskulturen in Norddeutschland,* edited by Janina Fuge, Rainer Hering, and Harald Schmid, 351–65. Göttingen: v&r unipress, 2014.

Meyer, Marcus, and Christel Trouvé. "Denkort Bunker Valentin. Eine erste Bilanz zwei Jahre nach der Eröffnung." *Gedenkstättenrundbrief* 188 (2017): 3–14.

Murphy, Robin R. *A Decade of Rescue Robots.* Abstract of a paper presented on the IEEE/RSJ International Conference on Intelligent Robots and Systems, Vilamoura, Algarve, Portugal, October 7–12, 2012. Accessed August 15, 2020. https://ieeexplore.ieee.org/stamp/stamp.jsp?arnumber=6386301.

Potree. "Bird-eye Exterior." Accessed October 14, 2020. http://robotics.jacobs-university.de/datasets/Valentin3D/3Dmodels/birdeye-exterior/visualization.html.

Potree. "Ruins Interior." Accessed October 14, 2020. http://robotics.jacobs-university.de/data sets/Valentin3D/3Dmodels/ruins-interior/visualization.html.

Puente, Iván, Mercedes Solla, Higinio González-Jorge, and Pedro Arias. "NDT Documentation and Evaluation of the Roman Bridge of Lugo Using GPR and Mobile and Static LiDAR." *Journal of Performance of Constructed Facilities* 29 (2013). Accessed September 5, 2020. doi: 10.1061/(ASCE)CF.1943–5509.0000531.

Schütz, Markus. "Potree: Rendering Large Point Clouds in Web Browsers." Diploma Thesis, Vienna University of Technology, 2016.

Sugarbaker, Larry J., Eric W. Constance, Hans Karl Heidmann, Allyson L. Jackson, Vicko Lukas, Davis L Saghy, and Jason M. Stoker. "The 3D Elevation Program Initiative: A Call for Action." *United States Geological Survey (USGS) Circular* 1399 (2014). Accessed October 6, 2020. doi: 10.3133/cir1399.

Videoray. "Videoray Pro 4 ROV." Accessed October 10, 2020. https://www.videoray.com/rovs/videoray-pro-4.html#!_SRC1370_sm.

Wasserstraßen- und Schifffahrtsverwaltung des Bundes. "Stammdaten Farge." Accessed October 25, 2020. http://www.pegelonline.wsv.de/gast/stammdaten?pegelnr=4950020.

Jannik Sachweh
Chapter 7
The National Socialist Prison System and the Illusive Appeal of Digital Maps

German Summary: Diese Kapitel diskutiert anhand eines landesgeschichtlichen Beispiels die Möglichkeiten und Fallstricke, die sich ergeben, wenn komplexe historischen Zusammenhänge zwischen unterschiedlichsten Orten in einer digitalen Karte als Teil einer Ausstellung der Öffentlichkeit präsentiert werden sollen.

Das Strafgefängnis Wolfenbüttel war während der Zeit des Nationalsozialismus die zentrale Haftanstalt des ehemaligen Freistaates Braunschweig. Im Land Braunschweig befanden sich jedoch zahlreiche weitere Orte des Strafvollzuges. Dies waren mehrere kleinere und größere Gefängnisse von Thedinghausen bei Bremen bis Blankenburg im Harz. Es waren aber auch Arbeitskommandos, die außerhalb der zentralen Haftanstalt in der Rüstungsindustrie oder beim Aufbau der Reichswerke Hermann Göring im Salzgitter-Gebiet eingesetzt wurden. Zusätzlich zählen beispielsweise Orte hinzu, an denen wehrmachtsgerichtliche Todesurteile vollstreckt wurden.

Neben der Geschichte des Strafvollzuges nimmt zusätzlich die Entwicklung der Zwangs- und Gefangenenarbeit in der Sphäre der Justiz einen wichtigen Stellenwert ein. Zentral ist dabei die Frage nach der Sichtbarkeit der nationalsozialistischen Justizverbrechen für die Bevölkerung im damaligen Land Braunschweig. Ausgehend von diesen historischen Fragestellungen zeigt dieses Kapitel die Chancen und Herausforderungen bei der Gestaltung einer interaktiven Karte. Hierbei wird insbesondere diskutiert, in welchen Formen Kartmaterial für eine Vermittlung passend ist, in welchem Umfang digitale Quellenzugänge sinnvoll eingesetzt werden können und welche Grenzen der digitalen Geschichtsvermittlung in diesem Format gegeben sind. Der Artikel zeigt, inwiefern ein digitaler und raumgeschichtlicher Zugang sinnig erscheint und wo die Grenzen der Vermittelbarkeit über interaktive digitale Karten liegen. Es wird deutlich, dass die Ausdehnung, Dichte und Tiefe des Netzwerkes des nationalsozialistischen Strafvollzuges mit einem landesgeschichtlichen Fokus eine derartige Komplexität erreicht, dass eine Abbildung in digitalen Karten zwangsläufig nur ausschnitthaft erfolgen kann und dadurch droht, missverständlich zu werden. Gleichzeitig bieten interaktive Karten allerdings auch didaktische Vorteile bei der Gestaltung einer Ausstellung, die mit herkömmlichen Ausstellungsmedien nicht zu erreichen sind.

1 Introduction

The system of imprisonment within the regular judiciary in National Socialist Germany is a comparatively new field of historical research. Even though the majority of the National Socialists' crimes, including the Shoa, where committed outside of the judiciary's sphere of influence, the judiciary had a key function in organizing the National Socialist regime of terror.[1] Even before their rise to power in 1933, the National Socialists had little respect for law and justice. After they installed their dictatorship, they modified laws that opposed their ideology and enacted new laws that turned their brutal and racist world view into applicable law. The judiciary became a powerful tool of their regime. A new legislation system emerged that put the request for a racially and politically put *Volksgemeinschaft* (national community) above the well-being of individuals.[2] Nikolaus Wachsmann has shown how the prisons and imprisonment changed within the years 1933 to 1945 and how fundamentally they were connected to the National Socialist ideology. Shortly after the National Socialists rose to power in 1933 judiciary prisons, as well as police prisons and early concentration camps, were a part of the terror and oppression against their political opponents like social democrats or communists. The use of the death penalty was enforced and newly organized in 1937, making some of the prisons centralized execution places. During World War II, prisons became part of National Socialist industrial endeavors and part of armament production. As Wachsmann has pointed out there was also fundamental cooperation between the police or Gestapo, the concentration camps, and the National Socialists' politics of annihilation.[3] The history of judiciary prisons in National Socialism is remembered and musealized in several places in Germany like the memorial Zuchthaus Brandenburg-Görden, the memorial Roter Ochse in Halle and the recently remodeled memorial inside the Wolfenbüttel prison. Displaying the diverse connections of a single prison to the National Socialist network of prosecution, oppression, and violence within an exhibition by the use of an interactive digital map seems an obvious choice for future exhibitions dealing with this subject. New digital

---

[1] Anett Dremel and Jens-Christian Wagner, "Strafvollzug im Nationalsozialismus. Ein Überblick," in *Recht. Verbrechen. Folgen. Das Strafgefängnis Wolfenbüttel im Nationalsozialismus*, ed. Martina Staats and Jens-Christian Wagner (Göttingen: Wallstein, 2019), 256.

[2] Michael Grüttner, *Brandstifter und Biedermänner: Deutschland 1933–1939* (Stuttgart: Klett-Cotta, 2015), 93–104.

[3] Most notably, this field of research was opened by Nikolaus Wachsmann. See Nikolaus Wachsmann, *Hitler's Prisons: Legal Terror in Nazi Germany* (New Haven, CT: Yale University Press, 2004).

tools enable museums to display not only a map with several marked places, but also to provide background information, pictures, or other source material to each and every one of those places within the network of a prison. Compared to the use of printed maps, that for a long time have been an analog tool used in museums and memorial places, a digital map suggests a more complex or more complete display of historical facts in a subliminal way.

This article will therefore examine the possibilities and disadvantages that come with the use of digital maps to display the vast variety of connections and interactions a single prison had in the years from 1933 to 1945. It will exemplarily focus on the prison of Wolfenbüttel in northern Germany close to Braunschweig as one of the centralized places where death penalties were executed from 1937 to 1945. A digital map is currently being developed by the Wolfenbüttel memorial for the new permanent exhibition.

2 Advantages of Digital Maps

Almost every memorial museum works with classic analog maps or models of the former National Socialist camp, prison, or other place of prosecution. The map—sometimes more and sometimes less accurate—is a classic medium of exhibition and explanation. While newer forms of digital reconstruction or display of demolished campsites or non-accessible places of National Socialist crimes make good use of augmented and virtual reality,[4] the use of digital maps is a more basic approach. The use of digital maps can aim at several points. First, a map can show a place in its whole extent. Digital maps also can use computer animated graphics to show the development of a site. If a digital map is used to display a wider area like a country or a state, visitors to an exhibition can locate the site they are visiting in a broader perspective and see it in relation or connection to other places. A physically limited analog map does not possess this ability to the same extent. In addition to these aspects of possible content, a digital map in most cases provides a more interactive use of the exhibition, for example by the use of a touch-screen. Browsing a map and accessing information on several places becomes a more intuitive and affective personal experience than just looking at a classic map. A digital map can offer a deeper engagement with the exhibition for the users and provide the impression of playing an active part in the exploration of historical information. The information on display is driven by the interest of its users. In

---

[4] See e.g. Jens-Christian Wagner, "Simulierte Authentizität? Chancen und Risiken von augmented und virtual reality an Gedenkstätten," *Gedenkstättenrundbrief* 196 (2019): 3–9.

this way digital access extends the classic exhibition beyond objects and descriptions by adding an interactive way of exploring history.

In the past decades the role of visitors to exhibitions of all kinds changed fundamentally. While the visitor was in the rather passive role of being an observer of information on display, visitors today often see themselves as users and people who interact with the objects and participate in the meaning-making processes involved in the understanding of history.[5]

3 How to Define the Content of a Digital Map?

While using digital maps, some curators might be tempted by the possibility to use the nearly endless capacity of digital storage to locate and mark more and more locations on a map and provide information on all of them.[6]

But how does the use of interactive maps add to the understanding of the history of the prison system in National Socialist Germany? This will be discussed following an example from the memorial inside the Wolfenbüttel prison where a new interactive map is in development to introduce a new exhibition. The Wolfenbüttel prison was the central imprisonment facility of the judiciary in the state of Brunswick.[7] But all over the state there were numerous other places that were part of the National Socialist prison system. There were other prisons, work deployment, and work and imprisonment camps. In addition, there were several places of collaboration with other participants in National Socialist prosecution and terror that can be taken into account, like a shooting range in the forest of Buchhorst close to the city of Braunschweig, where the Wehrmacht carried out death sentences.

These historical sites, some of which are still visible today, will be displayed on a digital map in the entrance hall of the Wolfenbüttel memorial's new exhibition building. The display shows a simplified map of central Germany with riv-

---

5 Chiel van den Akker and Susan Legêne, "Introduction," in *Museums in a Digital Culture: How Art and Heritage Become Meaningful*, ed. Chiel van den Akker and Susan Legêne (Amsterdam: Amsterdam University Press, 2016), 7–12.
6 For example the project "Views of Ghent" has identified and described over 3,500 locations in the City of Ghent alone. See Lars de Jaegher, Maria de Waele, and Véronique van Goethem, "The Use of Digital Media in a New Urban History Exhibition: STAM – Ghent City Museum," *18th International Conference on Virtual Systems and Multimedia, Milan, 2012*, 557–560, accessed 3 August, 2021, doi: 10.1109/VSMM.2012.6365976.
7 To prevent possible misunderstanding in this article the capital city will be referred to as "Braunschweig," while the state will be addressed as "Brunswick."

ers and mountains to provide some geographical orientation for the user. The only visible border is that of the state of Brunswick, as it was set to provide the spatial border for places to be included in the map. The map is designed specifically for this geographical and political area. Places are marked and accessible via a simple touch on the screen. A context box displays a short text containing more information about the chosen location and pictures or other historical sources—in cases where they are available. The installation is built on a content management system that allows changes to the context or the addition of new places over time as historical research might provide new views or information.

The following three examples will point out both the advantages and the disadvantages of the medium but will focus mainly on the pitfalls that accompany the presentation of complex historical situations and dependencies on a digital map within an exhibition. First, the example of the numerous prisons in the state of Brunswick is considered, followed by the work deployment of prisoners from Wolfenbüttel. Finally, focus turns to the special case of the Institute of Anatomy in Göttingen, which falls outside the proposed grid of places within the judiciary system.

During National Socialism, judiciary places of detention were operated under a variety of different names. However, a clear distinction can be made between remand prisons, court prisons, which also mainly housed prisoners on remand, and prisons for the accommodation of convicted prisoners. The term *Kreisgefängnis* (district prison), which is common in the state of Brunswick, denotes the regional jurisdiction, as does the name *Landesstrafanstalt* (state prison) referring to the Wolfenbüttel prison. The size of the prisons varied considerably. In addition to the two large prisons in Wolfenbüttel and Braunschweig, that were designed for an estimated number of roughly 1,000 and 300 prisoners, there were four district prisons, which had twenty-four to forty places of detention and also functioned as court prisons, as well as numerous court prisons, whose capacity was between two and seventeen prisoners. A total of twenty-three regular prisons can be identified in the state of Brunswick. In addition to the central state penal institution in Wolfenbüttel, the district- and remand prison in Braunschweig was the second largest prison. Furthermore, there were district prisons in Bad Gandersheim, Blankenburg, Goslar, Helmstedt, and Holzminden. In addition, there were smaller court prisons in Bad-Harzburg, Calvörde, Eschershausen, Greene, Hasselfelde, Königslutter, Lutter am Barrenberge, Salder, Schöningen, Schöppenstedt, Seesen, Stadtoldendorf, Thedinghausen, Vechelde, Vorsfelde, and Walkenried.

Imprisonment in the judicial prisons is distinguished from imprisonment in other places of detention, which during National Socialism were all part of the terror and persecution system. Inmates of a judicial prison usually were convicted by a court and sentenced to a certain period of imprisonment. The imprisonment itself was regulated by law. But the judiciary system collaborated closely with other bodies of persecution. For example, after being mistreated in the Gestapo prison in Braunschweig's Leopoldstraße, victims were taken to the police prison Wendenstraße. From there they were transferred to the district and remand prison and thus to the sphere of judiciary. From there, some prisoners were transported further, for example to the Alt-Moabit prison in Berlin before a trial at the *Volksgerichtshof* (people's court). Those sentenced to death were further transported from Berlin, among other places, to the prison in Brandenburg-Görden, where another of the central execution sites was located. Other prisoners were handed back to the Gestapo after their release from prison. They were further maltreated or taken to a concentration camp.[8] All in all no judiciary prison could be considered a more secure place of imprisonment for the victims of National Socialism. Even if mistreatment inside judiciary prisons might have been less common, some prisoners were handed over to other places and to severe physical abuse.

In addition, it is important to avoid the impression that convicted persons would have been imprisoned exclusively in prisons close to the places of their arrest. This becomes apparent, for example, when one looks at the origins of the Wolfenbüttel inmates in 1938, who came from the districts of the courts of Celle, Magdeburg, Hamm, Darmstadt, Hanover, Berlin, Leipzig, Düsseldorf, Frankfurt am Main, Munich, and Naumburg.[9] The question that arises when designing a digital map is: Which of the numerous prisons within the given frame of the state of Brunswick should be depicted? Is the number of places of detention decisive as far as which to include and which to exclude from the map or are the special crimes committed by the National Socialists in some prisons given special consideration? At the same time, the focus on judiciary prisons is deceiving: Gestapo prisons or their prison camps are not taken into account, even though many prisoners of justice were handed over to the Gestapo and vice

---

8 Der Oberlandesgerichtspräsident an den Braunschweigischen Minister des Inneren, 29.09. 1939, NLA WO 12 Neu 13 Nr. 15256 Polizeiliches Haftlokal in Braunschweig. The examples follow the imprisonment history of Wilhelm Keune. See Markus Gröchtemeier, *Fahnenwechsel: Nationalsozialismus und britische Besatzung in der Stadt Wolfenbüttel 1933–1948* (Hameln: CW Niemeyer Buchverlage, 2018), 136–48. On the Wolfenbüttel prison's collaboration with the Gestapo see Jannik Sachweh, "Von Wesermünde nach Wolfenbüttel. Orte der Justizverbrechen im nationalsozialistischen Strafvollzug," *Jahrbuch der Männer vom Morgenstern* 97 (2019): 15–16.
9 Wilfried Knauer, "… nicht hinter Mauern! Die Stadt und das Strafgefängnis Wolfenbüttel 1933–1945," in *Wolfenbüttel unter dem Hakenkreuz. Fünf Vorträge*, ed. Stadt Wolfenbüttel (Wolfenbüttel: Stadt Wolfenbüttel, 2000), 84.

versa. Of course, focusing on the prisons is already a narrowing of the perspective. The different courts could just as well be taken into consideration when it comes to giving an overview of the connections of a selected prison in the system of National Socialist persecution. For the final decisions on what sites to include on the digital map, it is important to strike a balance between a comprehensiveness (that can never be fully achieved) and the receptive capacity of the visitors.

During the entire period of National Socialism, there were more than seventy work detachments at the Wolfenbüttel prison, which were deployed inside and outside the prison. Prisoners in the prison itself usually worked from Monday to Saturday within the institution but were hardly paid. In addition to assignments in various commercial enterprises, prisoners were deployed spontaneously and briefly for transport or agricultural work. It is no longer possible today to give a complete list of these short-term assignments. In the course of preparations for war, the work deployment was expanded from 1938 onwards and almost all prisoners were employed. In the following years of the war, prisoners were also called upon to do work important to the war effort and were increasingly deployed outside the prison. If the places of work were near the prison, the prisoners were taken from the prison to work and back again in the evening. At more distant places, the prison set up several permanent external commands. The prisoners were mainly used for forced labor in the war economy. As a result, the number of sick prisoners and deaths rose significantly. During World War II, the penal system was to contribute to a German victory. The prisoners' manpower was increasingly exploited, while the food supply and medical care of the prisoners deteriorated increasingly. In Wolfenbüttel, as early as 1940, about 50 – 60 % of the prisoners were used exclusively for important war-related work at external commands.[10] This use of prisoners in permanent commands outside the prisons in the state of Brunswick has barely been researched to date.

Particularly during the last two years of the war, the judiciary prisoners could no longer be overlooked as workers in Brunswick's economy. In addition to foreign civilian and forced laborer's, Gestapo prisoners, the inmates of the concentration camps, prisoners of war, and Wehrmacht prisoners, the judiciary prisoners were often employed in the same company. The problem with displaying these details on a digital map is not so much marking the numerous different locations; rather, it is a challenge to distinguish between short-term and long-term deployments and to clearly differentiate between the deployment of judicia-

---

10 Jahresbericht über die Durchführung des Strafvollzuges und die Verwaltung des Strafgefängnisses Wolfenbüttel im Rechnungsjahr 1940, NLA WO 42 A Neu Fb. 3 Zg. 37/1983 Nr. 53 Einrichtung und Verwaltung der Vollzugsanstalten.

ry prisoners and the deployment of concentration camp inmates, for example. If this distinction is not made clearly, a digital map is in danger of suggestively equating the different forms of forced labor or of placing other forms of forced labor into the background.[11] This becomes clear in the example of the work deployment camps in the last months of the war. From the summer of 1944, the work deployment of prisoners outside the prison in Wolfenbüttel took on new dimensions. In nearby factories, armaments production was intensified once more and in large-scale projects, parts of the armaments production were to be moved underground and thus protected from air raids. The last months of National Socialist rule were also marked by murder, mass deaths, and the mass deportation of prisoners from prisons and camps. The front advancing ever further into the territory of the Reich led to "evacuations" of prisons to prevent the prisoners from falling into the hands of the Allies. The way in which the prisoners were treated varied greatly from place to place. However, clear differences can be seen when comparing the evacuations of the concentration camps.[12] Especially within the framework of the *Jägerprogramm* (production of fighter airplanes), prisoners from Wolfenbüttel were called upon to work on underground relocations of the armament industry alongside prisoners of war and concentration camp inmates. Thus, three new permanent field commands were created in the final phase of the war: one in Walbeck for the company Büssing NAG Flugmotorenwerke from Braunschweig-Querum, and two in Blankenburg for the Oda-Werke and the Klosterwerke. For the two underground relocations in Blankenburg, the prison worked directly with the construction management of Organisation Todt,[13] which coordinated the work. In accordance with the legal regulations, Organisation Todt could not place judiciary prisoners in the same work camps as the concentration camp prisoners it also used for the underground relocations.[14] This causes a problem for a digital map focusing on judi-

---

11 On the differentiation between forms of forced labour see Marc Buggeln, "Unfreie Arbeit im Nationalsozialismus. Begrifflichkeiten und Vergleichsaspekte zu den Arbeitsbedingungen im Deutschen Reich und in den besetzten Gebieten," in *Arbeit im Nationalsozialismus*, ed. Marc Buggeln and Michael Wildt (Munich: Oldenbourg Verlag, 2014), 231–52.
12 Christoph Bitterberg and Silvia de Pasquale, "Mord, Massensterben und 'Rückführungen'. Die letzten Kriegsmonate im nationalsozialistischen Strafvollzug," in *Kriegsendverbrechen zwischen Untergangschaos und Vernichtungsprogramm*, ed. Detlef Garbe and Günther Morsch (Berlin: Metropol-Verlag, 2015), 81–96.
13 In the late phase of the Third Reich, Organisation Todt (OT) administered the construction of concentration camps and the supply of forced labor to the war industry.
14 Nachweisung der ständigen Außenarbeitsstellen bei den Vollzugsanstalten Bezirk Braunschweig, 08.01.1945, NLA WO 42 A Neu Fb. 3 Zg. 37/1983 Nr. 22 Belegungs- und Beschäftigungsübersichten der Vollzugsanstalten; betr. Belegungsübersichten. And: OT-Einsatzgruppe IV "Kyffhäus-

ciary prisons' inmates. There were more prisoners in this system of forced labor but not all would be represented on the map.

The historical investigation of the external commands of the Wolfenbüttel prison in the last months of World War II is made more difficult by the fact that parts of the files of the prison and the responsible Brunswick Prosecutor General's Office were destroyed. In addition, both in contemporary records as well as in post-war documents, the assignments of different camps to the respective organizations to which they were subject are not clear and often simply incorrect. For example, in a post-war trial in Belgium against prison officials, not only was witness testimony on the justice camps evaluated but reports from survivors of the Buchenwald concentration camp's external commands were also taken into account. The fact that Blankenburg, like many places, had a large number of different camps was hardly recognized.[15] It is obviously a great challenge to transfer this distinction, which has not yet been conclusively clarified in historical research, into a digital map without concealing important information or aspects of forced labor in these places.

The third example will deal with the case of a place that was closely connected to the Wolfenbüttel prison but was administrated by a university. There was a connection between an increased number of executions under National Socialism and anatomical research at German universities. In February 1939, the distribution of the bodies of executed persons was organized by permanently assigning the execution sites to different anatomical institutes. Those killed in the Wolfenbüttel prison were now firmly assigned and regularly offered to the Anatomical Institute in Göttingen.[16] For at least 217 of the 783 bodies recorded in Göttingen for the period 1933–1945, the Wolfenbüttel prison was the place of origin. Thus, the prison was the largest place of origin of the bodies handed over to the Anatomical Institute. Due to the increased application of the death penalty during National Socialism, all anatomical institutes found themselves in a situation that allowed them almost unlimited access to the desired "material."[17] In some instances, only

---

er" S-Bauleitung Osterode/ Hz. An das Strafgefängnis Wolfenbüttel, 22.02.1945, NLA WO 42 A Neu Fb. 3 Zg. 37/1983 Nr. 14 Ersatzgefangene für Gefangenenlager und Auffüllung von Strafanstalten.
15 Commissariat de police, ville de Liège, 13.11.1946, State Archives of Belgium, Cour Militaire de Bruxelles, Prosecutor v. Lupfer et al., case 182/B/1950, 05.12.1950, Nr. 58.
16 Der Reichsminister für Wissenschaft, Erziehung und Volksbildung (i.A. Mentzel) an das Universität-Kuratorium Göttingen, 18.02.1939, UniAGött Kur. 0987 Anatomie Leichen 1939–1958.
17 Sabine Hildebrandt, *The Anatomy of Murder: Ethical Transgressions and Anatomical Science during the Third Reich* (New York: Berghahn Books, 2016). And: UniAGött Kur. 0986 Anatomie Leichen bis 1938; UniAGött Kur. 0987 Anatomie Leichen 1939–1958.

parts of the bodies were transferred from Wolfenbüttel to Göttingen. The funeral company Frieden, which in some cases represented the Göttingen medical staff in Wolfenbüttel when taking over the bodies, received order lists with the desired body parts. For example, in some cases only the severed heads of the bodies were to be brought to Göttingen by train.[18] The prison in Wolfenbüttel also differed from the other places of origin of the bodies in that samples were taken on site and physicians worked with the bodies in a special room set up for this purpose right next to the guillotine in Wolfenbüttel.[19] The bodies of the executed persons were used in university teaching for dissection courses and for the production of permanent show specimens.[20] Thus, the Institute of Anatomy in Göttingen was an institution directly and immediately connected with the prison in Wolfenbüttel. The bodies of the victims of the National Socialists executed there became "research material." A cartographic representation should hardly hide such a close connection between two places in the system of National Socialist persecution. Nevertheless, the Institute of Anatomy was not an institution of the judiciary and was located outside the state of Brunswick. If this connection is taken into account and displayed on the map, it is difficult to explain why other connections, such as those to the Gestapo, might be omitted from a map.

It becomes clear that the selection of the places to be depicted is quite difficult. It is a process of weighing up direct connections between the prison in Wolfenbüttel and other places and the relevance of the respective connections. Not even a digital map, which could theoretically depict every conceivable connection, can flood exhibition visitors with such a wealth of information and at the same time hope that the visitors will actively engage with the information.

4 Conclusion

Digital maps can be used to show the development and expansion of a singular place towards a more connected structure. They cannot show the whole complexity of the National Socialists' system of oppression, violence, and terror and its development over the whole period of the National Socialist regime from 1933 to 1945 in a way that is easily accessible for exhibition visitors. In re-

---

18 Anatomisches Institut Göttingen an Beerdigungsinstitut "Frieden," 31.10.1942, ZAUGA – B 1, Kuratorium Leichen.
19 Anatomisches Institut Göttingen an den Vorstand des Strafgefängnisses Wolfenbüttel, 27.07.1943, ZAUGA – B 1, Kuratorium Leichen.
20 Erich Blechschmidt an den Kurator der Universität Göttingen, 17.06.1942, UniAGött Kur. 2602 Bausachen Anatomie.

ality, the prison system was only one of many ways the National Socialists terrorized and persecuted their political opponents and those who were not seen as part of the so-called *Volksgemeinschaft*. The legal prison system was intertwined with other sorts of places of imprisonment like concentration camps or police prisons, and depended on bigger structures like local, regional, and national courts and the ministry of justice in Berlin. Focusing on the legal prison system and displaying it on a digital map therefore will always necessarily leave some blind spots for exhibition visitors, even if the map aims to display all elements of the prison system within a given region. Nevertheless, digital maps are a meaningful tool to show the density of the prison system within the German state and in the occupied territories. But eventually a map cannot replace a visit to the historical sites. As in all cases, maps have to be used very carefully and the information on display should help those who view it to gain insight into the more complex structures while maintaining awareness of its limited contents and its constructed character.

Compared to other ways of including digital media into an exhibition, like virtual- or augmented-reality applications, a map still is a more basic tool. But all in all, the digital presentation of information on a map can be seen as highly significant or even necessary to future exhibitions that deal with a certain space in a certain period. By showing its extension and development the digital map addresses the audience's expectations for participation and interaction that have emerged in recent years and will most likely emerge even further and can even be considered a "product of digital identity."[21]

By exploring this example of a rather neglected part of the history of National Socialist crimes, it became clear that the use of digital tools increases the feasibility to make more information on a network accessible within an exhibition. On the other hand, this way of "doing history digitally" also carries some potential dangers. It must be based on a thorough historical investigation of the individual sites and needs to be carefully applied so as to not overwhelm the audience with the vast number of places and immense possibilities for including information on those sites as well as all the connections maintained by a prison in National Socialist Germany.

---

[21] Tula Giannini and Jonathan P. Bowen, "Museums and Digitalism," in *Museums and Digital Culture: New Perspectives and Research*, ed. Tula Giannini and Jonathan P. Bowen (Cham: Springer Nature, 2019), 30.

Bibliography

Akker, Chiel van den, and Susan Legêne. "Introduction." In *Museums in a Digital Culture: How Art and Heritage Become Meaningful*, edited by Chiel van den Akker and Susan Legêne, 7–12. Amsterdam: Amsterdam University Press, 2016.

Bitterberg, Christoph, and Silvia de Pasquale. "Mord, Massensterben und 'Rückführungen'. Die letzten Kriegsmonate im nationalsozialistischen Strafvollzug." In *Kriegsendverbrechen zwischen Untergangschaos und Vernichtungsprogramm*, edited by Detlef Garbe and Günther Morsch, 81–96. Berlin: Metropol-Verlag, 2015.

Buggeln, Marc. "Unfreie Arbeit im Nationalsozialismus. Begrifflichkeiten und Vergleichsaspekte zu den Arbeitsbedingungen im Deutschen Reich und in den besetzten Gebieten." In *Arbeit im Nationalsozialismus*, edited by Marc Buggeln and Michael Wildt, 231–52. Munich: Oldenbourg Verlag, 2014.

Dremel, Anett, and Jens-Christian Wagner. "Strafvollzug im Nationalsozialismus. Ein Überblick." In *Recht. Verbrechen. Folgen: Das Strafgefängnis Wolfenbüttel im Nationalsozialismus*, edited by Martina Staats and Jens-Christian Wagner, 254–63. Göttingen: Wallstein, 2019.

Giannini, Tula, and Jonathan P. Bowen. "Museums and Digitalism." In *Museums and Digital Culture: New Perspectives and Research*, edited by Tula Giannini and Jonathan P. Bowen, 27–46. Cham: Springer Nature, 2019.

Gröchtemeier, Markus. *Fahnenwechsel: Nationalsozialismus und britische Besatzung in der Stadt Wolfenbüttel 1933–1948*. Hameln: CW Niemeyer Buchverlage, 2018.

Grüttner, Michael. *Brandstifter und Biedermänner: Deutschland 1933–1939*. Stuttgart: Klett-Cotta, 2015.

Hildebrandt, Sabine. *The Anatomy of Murder: Ethical Transgressions and Anatomical Science during the Third Reich*. New York: Berghahn Books, 2016.

Jaegher, Lars de, Maria de Waele, and Véronique van Goethem. "The Use of Digital Media in a New Urban History Exhibition: STAM – Ghent City Museum." *18th International Conference on Virtual Systems and Multimedia, Milan, 2012*, 557–560. Accessed 3 August, 2021. doi: 10.1109/VSMM.2012.6365976.

Knauer, Wilfried. "… nicht hinter Mauern! Die Stadt und das Strafgefängnis Wolfenbüttel 1933–1945." In *Wolfenbüttel unter dem Hakenkreuz: Fünf Vorträge*, edited by Stadt Wolfenbüttel, 81–102. Wolfenbüttel: Stadt Wolfenbüttel, 2000.

Sachweh, Jannik. "Von Wesermünde nach Wolfenbüttel. Orte der Justizverbrechen im nationalsozialistischen Strafvollzug." *Jahrbuch der Männer vom Morgenstern* 97 (2019): 13–31.

Wachsmann, Nikolaus. *Hitler's Prisons: Legal Terror in Nazi Germany*. New Haven, CT: Yale University Press, 2004.

Wagner, Jens-Christian. "Simulierte Authentizität? Chancen und Risiken von augmented und virtual reality an Gedenkstätten." *Gedenkstättenrundbrief* 196 (2019): 3–9.

Christian Günther
Chapter 8
Authenticity and Authority in German Memorial Sites

German Summary: Im Workshop und in den Beiträgen in diesem Buch wurden methodische und ethische Fragen zum Umgang mit digitalen Quellen zur NS-Geschichte aufgeworfen. Eine wiederkehrende Fragestellung ist die nach dem Rollenverständnis von Einrichtungen bei der Geschichtsvermittlung: Wie stark sollen Besucher*innen durch Gedenkstätten in der Rezeption von Medien gelenkt werden? Die Weiterverarbeitung der Daten durch das Forschungsprojekts „Valentin3D" in ein VR-Projekt konnte im zeitlichen Rahmen des Workshops leider nicht mehr diskutiert werden. Aus der Sicht des Autors dieses Kapitels verdichten sich jedoch die skizzierten Fragen in der Gestaltung von VR-Projekten: Sie versprechen den Nutzer*innen oft ein selbstbestimmtes und möglichst „authentisches" Erlebnis und sind damit in mehrfacher Hinsicht problematisch. Ausgehend vom Begriff der Authentizität, wie er im Gedenkstättenkontext genutzt wird, werden in diesem Kapitel Theorien aus den Game Studies adaptiert, um Virtual-Reality-Angebote theoretisch besser beschreiben zu können. Darauf aufbauend folgen Überlegungen zu einem Rollenwechsel von Gedenkstätten in einer digitalisierten Welt.

1 Virtual Reality as a Challenge for Memorial Sites

During the editors' workshop in 2019 that was the starting point for this book, I started thinking about what kind of educational experience could emerge from the research project "Valentin3D."[1] Could the collected data be used to create a Virtual Reality experience?[2] Would it be possible to show the conditions on the construction site from summer 1943 to spring 1945 using digital tools—that is, the mass use of forced civilian laborers and their living conditions? How could the educational work of the memorial site Denkort Bunker Valentin benefit from this?

---

[1] For a more detailed discussion of this project, see Chapter 6 in this book.
[2] In a nutshell, I am talking about an artificial world that is created using special software and hardware.

OpenAccess. © 2022 Christian Günther, published by De Gruyter. This work is licensed under the Creative Commons Attribution 4.0 International License.
https://doi.org/10.1515/9783110714692-011

Virtual Reality is often described as a ground-breaking technology; but in fact, as Christian Bunnenberg has pointed out, Virtual Reality is not that new.³ Introduced in the 1960s, it was limited to industry, science, and research until the 1980s, opened to the public through games in the 1990s, and finally found its way to general public usage through the mass distribution of smartphones in the last few years.⁴ Bunnenberg claims that "the virtual realities and the 360° films of the present time represent the technically further developed panoramas of the 21st century."⁵ I consider this comparison to be very helpful because it covers the aspect of the promised "authentic experience" very clearly. This aspect will be an important part of this chapter.⁶

The concept of Virtual Reality is an umbrella term that has not been clearly defined yet. From a technological point of view, it comprises Mixed Reality, Augmented Reality, and full dive Virtual Reality. Sometimes, also for marketing reasons, it is used to advertise 360° films such as "Inside Auschwitz."⁷ The Virtual Reality continuum designed by the engineer Paul Milgram offers a good way to distinguish the individual technologies.⁸ According to this, the technologies mentioned are characterized by gradual differences in their virtuality. The span of the continuum ranges from complete reality to complete virtuality. In this process, the degree of virtuality increases continuously, while that of reality decreases further. Mixed Reality (MR) describes a hybrid in which real environment and virtual elements merge with each other in real time. The term includes both Virtual Reality (VR) and Augmented Reality (AR).

AR, according to Ronald T. Azuma, can be described by three defining characteristics: (1) The real environment is extended by digital elements such as videos or graphics; (2) The resulting application is real time and interactive; (3) The virtual objects are registered three-dimensionally. AR systems are thus also characterized by spatial independence. They are not tied to a fixed location and can

---

3 Christian Bunnenberg, "Virtual Time Travels? Public History and Virtual Reality," *Public History Weekly* 6, no. 3 (2018), accessed September 15, 2020, doi: 10.1515/phw-2018–10896.
4 Bunnenberg, "Virtual Time Travels?"
5 Bunnenberg, "Virtual Time Travels?"
6 For better readability, I decided to translate titles of German publications as well as some selected passages into English. This is marked with [TAA]=Translated by the author of the article.
7 INSIDE AUSCHWITZ – Das ehemalige Konzentrationslager in 360° | WDR, accessed October 12, 2020, https://www.youtube.com/watch?v=QwC5d75iTcA.
8 Paul Milgram et al., "Augmented Reality: A Class of Displays on the Reality-Virtuality Continuum," in *Proceedings of SPIE – The International Society for Optical Engineering* 2351 (January 1994), accessed September 10, 2020, doi: 10.1117/12.197321.

therefore be used mobile and outdoors.⁹ Virtual Reality (VR), according to Milgram, means a Virtual Reality completely simulated by the computer, in which one can move around with the help of terminals such as 3D glasses and controllers. This definition allows a clear distinction to be made between Virtual Reality and 360° films such as the aforementioned "Inside Auschwitz" or "The Eva Experience."¹⁰ They differ above all in the degree of freedom of movement that they allow the user. While recorded 360° films only allow movements in three axes of rotation and only very limited possibilities for action, the three-dimensional spaces of a VR application are calculated in real time and thereby not only allow complete freedom of movement in the simulation but also offer possibilities for interaction. However, the degree of immersion cannot be used here for further comparison between those types, since immersion is based on subjective feelings and there are no recipient surveys on this topic when it comes to memorials.¹¹

VR represents a challenge for memorial sites.¹² On the one hand, it enables users to have a different, more interactive access to history that cannot be pro-

---

9 Ronald T. Azuma, "A Survey of Augmented Reality," *Presence: Teleoperators and Virtual Environments* 6, no. 4 (1997): 355–85, accessed September 10, 2020, doi: 10.1162/pres.1997.6.4.355.
10 The Eva Experience – VR Exhibit, accessed October 12, 2020, https://www.oculus.com/experiences/go/2265625690131356/. Another example is the 360-degree panoramic tour of the Neuengamme concentration camp memorial site, accessed October 12, 2020, https://www.kz-gedenkstaette-neuengamme.de/360tour/.
11 The term "immersion" was introduced into the discourse in 1938 by Bela Balasz in the context of films and further developed in the field of game studies: see Simon Huber, "Zur Geschichte der Cutscenes: Versuch einer Medienarchäologie kommerzieller Videospiele," in *Frühe Neuzeit im Videospiel*, ed. Florian Kerschbaumer and Tobias Winnerling (Bielefeld: transcript Verlag, 2014), 84. Immersion can be described as "the sensation of being surrounded by a completely other reality, as different as water is from air that takes over all of our attention, or whole perceptual apparatus," Janet Horowitz Murray, *Hamlet on the Holodeck: The Future of Narrative in Cyberspace* (Cambridge, MA: MIT Press, 1998), 98. However, there are projects in progress aiming to conduct such surveys: See Ruhr Universität Bochum, Geschichtsdidaktik. "ViRaGe – Virtuelle Realitäten als Geschichtserfahrung," accessed September 10, 2020, https://www.ruhr-uni-bochum.de/jpgeschichtsdidaktik/forschung/virage.html.de; see Grimme-Forschungskolleg an der Universität zu Köln, accessed September 10, 2020, https://www.grimme-forschungskolleg.de/portfolio/witness-auschwitz-2020/.
12 I follow Habbo Knoch here: "A 'memorial site' today is understood in a broader sense to be an institution (usually state or state-sponsored) at a historical site of state, terrorist or catastrophic violence, whose primary task is to remember those people who suffered or died there. Memorials in the narrower sense of the word commemorate the victims of past state mass crimes. ... Through material remains, personal testimonies, and the spatial impression of places distinguished from the everyday world, memorials open up an emotionally intense, multi-sensory, and experience-oriented approach to history that has an attachment to cognitive

vided by other media. On the other hand, VR systems carry the risk of overwhelming their users and thereby violating the basic principles of the Beutelsbach Consensus.[13] Jens-Christian Wagner has put forward several theses for discussion on this matter.[14] In his article, he articulates ideas on the circumstances under which Augmented Reality can be used in educational work on the history of National Socialism. He considers the use of VR more carefully, as it "simulates emotional approaches to history."[15] But as I would like to show in the following, the development of a VR experience for a memorial is not only a challenge to the educational work, but also to the self-image, the role, and the working culture of individual memorial sites. It also requires reflection on how to deal with (digital) visitors. Users make an immersive experience in VR that is only seemingly self-determined. In the background are carefully curated narratives which would have to be made transparent in the further development of the Beutelsbach Consensus. That would imply that the sources underlying the virtual world and their interpretation would have to be presented. Furthermore, the spatial and temporal distance bridged in VR would have to be restored. In addition, the history of events and complexities of actions, which is told in memorials through media-specific possibilities, is decoupled from its geographical localization and thus its authentication in VR.

---

and reflexive approaches. [TAA]" Habbo Knoch, "Gedenkstätten," *Docupedia-Zeitgeschichte*, September 11, 2018, accessed September 15, 2020, doi: 10.14765/zzf.dok.2.1221.v1.

13 The Beutelsbach Consensus was developed in 1976 and is still the baseline for political-historical education in memorial sites in Germany. It is based on three fundamental rules: a ban on indoctrination, a requirement to present politically controversial issues in a controversial way, and an aim to enable students to make an independent judgment on political topics. ("Beutelsbacher Konsens," Landeszentrale für politische Bildung Baden-Württemberg, accessed September 15, 2020, https://www.lpb-bw.de/beutelsbacher-konsens/.) As Helmut Däuble points out, those points are void of content. The actual function of the Beutelsbach Consensus provides more of a reference frame within which one can discuss the goals of political-historical education: see Helmut Däuble, "Der fruchtbare Dissens um den Beutelsbacher Konsens," *GWP* 4 (2016): 449–58, accessed September 15, 2020, doi: 10.3224/gwp.v65i4.05.

14 Jens-Christian Wagner, "Simulierte Authentizität, Chancen und Risiken von Augmented und Virtual Reality an Gedenkstätten," *Gedenkstättenrundbrief* 196, accessed August 15, 2020, https://www.gedenkstaettenforum.de/nc/gedenkstaettenrundbrief/rundbrief/news/simulierte_authentizitaet_chancen_und_risiken_von_augmented_und_virtual_reality_an_gedenkstaetten.

15 [TAA]. Wagner, "Simulierte Authentizität." See Christian Bunnenberg analyses this problem from a historical-didactic perspective: Christian Bunnenberg, "Mittendrin im historischen Geschehen? Immersive digitale Medien (Augmented Reality, Virtual Reality, 360°-Film) in der Geschichtskultur und Perspektiven für den Geschichtsunterricht," *geschichte für heute* 4 (2020): 45–58.

2 About Authenticity in Memorial Sites

According to the title of an article by Drecoll, Schaarschmidt, and Zündorf, authenticity may be the "asset of historical places."[16] The authors point out that historical places are authentic because they are able to locate history concretely and make it tangible through the presence of architectural remains. This view coincides with the concept for memorial sites promulgated by the German Federal government, which declares an institution a memorial site if, among other things, it has an unmistakable profile that refers to the "authenticity of the site."[17] In this context, Jens-Christian Wagner points out that the use of material relics in memorial sites also has generational reasons. According to Wagner, after passing the Era of Witnesses, structural relics will become "stone evidence, documentary evidence."[18] Through this argument, Wagner relates the term authenticity to its Greek origin αυθεντικός or authentikós (lat: authenticus) and defines it as "genuine" or "warranted." This definition has consequences for memorial sites because it assigns them the function of serving as evidence for the crimes that took place on the site. As Alexandra Klei states, buildings are information carriers:

> They can be used to make statements about materiality, for example about the conditions of accommodation for captives, the relationship between buildings with different functions, about paths, boundaries, visible surfaces, visual relationships, points of contact with the surrounding villages, etc.[19]

Following the logic that memorials are evidence, the ban on reconstruction follows as a consensus among memorial sites; after all, "no detective at a crime

---

[16] [TAA]. Axel Drecoll, Thomas Schaarschmidt, and Irmgard Zündorf, "Authentizität als Kapital historischer Orte?" in *Authentizität als Kapital historischer Orte? Die Sehnsucht nach dem unmittelbaren Erleben von Geschichte*, ed. Axel Drecoll, Thomas Schaarschmidt, and Irmgard Zündorf (Göttingen: Wallstein Verlag, 2019), 7–17.
[17] Konzeption der künftigen Gedenkstättenförderung des Bundes, BT-Drucksache 14/1569, July 27, 1999, 3–6, accessed September 15, 2020, http://dip21.bundestag.de/dip21/btd/14/015/1401569.pdf.
[18] Wagner, "Simulierte Authentizität." See also: Olaf Mussmann, "Die Gestaltung von Gedenkstätten im historischen Wandel," in *Museale und mediale Präsentationen in KZ-Gedenkstätten*, Beiträge zur Geschichte der nationalsozialistischen Verfolgung in Norddeutschland 6, ed. Herbert Diercks (Bremen: Ed. Temmen, 2001), 14–33.
[19] [TAA]. Alexandra Klei, *Der erinnerte Ort* (Berlin: De Gruyter, 2011), 30; see also Habbo Knoch, "'Ferienlager' und 'gefoltertes Leben'. Periphere Räume in ehemaligen Konzentrationslagern," in *Sanierung – Rekonstruktion – Neugestaltung: Zum Umgang mit historischen Bauten in Gedenkstätten*, ed. Gabriele Hammermann and Dirk Riedel (Göttingen: Wallstein Verlag, 2014), 32–49.

scene would (hopefully) get the idea of reproducing evidence."[20] This "ban" is not a formal decision in a legal sense but rather a consensus that has been acted on in recent years when memorial sites in Germany are opened or redesigned.[21]

Thomas Lutz demonstrates the contradiction that arises from fixating on a certain point in time and blocking out subsequent periods. As he points out, sites of mass violence not only underwent dynamic changes during the Nazi regime, but also in the post-war period, when they were often used in different ways.[22] Detlev Hoffman speaks in his book *Memory of Things*[23] about different interdependent layers that must be related to each other in a process which is like "tracing." The "concept of tracing"[24] is an attempt to resolve the aforementioned contradiction in exhibitions. Architectural relics are conserved by means of glass and, in this way, presented to the visitors inside a sort of "time window." These windows are integrated into the exhibition in a larger ensemble including different design elements, documents, media, and objects. Visitors thus have the opportunity to engage with the multidimensionality and multi-temporality of the site and its constructional character. This changes the authentication strategy of memorial sites. The structural relics are additionally authenticated by the exhibition through the use of media or objects. Just like sites, the objects must be contextualized as they alone can tell observers little about their creation and usage. This would mean that their value as evidence of authenticity would be determined solely by their provenance and age. Photographs are often given spe-

---

20 [TAA]. Jens-Chirstian Wagner, "Lernen mit Sachquellen in Museen und Gedenkstätten. Fragen und Antworten einer interdisziplinären Tagung," *Lernen aus Geschichte*, January 31, 2018, accessed September 15, 2020, http://lernen-aus-der-geschichte.de/Lernen-und-Lehren/content/13865.
21 This is clearly shown in the following conference publications: Hammermann and Riedel, *Sanierung – Rekonstruktion – Neugestaltung*; Wolfgang Brandes, *Tagungsbericht: Neue Ansätze zur Präsentation regionaler NS-Geschichte in Museen, Dokumentations- und Gedenkstätten* (Hannover: 2012), accessed September 20, 2020, http://hsozkult.geschichte.hu-berlin.de/tagungsberichte/id=4410. In this context, Habbo Knoch also points out that the handling of crime scenes has become more scientific (Knoch, "Gedenkstätten"). Quite interestingly, this is also accounted for in virtual environments like those provided for the Bergen-Belsen concentration camp, which have a "forensic, respectively a historical view on the camps" in common, as Steffi de Jong points out in her article "Witness Auschwitz? How VR Is Changing Testimony," *Public History Weekly* 8, no. 4 (2020), accessed September 1, 2020, doi: 10.1515/phw-2020 – 15689.
22 Thomas Lutz, "Materialisierte Authentifizierung: Die Bedeutung authentischer Gebäude und Objekte in Gedenkstätten und Dokumentationszentren der NS-Verbrechen," in Drecoll et al., *Authentizität*, 57–76.
23 [TAA, Das Gedächtnis der Dinge]. Detlef Hoffmann, *Das Gedächtnis der Dinge: KZ-Relikte und KZ-Denkmäler 1945–1995* (Frankfurt am Main: Campus Verlag, 1998).
24 [TAA, "Konzept der Spurensuche"].

cial space in exhibitions. Only a few permanent exhibitions, however, reveal their perspective, the context of their origin (staging), and most provide only limited information about events depicted on the photographs. As a substitute for non-existing photographs from the victims' perspective, drawings of captives are often used as authentic testimonies. These, however, can only reveal a subjective perception of an individual person. Similar to the contemporary witnesses their authenticity is based on the power of the narratives of their experience. This is not primarily judged by credibility or truthfulness, but by how the depiction is experienced. Therefore, in the exhibition, two different fields of attribution of the authentic get entangled: that of authentic testimony and that of authentic experience.[25]

Irrespective of the discussion in historical studies about authenticity, the authenticity character, and multidimensionality of such relics, memorials are also symbolic and mediatized places. Visitors bring their own expectations and ideas with them which can complement or transform the perception of the physical site. On the visitor's part there is a subjective expectation of a place to be authentic. According to Gottfried Korf, this expectation refers to the "quality of impression"[26] of a historical place, an object, or an ensemble of objects. The latter refers to a concrete moment or event in the past to which an emotional connection can be established. The "authentic feeling" is a kind of collaborative hallucination[27] between the institution, the exhibition organizer, and the visitor. Therefore, it seems to make sense to understand this pact as a communication structure and to further analyze it.[28] Another facet of the concept of authenticity contributes to this: Joachim Saupe has pointed out the ambiguity of the stem of the Greek word for authenticity, which also includes the Greek words for "doer" and "murderer" in its meaning, thus linking the concept of authenticity to that of authority, or "authorization."[29] In other words, architectural remains are not authentic in themselves, but rather undergo a certain process in which

---

25 As there is a lack of empirical studies on this issue, statements about visitors' authenticity perception are rather in the area of speculation.
26 [TAA, Anmutungsqualität]. Gottfried Korff, "Die Eigenart der Museums-Dinge: Zur Materialität und Medialität des Museums," in *Handbuch der museumspädagogischen Ansätze*, ed. Kirsten Fast (Wiesbaden: VS Verlag für Sozialwissenschaften, 1995), 17–28.
27 Barbara Kirshenblatt-Gimblett, *Destination Culture: Tourism, Museums, and Heritage* (Berkeley: University of California Press, 1998), 314.
28 Helmut Lethen, "Versionen des Authentischen: Sechs Gemeinplätze," in *Literatur und Kulturwissenschaften: Positionen, Theorien, Modelle*, ed. Hartmut Böhme and Klaus R. Scherpe (Reinbek bei Hamburg: Rowohlt-Taschenbuch-Verlag, 1996), 209.
29 Achim Saupe, "Authenticity," *Docupedia-Zeitgeschichte*, April 12, 2016, accessed September 1, 2020, doi: 10.14765/zzf.dok.2.645.v1.

they are verified as "authentic" by authorities. Julia Röttjer has vividly described this in her article which shows how UNESCO, as the authorizing authority—that is, as an "authentication agency,"[30] reacted to the Polish government's application in the late 1970s to have Auschwitz-Birkenau declared a world cultural heritage site.[31] She emphasizes that the communication between the institution, the exhibition's organizers, and the visitors is strongly characterized by hierarchies and authority.

3 Memorials and Working Culture

The memorial sites themselves are usually self-contained units that still function according to the nineteenth-century principle of cooperative work. This means that the individual units of the institution, such as research, education, and library, usually only communicate with each other for specific purposes. Projects are worked on based on a division of labor, tasks are delegated according to competence, and missing knowledge is externally purchased. Information, knowledge, and skills are usually only shared on a project-related basis for a limited time. The actual work processes are not transparent and not comprehensible to external spectators.

The potential visitors to memorial sites are seldom involved in the process. They are usually confronted with an exhibition that on the one hand has to do justice to the triad of commemoration, politics of history, and science,[32] but on the other hand also has to meet the visitors' expectations.

This working culture was compatible with the realization of exhibition projects in an analog space. However, in a "culture of digitality,"[33] in which the culture of communication and the reception of media is undergoing massive changes, this process cannot survive in the long term. The digitalization of processes and communication is not a purely technical issue, but also a matter of an open and changed work culture. It affects all employees. Memorial sites have to decide how open and participative they want to be. Their attitude towards digitality and the value of digital visitors should ideally be reflected in a mission statement published on the memorial sites' website.

---

30 [TAA, Authentifizierungsagentur].
31 Julia Röttjer, "Authentizität Im UNESCO-Welterbe-Diskurs: Das Konzentrations- und Vernichtungslager Auschwitz-Birkenau," in Drecoll et al., *Authentizität*, 35.
32 Knoch, "Gedenkstätten."
33 See Felix Stalder, *Kultur der Digitalität* (Berlin: Suhrkamp, 2016).

Such a demand also means that memorial sites must actively face the challenges of the digital transformation. So far, however, I am not aware of any strategy paper published by a German memorial site that addresses digitalization, analyses its own current status in this regard, sets goals for a digital strategy, and defines the resources required for this. It is noteworthy that memorials are remarkably unobtrusive in this regard, in contrast to at least some museums, where some of the things listed above have already been done and some calls for digital curators have been published. If one can draw a conclusion from the job offers published so far in the area, it is that the budget for digital projects in memorial sites is marginal. The digital collections of memorial sites (with the exception of the Arolsen Archive) are exclusively recorded in non-public databases.[34] Furthermore, the websites of memorial sites are usually technically outdated, visually unappealing, and rarely consider the needs of visitors, and this despite the fact that a website is usually the heart of every digital presence. In my estimation, no memorial site would actually be capable of making qualified statements about its digital visitors, their interests, and usage behavior.[35] The appreciation of the importance of PR for memorials has increased enormously in recent years. The digital space has dramatically increased the opportunities and options for making contact with visitors and experts. For a long time, memorial site communication was output-oriented and focused on newsletters, the local press, and accompanying publications. Meanwhile several memorials are present in social networks.[36] However, their presence in social networks shows that online communication requires specially adapted concepts. Accelerated communication means that the transitions between individual departments must be smoother, because all departments must contribute content on an equal footing in order to generate public resonance.[37] At the same time, however, it also becomes clear that the digital space extends far beyond the physical space of the memorial site and is no longer controllable by the institution. In addition to the memorial sites, other actors of remembrance[38] offer interpretation and access to the

---

34 This term refers to databases that are not following the FAIR principles: Findability, Accessibility, Interoperability, and Reuse of digital assets. "FAIR Principles," Go Fair, accessed September 15, 2020, https://www.go-fair.org/fair-principles/.
35 This is of course only a reasonable assumption based on the fact that to my knowledge there is no published digital strategy for a memorial site and that the museum world is still debating the value of digital visitors and how to count them.
36 "Raus aus dem Elfenbeinturm," Arolsen Archives, accessed October 13, 2020, https://arolsen-archives.org/lernen-mitwirken/lernen-mit-dokumenten/gedenkstaettenseminar/.
37 See Hartmut Rosa, *Resonanz – Eine Soziologie der Weltbeziehung* (Berlin, Suhrkamp, 2016).
38 Such as archives or historical societies, but also history instructors on YouTube or serious games.

history of perpetrators and persecution under National Socialism, which calls into question the sovereignty of interpretation of memorial sites. Particularly in the Digital Age and especially in social media, authenticity, attention, and knowledge are structured, hierarchized, and organized according to other mechanisms. Similar to the "collaborative hallucination" in the real world, a different pact between the institution, the exhibition organizer, and the visitor must be made for digital projects, and relatedly, a different authentication strategy must be developed.

4 Preserved "Era of Witnesses"?

An authentication strategy for AR or MR projects is to tie in with the "Era of Witnesses" or to digitally preserve witnesses' testimonies. With the project "New Dimensions in Testimony" (2012), the USC Shoah Foundation (USC SF) wants to create an interactive collection of video interviews with witnesses of the Holocaust and genocide survivors. The type of recording is meant to make it possible to display the interviews in the form of a hologram at a later date. During the interview, the witnesses can be asked up to 2,000 questions, the answers to which are stored in individual sequences in a database. Users can ask the digitized witnesses questions, which are then translated by speech recognition software into corresponding search terms and assigned to individual answers. This is intended to simulate a conversation in real time. Steffi De Jong describes this as an attempt to halt the decline of communicative memory by means of "memory cyborgs"[39] and thus to maintain an empathy-centered culture of remembrance.[40] The parts of this project that have already been realized are used in museums, memorials, and schools. The type of presentation and integration is controlled by the USC SF. It is not clear from the information provided by this organization whether the questions and the framework conditions of the interviews will also be recorded and can be viewed by users. The first German-language interview was conducted in 2019 with Auschwitz survivor Anita Lasker-Wallfisch. It has been on display in a beta test phase at the Deutsches Technikmuseum (German Museum of Technology) in Berlin since February 2020.[41]

---

39 [TAA, Erinnerungscyborg]. Steffi de Jong, "Von Hologrammen und sprechenden Füchsen – Holocausterinnerung 3.0," *Tagung #erinnern_kontrovers*, accessed September 15, 2020, https://erinnern.hypotheses.org/465.
40 Jong, "Hologrammen."
41 A similar project called 'LediZ' exists at the LMU München: "Lernen mit digitalen Zeugnissen," accessed October 13, 2020, https://www.lediz.uni-muenchen.de/.

In the VR project "The Last Goodbye," realized by the USC SF in 2017, users can accompany Holocaust survivor Pinchas Gutter on a tour of the former concentration and extermination camp Lublin-Majdanek. Up to now, this VR tour could only be visited in several museums in the USA. According to information from USC SF, however, the tour has been available on the VR headset Oculus since September 2020. This would enable users to access the project without having to visit a museum. Also available on Oculus Go is the project "Anne Frank VR." The company Force Field realized this project in 2018 for the Anne Frank House in Amsterdam. After a short historical introduction, the simulation starts in front of the entrance to the rear building of the Anne Frank House. However, in contrast to the museum, the interior was reconstructed here. The users can only move around the building by using jump marks.[42] That also means that the respective perspective is restricted, and that free movement is not possible. The exploration of the rooms is supplemented by entries from Anne Frank's diary, which are presented by dubbing actors and can be heard when running the simulation.

As discussed above, it is possible that memorial sites lose the sovereignty of interpretation when historical places or parts of them are digitized. This is illustrated by announcements from various studios to reconstruct the Auschwitz-Birkenau extermination camp using VR. In 2019, the developers of the Polish Real Invented Studio failed in their kick-start-campaign-driven attempt to raise funds for the "Auschwitz VR" project. Only $545 of the targeted $ 7,000 were achieved. The studio's aim was to use plans, photographs, and reports to make the camp's condition between 1940 and 1945 accessible and to enable people to move around freely in the created digital environment. In March 2020 the studio updated its homepage on this project with a screenshot of the reconstruction of the gatehouse.[43] A different project is called "Witness Auschwitz."[44] Its initiator, the Italian studio 101%, announced that it would make its experience of the Auschwitz-Birkenau extermination camp as "authentic" as possible by implementing photos and construction plans as well as conversations with contemporary witnesses. Users were asked to dig graves, playing the role of an inmate of the concentration camp. Since studio 101% presented a trailer at Gamescom in 2017, which attracted a lot of negative attention, the project seems to have come to a halt.

---

42 Probably to prevent the VR sickness that, among other things, can cause nausea.
43 Real Invented Studio, Auschwitz-Birkenau, Historical VR Reconstruction, accessed October 12, 2020, https://auschwitz-vr.pl/.
44 101% Studios and I Say Web, Witness Auschwitz, accessed October 12, 2020, http://witnesauschwitz.com/.

In May 2020 *The New York Times* reported on the plans of director Ilya A. Khrzhanovsky to develop a VR exhibition for the Babyn Yar Memorial which is scheduled to open in 2025. After visitors complete a psychological test and the system has gathered information from their social media accounts, an algorithm assigns a role to each user. For example, you can be asked to take the role of an executioner or of a victim in the context of the Babyn Yar massacre. The exhibition intends to be a "a challenging and sometimes shocking emotional journey with ethical choices at its core."[45] The above-mentioned projects have in common that they have been massively criticized for their intention to offer the "most authentic experiences" in their given historical settings, thereby overwhelming the users emotionally. A discussion on whether the sovereignty of interpretation, intergenerational conflicts, ethical norms, or a paradigm shift in the culture of memory have become apparent in these projects would, at this point, lead too far. However, the promise to users to create the most accurate replica of objects possible and thereby to offer an authentic experience of the past shows another interesting aspect of the topic at hand. This promise is reminiscent of the marketing strategies employed for digital historical games. The debates about authenticity and the use of digital games in the didactics of history have long since arrived in historical game studies, and the theory formation around these terms can be fruitfully used for further analysis here.[46]

5 Virtual Reality Applications as Digital Games?

From my point of view, VR applications as described here can be understood as digital games in the broadest sense. With this, I build on the definition developed by Eugen Pfister and Tobias Winnerling: They are digital and—admittedly restricted—interactive programs on electronic systems, which can be operated via specific input devices. Following this train of thought, I would go one step further by applying Felix Zimmermann and Christian Hubert's reflections on ambience action games to VR applications:

---

[45] Andrew E. Kramer and Maria Varenikova, "Victim or Executioner? Let the Computer Decide," *The New York Times*, May 11, 2020, accessed August 30, 2020, https://www.nytimes.com/2020/05/11/world/europe/ukraine-holocaust-babyn-yar.html.
[46] It is of course also important to discuss the ethical limits of this technology. However, as there is not enough space for that in this article, I would like to refer to the already mentioned contributions by Wagner (footnote 14) and Eugen Pfister (footnote 56) and the project page Digital Holocaust Memory by Victoria Grace Walden.

When the ambience action game brings the player into a latent state of pause, it fills the emerging void with the action of the game world, the ambience act. For some players, this might seem like a humiliating idea, being less important than the world around them. But it mustn't be.[47]

Digital games, as Zimmermann pointedly states, can never be authentic in the sense of object authenticity because every object, no matter how detailed it is presented, always remains a simulation. Nevertheless, the term authenticity is used as a "marketing buzzword" which is employed to advertise that the games aim to provide a direct access to the past. The created world gains credibility for the players through the accurate representation of verified objects or facts. Zimmermann describes this as "atmosphere." For him, atmosphere is a medium that can produce certain feelings in certain contexts, such as authenticity. Atmospheres of the past are a specific manifestation of said medium that can satisfy a need for authenticity. According to Zimmermann, sounds are invaluable in this context because the players have certain expectations not only of the appearance of the past but also of its sound. The atmosphere in the gaming situation can only be perceived as a total impression (*Totaleindruck*) and only later be broken down into individual impressions.[48] Tobias Winnerling has introduced

---

[47] Felix Zimmermann and Christian Huberts, "From Walking Simulator to Ambience Action Game: A Philosophical Approach to a Misunderstood Genre," *Press Start* 5, no. 2 (2019), accessed September 20, 2020, https://press-start.gla.ac.uk/index.php/press-start/article/view/126.

[48] Felix Zimmermann, *"Historical Digital Games as Experiences: How Atmospheres of the Past Satisfy Needs of Authenticity,"* in *Game | World | Architectonics – Transdisciplinary Approaches on Structures and Mechanics, Levels and Spaces, Aesthetics and Perception*, ed. Marc Bonner (Heidelberg: Heidelberg University Publishing, 2020), 19–34. In game studies, there are other concepts besides the mentioned concepts for authenticity. To present them here would go beyond the scope of this article. For a quick glance, I recommend the doctoral theses of Manuel Alejandro Cruz Martínez, "The Potential of Video Games for Exploring Deconstructionist History" (PhD diss., University of Sussex, 2020), accessed September 10, 2020, http://sro.sussex.ac.uk/id/eprint/90194. Also to be mentioned, because they fit especially well into this context, are the considerations of Andrew J. Salvati and Jonathan M. Bullinger on selective authenticity. The selective authenticity creates a "narrative licence" (p. 154) that allows players to play interactively with the past in numerous variations. The impression of authenticity is thereby based on three categories: "technology fetishism" (which means a precise representation of objects), "cinematic conventions" (which in this context would mean orienting oneself on iconographic film models), and "documentary authority" (using documents and photographs which were, for example, used as advertisements for "Witness Auschwitz"). Andrew J. Salvati and Jonathan M. Bullinger, "Selective Authenticity and the Playable Past," in *Playing with the Past: Digital Games and the Simulation of History*, ed. M. Kappell and Andrew B. R. Elliott (London: Bloomsbury, 2013), 153–68. From my perspective, the concept of "atmosphere" fits particularly well with the immersive effect of VR.

the concept of "affective historicity" which he distinguishes from "factual history."[49] With reference to Kevin Schut, he describes history as not identical with the past as it only approaches the real past by assembling remnants into a picture that is consistent for us. Although it is necessarily interpretative in nature, it follows comprehensible procedures and arguments. In contrast, he defines "affective historicity" as the attempt to convey a "feeling of (representations of) the past."[50] In doing so, it tends to follow aesthetic and imaginative procedures. According to Winnerling, both types of history can refer to each other.[51]

6 "Dark Nostalgia" or "Prosthetic Witnessing"?

With regard to the presentation of the history of Nazi crimes in Virtual Reality, it becomes clear that projects that advertise an authentic experience are potentially more appealing because they tie in with a need described as "dark nostalgia" by Silke Arnold-de Simine.[52] Her term refers to an empathy-centered form of memory that enables an extreme experience that lies outside one's own horizon of experience.[53] From the perspective of memorial and history didactics, the problems of such offerings are numerous: Users run the risk of being emotionally overwhelmed by what is shown, in each user's case contextualization of the images can be problematic, and the depictions could unthinkingly be integrated into the user's own view of history.[54] In addition, what is experienced in VR is presumably limited to a certain point in time, because it is unlikely to have enough data to cover a longer period. Therefore, the dynamic developments that affected the Nazi regime and thus also the everyday life of camp inmates are outside the realm of user experience.

---

49 Tobias Winnerling, "The Eternal Recurrence of All Bits. How Historicizing Video Games' Series Transform Factual History into Affective Historicity," in *Eludamos: Journal for Computer Game Culture* 8 (2014): 151–170.
50 Winnerling, "Eternal Recurrence."
51 Winnerling, "Eternal Recurrence."
52 See Silke Arnold-de Simine, *Mediating Memory in the Museum* (Basingstoke: Palgrave Macmillian 2013); Richard Sharpley and Philipp R. Stone, *The Darker Side of Travel: The Theory and Practice of Dark Tourism* (Bristol: Channel View, 2009).
53 This thesis is supported on the one hand by the success of re-enactment projects such as "Gefrierfleischorden 1942" or "Die Endlösung der Zigeunerfrage. Ein fiktives internationales Symposion, Berlin 1941," and by the image of National Socialism shaped by mass media on the other hand, which leads to the fact that scenes of National Socialist crimes are highly charged.
54 To be clear, it would be insolent to believe that with the help of VR one could really understand what victims must have felt.

A discussion of Nazism-themed virtual game environments is outside the scope of this chapter. However, some observations from the corresponding literature are interesting and can be integrated here. Specifically, two main categories can be identified in this area: firstly, settings in which the Holocaust is somehow obfuscated;[55] secondly, games using the visual codes of paradigm shift movies like *Schindler's List*.[56] This last category can again be divided into sub-categories: alternative history settings like the *Wolfenstein* franchise,[57] AAA games like *Call of Duty: WWII*,[58] and serious games like *Through the Darkest of Times*,[59] which try to show new ways of engaging with the past. As Wulf Kansteiner states:

> [T]he Holocaust memory establishment cannot imagine how they could successfully transfer their didactic and political mission into simulative and interactive ludic digital environ-

---

55 For example, *Brothers in Arms: Hell's Highway* (Ubisoft Entertainment, 2008), *Company of Heroes: Opposing Fronts* (THQ, 2007), *Battle of the Bulge* (Shenandoah Studio, 2012), *Memoir '44* (Borg, 2004), *World War II Online: Battleground Europe* (Cornered Rat, 2009), see Adam Chapman and Jonas Linderoth, "Exploring the Limits of Play: A Case Study of Representations of Nazism in Games," in *The Dark Side of Game Play: Controversial Issues in Playful Environments*, ed. Torill Elvira Mortensen, Jonas Linderoth, and Ashley M. L. Brown (London: Routledge, 2015), 137–53.
56 Eugen Pfister, "Das Unspielbare spielen – Imaginationen des Holocaust in Digitalen Spielen," *Zeitgeschichte* 4 (2016): 250–63; Eugen Pfister, "'Of Monsters and Men' – Shoah in Digital Games," *Public History Weekly* 6, no. 23 (2018), accessed September 20, 2020, doi: 10.1515/phw-2018–12271.
57 Felix Zimmermann, "Wider die Selbstzensur – Das Dritte Reich, nationalsozialistische Verbrechen und der Holocaust im Digitalen Spiel," *gespielt | Blog des Arbeitskreises Geschichtswissenschaft und Digitale Spiele*, August 27, 2017, accessed October 12, 2020, https://gespielt.hypotheses.org/1449.
58 Pfister, "Das Unspielbare spielen"; Pfister, "Of Monsters and Men"; see also Tabea Widman, "Playing Memories? Digital Games as Memory Media," *Digital Holocaust Memory*, September 17, 2020, accessed September 20, 2020, https://digitalholocaustmemory.wordpress.com/2020/09/17/playing-memories-digital-games-as-memory-media/.
59 Bastian Dawitz, "Krieg bleibt immer gleich!? – Ein Plädoyer wider die Meistererzählung in Spielen zum 2. Weltkrieg," *gespielt | Blog des Arbeitskreises Geschichtswissenschaft und Digitale Spiele*, June 4, 2020, accessed October 12, 2020, https://gespielt.hypotheses.org/3701. See The current project "Pitch Jam: Memory Culture with Games" wants to explore possibilities of how and where interactive, digital media such as video and computer games can be used within the framework of the culture of remembrance. Pitch Jam: Memory Culture with Games, accessed October 12, 2020, https://www.stiftung-digitale-spielekultur.de/project/pitch-jam-memory-culture-with-games/.

ments and have therefore concluded that video games and their brand of genocide/human rights education are simply incompatible with each other.[60]

In accordance with Kantsteiner, I would argue that this field offers immense possibilities. For example, as Tabea Widmann argues with recourse to Alison Landsberg, "the act of playing ... becomes an act of [prosthetic] witnessing."[61] Just like in memorial sites, the player is enabled to "move around freely in the constructed space, looking at what she chooses to, experiencing the space in her own pace and order."[62]

7 Pierce the Atmosphere

I would argue that abstract or defamiliarized reconstructions of memorial sites are visually too unattractive to users to be able to compete with projects like "Auschwitz VR." In order not to yield the floor to ethically questionable commercial projects and offer an alternative with higher educational standards, memorial sites should make better use of the possibilities VR offers while still abiding by the Beutelsbach Consensus. For example, VR could be used to make "prosthetic witnessing" possible if the general conditions are appropriate. Similar to an exhibition in the analog world, written and visual sources could complement a virtual ensemble and even open it up in multiple perspectives. The simulation could be provided with an off-commentary by the curators to break through the created atmosphere. Following up on the "concept of tracing,"[63] this could also be transferred to VR through the possibility of visual superimposition, if sufficient material is available.[64] In VR applications of museums, this is for example used to make different degrees of restoration or underpainting in oil paintings visible. The main idea that

---

60 Wulf Kansteiner, "Transnational Holocaust Memory, Digital Culture," in *The Twentieth Century in European Memory and the End of Reception Studies*, ed. Tea Sindbæk Andersen and Barbara Törnquist-Plewa (Leiden: Brill, 2017), 305–43, accessed September 20, 2020, doi: https://doi.org/10.1163/9789004352353_014.
61 Widman, "Playing Memories?"; see also Jong, "Witness Auschwitz?"
62 Widman, "Playing Memories?"
63 [TAA, Konzept der Spurensuche].
64 Harold Marcuse points out that the deliberate destruction of testimonies should not only be seen as "traces of time" but also as manipulations by past communities. Harold Marcuse, "Thesen zur Neugestaltung des Kräutergartens," in Hammermann and Riedel, *Sanierung – Rekonstruktion – Neugestaltung*, 59. Also accessible online: University of California Santa Barbara, Department of History, accessed September 29, 2020, http://marcuse.faculty.history.ucsb.edu/publications/articles/59Marcuse2014NichtRekonstruierenSondernRezeptionsspuren.pdf.

I would like to convey from my brief discussion of game studies into the conversation about the use of VR in memorial sites regards the role of the users, their expectations and their ideas of authenticity, and their possible role in the digital culture of memory. The virtualization of memory has a fundamental impact on the culture of remembrance. Referring to Andrew Hoskins, digital memory culture is either more settled and regimented, neatly controlled by institutions, or more fluid and fragmented.[65] This statement can easily be illustrated with the abovementioned VR projects, but also with examples like the practice of taking selfies at historical sites of violent crimes[66] or the #pov challenge on TikTok,[67] in which a user "demonstrates something that is very valuable in these times of growing distance to the past events: interest, dedication, creativity, and the effort to integrate the memories from the past in present (social media) lives."[68] These examples also show how quickly the discussion about digital Holocaust education can be extended, for example by including the importance of geographical particularities or intergenerational conflicts in the shaping of memory culture.

8 From Gatekeepers to Facilitators

Faced with these challenges, memorials should transform into creative organizations and review their current working culture. In a digitization survey carried out by the Topography of Terror Documentation Center in Berlin, memorial sites self-critically recognized their limited knowledge with regard to providing digital presentations.[69] Especially for smaller institutions, the available technical

---

65 Andrew Hoskins, "The Right to Be Forgotten in Post-Scarcity," in *The Ethics of Memory in a Digital Age: Interrogating the Right to Be Forgotten*, ed. Alessia Ghezzi, Ângela Pereira, and Lucia Vesnic-Alujevic (New York: Palgrave Macmillian, 2014), 60. See also Andrew B. R. Elliott, "Simulations and Simulacra: History in Video Games," *Práticas da História* 5 (2017): 11–41.
66 Stefanie Samida, "Doing Selfies in Auschwitz?" *Public History Weekly* 7, no. 25 (2019), accessed September 23, 2020, doi: 10.1515/phw-2019–14095.
67 Carmelle Stephens, "The Holocaust on TikTok: The Importance of Context," *Virtual Memory – The Evolution of Holocaust Memory in the Digital Age*, accessed October 12, 2020, https://memoscape.net/the-holocaust-on-tiktok-the-importance-of-context/.
68 Tobias Ebbrecht Hartmann, Twitter Thread, August 30, 2020, accessed October 12, 2020, https://twitter.com/te_hartmann/status/1300187822972973058?s=20. See The whole thread is saved on: Thread reader: https://threadreaderapp.com/thread/1300187787304546309.html.
69 Sven Hilbrandt, "Wahrnehmbarkeit, Fortbildung, Vernetzung," *Gedenkstättenrundbrief* 199 (2020): 22–31, accessed September 20, 2020, https://www.gedenkstaettenforum.de/nc/gedenkstaettenrundbrief/rundbrief/news/wahrnehmbarkeit_fortbildung_vernetzung/. The raw data of the study are apparently not available.

equipment is inadequate, devices are outdated, and a wireless network is rarely available. The memorial sites run by volunteers often do not even have databases. A report by Sven Hilbrandt based on a survey by the Topography of Terror mentions the platform www.gedenkstätte-digital.de, which is to be created and which is planned to contain a database that can be used by memorial sites—this creation and its usage opportunities would follow the model of www.museum-digital.de. However, the objects collected on museum-digital are merely presented on the website. Their data are not interoperable or reusable. Ideally, memorial sites (but also museums) should take on the role of facilitators, not that of gatekeepers. Their own data should be provided with metadata and stored in an open format in a publicly accessible repository so that they can be used by everybody.[70] A good example of a successful change of role from gatekeepers to facilitators is the Coding da Vinci Hackathons, in which the Dachau Memorial and the Arolsen Archive have already participated as data providers.[71] The latter's project, "Every Name Counts,"[72] which started during the Covid-19 pandemic, has engaged thousands of volunteers for indexing names, birth dates, and captive's numbers in the online database and makes it possible to "take part in active remembrance without leaving the house."[73]

By opening up the data, users could also be invited to participate as active partners in VR projects and help shape them. Such an attitude would mean a shift towards a participatory memorial—that is, the visitor's role would change from recipient to prosumer. But this requires a digitization strategy to address not only technical aspects, such as the digitization of objects and the standardization and provision of data, but also digitization as a cultural change. Digital literacy skills should ideally neither be outsourced, nor centered only on a single person or a small group of people. Rather, the aim should be to involve all employees through further training opportunities. The digital should not be seen as a technological innovation, but as a cultural change that affects the entire practice of the memorial site. At the organizational level, such an approach would be

---

[70] I am aware of the fact that such implementation is difficult given that for these tasks often only small financial resources are available to memorial sites.
[71] Barbara Fischer, "Coding da Vinci," in *Der digitale Kulturbetrieb*, ed. Lorenz Pöllmann and Clara Herrmann (Wiesbaden: Springer Gabler, 2019), accessed September 20, 2020, doi: 10.1007/978-3-658-24030-1_19.
[72] Andrew Curry, "How Crowdsourcing Aided a Push to Preserve the Histories of Nazi Victims," *The New York Times*, June 3, 2020, accessed September 15, 2020, https://www.nytimes.com/2020/06/03/world/europe/nazis-arolsen-archive.html.
[73] "Help Us Build a Unique Digital Monument," Arolsen Archives, accessed September 20, 2020, https://arolsen-archives.org/en/learn-participate/interactive-archive/everynamecounts/.

more sensible since innovations do not have to be implemented with great effort by (single) individuals and with dubious success. The dissolution of traditional practices would create the possibility of an open dialogue which could be conducted both in own offerings—for example, websites, blogs, streams—and on external social media platforms. It would be important that the memorial site understands the internet less as a marketing instrument for tapping into new groups of visitors but rather uses it primarily to initiate dialogic processes. A memorial acting in such manner could thus take on a leading role in a digital public sphere that positions itself against historical revisionism[74] and historical hate speech. With its expert knowledge and resources, it would create a global social meeting space that could serve as a forum for exchange at eye level, forming a co-creational memory of the Holocaust. In such a collaborative and networked environment, users would be encouraged to share their knowledge and enter into discourse with one another.

Bibliography

Arnold-de Simine, Silke. *Mediating Memory in the Museum*. Basingstoke: Palgrave Macmillian, 2013.
Arolsen Archives. "Raus aus dem Elfenbeinturm." Accessed October 13, 2020. https://arolsen-archives.org/lernen-mitwirken/lernen-mit-dokumenten/gedenkstaettenseminar/.
Azuma, Ronald T. "A Survey of Augmented Reality." *Presence: Teleoperators and Virtual Environments* 6, no. 4 (1997): 355–85. Accessed September 10, 2020. doi: 10.1162/pres.1997.6.4.355.
Brandes, Wolfgang. *Tagungsbericht: Neue Ansätze zur Präsentation regionaler NS-Geschichte in Museen, Dokumentations- und Gedenkstätten* (Hannover: 2012). Accessed September 20, 2020. http://hsozkult.geschichte.hu-berlin.de/tagungsberichte/id=4410.
Bunnenberg, Christian. "Mittendrin im historischen Geschehen? Immersive digitale Medien (Augmented Reality, Virtual Reality, 360°-Film) in der Geschichtskultur und Perspektiven für den Geschichtsunterricht." *geschichte für heute* 4 (2020): 45–58.
Bunnenberg, Christian. "Virtual Time Travels? Public History and Virtual Reality." *Public History Weekly* 6, no. 3 (2018). Accessed September 15, 2020. doi: 10.1515/phw-2018–10896.
Chapman, Adam, and Jonas Linderoth. "Exploring the Limits of Play: A Case Study of Representations of Nazism in Games." In *The Dark Side of Game Play: Controversial Issues in Playful Environments*, edited by Torill Elvira Mortensen, Jonas Linderoth, and Ashley M. L. Brown, 137–53. London: Routledge, 2015.

---

[74] A good example of such an intervention was, for example, a reaction of the Arolsen Archive on Twitter to an article published on *Spiegel Online* about the DER Touristik Association. Arolsen Archives, December 11, 2019, accessed September 20, 2020, https://twitter.com/ArolsenArchives/status/1204697832952713217?s=20.

Cruz Martínez, Manuel Alejandro. "The Potential of Video Games for Exploring Deconstructionist History." PhD diss., University of Sussex, 2020. Accessed September 10, 2020. http://sro.sussex.ac.uk/id/eprint/90194.

Curry, Andrew. "How Crowdsourcing Aided a Push to Preserve the Histories of Nazi Victims." *The New York Times*, June 3, 2020. Accessed September 15, 2020. https://www.nytimes.com/2020/06/03/world/europe/nazis-arolsen-archive.html.

Däuble, Helmut. "Der fruchtbare Dissens um den Beutelsbacher Konsens." *GWP* 4 (2016): 449–58. Accessed September 15, 2020. doi: 10.3224/gwp.v65i4.05.

Dawitz, Bastian. "Krieg bleibt immer gleich!? – Ein Plädoyer wider die Meistererzählung in Spielen zum 2. Weltkrieg." *gespielt | Blog des Arbeitskreises Geschichtswissenschaft und Digitale Spiele*, June 4, 2020. Accessed October 12, 2020. https://gespielt.hypotheses.org/3701.

Drecoll, Axel, Thomas Schaarschmidt, and Irmgard Zündorf. *Authentizität als Kapital historischer Orte? Die Sehnsucht nach dem unmittelbaren Erleben von Geschichte*. Göttingen: Wallstein Verlag, 2019.

Elliott, Andrew B. R. "Simulations and Simulacra: History in Video Games." *Práticas da História* 5 (2017): 11–41.

Fischer, Barbara. "Coding da Vinci." In *Der digitale Kulturbetrieb*, edited by Lorenz Pöllmann and Clara Herrmann, 415–30. Wiesbaden: Springer Gabler, 2019.

Grace Walden, Victoria. Digital Holocaust Memory, Accessed June 15, 2021. https://reframe.sussex.ac.uk/digitalholocaustmemory/.

Hammermann, Gabriele, and Dirk Riedel, eds. *Sanierung – Rekonstruktion – Neugestaltung. Zum Umgang mit historischen Bauten in Gedenkstätten*. Göttingen: Wallstein Verlag, 2014.

Hartmann, Tobias Ebbrecht. Twitter. August 30, 2020. Accessed October 12, 2020. https://twitter.com/te_hartmann/status/1300187822972973058?s=20.

Hilbrandt, Sven. "Wahrnehmbarkeit, Fortbildung, Vernetzung." *Gedenkstättenrundbrief* 199 (2020): 22–31. Accessed September 20, 2020. https://www.gedenkstaettenforum.de/nc/gedenkstaettenrundbrief/rundbrief/news/wahrnehmbarkeit_fortbildung_vernetzung/.

Hoffmann, Detlef. *Das Gedächtnis der Dinge: KZ-Relikte und KZ-Denkmäler 1945–1995*. Frankfurt am Main: Campus Verlag, 1998.

Horowitz Murray, Janet. *Hamlet on the Holodeck: The Future of Narrative in Cyberspace*. Cambridge, MA: MIT Press, 1998.

Hoskins, Andrew. "The Right to Be Forgotten in Post-Scarcity." In *The Ethics of Memory in a Digital Age: Interrogating the Right to Be Forgotten*, edited by Alessia Ghezzi, Ângela Pereira, and Lucia Vesnic-Alujevic, 50–64. New York: Palgrave Macmillian, 2014.

Huber, Simon. "Zur Geschichte der Cutscenes: Versuch einer Medienarchäologie kommerzieller Videospiele." In *Frühe Neuzeit im Videospiel*, ed. Florian Kerschbaumer and Tobias Winnerling, 71–86. Bielefeld: transcript Verlag, 2014.

Jong, Steffi de. "Von Hologrammen und sprechenden Füchsen – Holocausterinnerung 3.0." *Tagung #erinnern_kontrovers*. Accessed September 15, 2020. https://erinnern.hypotheses.org/465.

Jong, Steffi de. "Witness Auschwitz? How VR Is Changing Testimony." *Public History Weekly* 8, no. 4 (2020). Accessed September 1, 2020. doi: 10.1515/phw-2020-15689.

Kansteiner, Wulf. "Transnational Holocaust Memory, Digital Culture." In *The Twentieth Century in European Memory and the End of Reception Studies*, edited by Tea Sindbæk Andersen

and Barbara Törnquist-Plewa, 305–43. Leiden: Brill, 2017. Accessed September 20, 2020. doi: 10.1163/9789004352353_014.
Kirshenblatt-Gimblett, Barbara. *Destination Culture: Tourism, Museums, and Heritage*. Berkeley: University of California Press, 1998.
Klei, Alexandra. *Der erinnerte Ort*. Berlin: De Gruyter, 2011.
Knoch, Habbo. "'Ferienlager' und 'gefoltertes Leben': Periphere Räume in ehemaligen Konzentrationslagern." In *Sanierung – Rekonstruktion – Neugestaltung: Zum Umgang mit historischen Bauten in Gedenkstätten*, edited by Gabriele Hammermann and Dirk Riedel, 32–50. Göttingen: Wallstein Verlag, 2014.
Knoch, Habbo. "Gedenkstätten." *Docupedia-Zeitgeschichte*, September 11, 2018. Accessed September 15, 2020. doi: 10.14765/zzf.dok.2.1221.v1.
Korff, Gottfried. "Die Eigenart der Museums-Dinge: Zur Materialität und Medialität des Museums." In *Handbuch der museumspädagogischen Ansätze*, edited by Kirsten Fast, 17–28. Wiesbaden: VS Verlag für Sozialwissenschaften, 1995.
Kramer, Andrew E. and Maria Varenikova. "Victim or Executioner? Let the Computer Decide." *The New York Times*, May 11, 2020. Accessed August 30, 2020. https://www.nytimes.com/2020/05/11/world/europe/ukraine-holocaust-babyn-yar.html.
Lethen, Helmut. "Versionen des Authentischen: Sechs Gemeinplätze." In *Literatur und Kulturwissenschaften. Positionen, Theorien, Modelle*, edited by Hartmut Böhme and Klaus R. Scherpe, 205–32. Reinbek bei Hamburg: Rowohlt-Taschenbuch-Verlag, 1996.
Lutz, Thomas. "Materialisierte Authentifizierung: Die Bedeutung authentischer Gebäude und Objekte in Gedenkstätten und Dokumentationszentren der NS-Verbrechen." In *Authentizität als Kapital historischer Orte? Die Sehnsucht nach dem unmittelbaren Erleben von Geschichte*, edited by Axel Drecoll, Thomas Schaarschmidt, and Irmgard Zündorf, 57–77. Göttingen: Wallstein Verlag, 2019.
Marcuse, Harold. "Thesen zur Neugestaltung des Kräutergartens." In *Sanierung – Rekonstruktion– Neugestaltung. Zum Umgang mit historischen Bauten in Gedenkstätten*, edited by Gabriele Hammermann and Dirk Riedel, 50–64. Göttingen: Wallstein Verlag, 2014.
Milgram, Paul, Haruo Takemura, Akira Utsumi, and Fumio Kishino. "Augmented Reality: A Class of Displays on the Reality-Virtuality Continuum." In *Proceedings of SPIE – The International Society for Optical Engineering* 2351 (January 1994). Accessed September 10, 2020. doi: 10.1117/12.197321.
Mussmann, Olaf. "Die Gestaltung von Gedenkstätten im historischen Wandel." In *Museale und mediale Präsentationen in KZ-Gedenkstätten*, Beiträge zur Geschichte der nationalsozialistischen Verfolgung in Norddeutschland 6, edited by Herbert Diercks, 14–33. Bremen: Ed. Temmen, 2001.
Pfister, Eugen. "Das Unspielbare spielen – Imaginationen des Holocaust in Digitalen Spielen." *Zeitgeschichte* 4 (2016): 250–65.
Pfister, Eugen. "'Of Monsters and Men' – Shoah in Digital Games." *Public History Weekly* 6, no. 23 (2018). Accessed September 20, 2020. doi: 10.1515/phw-2018–12271.
Röttjer, Julia. "Authentizität Im UNESCO-Welterbe-Diskurs. Das Konzentrations- und Vernichtungslager Auschwitz-Birkenau." In *Authentizität als Kapital historischer Orte? Die Sehnsucht nach dem unmittelbaren Erleben von Geschichte*, edited by Axel Drecoll, Thomas Schaarschmidt, and Irmgard Zündorf, 35–57. Göttingen: Wallstein Verlag, 2019.
Rosa, Hartmut. *Resonanz – Eine Soziologie der Weltbeziehung*. Berlin, Suhrkamp, 2016.

Salvati, Andrew J., and Jonathan M. Bullinger. "Selective Authenticity and the Playable Past." In *Playing with the Past: Digital Games and the Simulation of History*, edited by M. Kappell and Andrew B. R. Elliott, 153–67. London: Bloomsbury, 2013.

Samida, Stefanie. "Doing Selfies in Auschwitz?" *Public History Weekly* 7, no. 25 (2019). Accessed September 23, 2020. doi: 10.1515/phw-2019-14095.

Saupe, Achim. "Authenticity." *Docupedia-Zeitgeschichte*, April 12, 2016. Accessed September 1, 2020. doi: 10.14765/zzf.dok.2.645.v1.

Sharpley, Richard, and Philipp R. Stone. *The Darker Side of Travel: The Theory and Practice of Dark Tourism*. Bristol: Channel View, 2009.

Stalder, Felix. *Kultur der Digitalität*. Berlin: Suhrkamp, 2016.

Stephens, Carmelle. "The Holocaust on TikTok: The Importance of Context." *Virtual Memory – The Evolution of Holocaust Memory in the Digital Age*. Accessed October 12, 2020. https://memoscape.net/the-holocaust-on-tiktok-the-importance-of-context/.

Wagner, Jens-Chirstian. "Lernen mit Sachquellen in Museen und Gedenkstätten. Fragen und Antworten einer interdisziplinären Tagung." *Lernen aus Geschichte*, January 31, 2018. Accessed September 15, 2020. http://lernen-aus-der-geschichte.de/Lernen-und-Lehren/content/13865.

Wagner, Jens-Christian. "Simulierte Authentizität? Chancen und Risiken von Augmented und Virtual Reality an Gedenkstätten." *Gedenkstättenrundbrief* 196. Accessed August 15, 2020. https://www.gedenkstaettenforum.de/nc/gedenkstaettenrundbrief/rundbrief/news/simulierte_authentizitaet_chancen_und_risiken_von_augmented_und_virtual_reality_an_gedenkstaetten.

Widman, Tabea. "Playing Memories? Digital Games as Memory Media." *Digital Holocaust Memory*, September 17, 2020. Accessed September 20, 2020. https://digitalholocaustmemory.wordpress.com/2020/09/17/playing-memories-digital-games-as-memory-media/.

Winnerling, Tobias. "The Eternal Recurrence of All Bits: How Historicizing Video Games' Series Transform Factual History into Affective Historicity." In *Eludamos: Journal for Computer Game Culture* 8 (2014): 151–70.

Zimmermann, Felix. "Historical Digital Games as Experiences: How Atmospheres of the Past Satisfy Needs of Authenticity." In *Game | World | Architectonics – Transdisciplinary Approaches on Structures and Mechanics, Levels and Spaces, Aesthetics and Perception*, edited by Marc Bonner, 19–34. Heidelberg: Heidelberg University Publishing, 2020.

Zimmermann, Felix. "Wider die Selbstzensur – Das Dritte Reich, nationalsozialistische Verbrechen und der Holocaust im Digitalen Spiel." *gespielt | Blog des Arbeitskreises Geschichtswissenschaft und Digitale Spiele*, August 27, 2017. Accessed October 12, 2020. https://gespielt.hypotheses.org/1449.

Zimmermann, Felix, and Christian Huberts. "From Walking Simulator to Ambience Action Game: A Philosophical Approach to a Misunderstood Genre." *Press Start* 5, no. 2 (2019). Accessed September 20, 2020. https://press-start.gla.ac.uk/index.php/press-start/article/view/126.

Further Readings on Writing the Digital History of Nazi Germany and Topics in This Book: A Selection of Academic Scholarship and Online Resources

1 Academic Scholarship

Arguing with Digital History Working Group. "Digital History and Argument." White paper, Roy Rosenzweig Center for History and New Media. November 12, 2017. Accessed October 24, 2020. https://rrchnm.org/argument-white-paper.

This white paper emerged from a 2017 workshop convened to promote digital history. The paper's expressed goal is "to help bridge the argumentative practices of digital history and the broader historical profession," by showing how digital historians contribute arguments in new forms while also discussing how they can better integrate their scholarship into broader larger historiographical discourses. The paper also considers the implications of the growth of digital history for analog history and the ethical questions it raises. It covers five topics, namely digital collections, digital public history, visualization, computational digital history, and methodological questions, and for each topic includes a discussion of practical examples, mostly online projects.

Bondzio, Sebastian, and Christoph Rass. "Data Driven History: Methodische Überlegungen zur Osnabrücker Gestapo-Kartei als Quelle zur Erforschung datenbasierter Herrschaft." *Archiv Nachrichten Niedersachsen* 22 (2018): 124–38.

This article asks the question how we can efficiently include large card files and other sets of serial sources into historical research. Bondzio and Rass describe the process used to digitize the entire Osnabrück Gestapo card file and, in so doing, present a cost- and time-effective workflow that could open up large sources for historical research. Bondzio and Ross discuss research questions that only become possible when such a digital replica of a card file is created, pointing out the new research options such digitization gains for historians.

Note: The editors would like to thank the contributors to this book for recommending titles that further develop topics explored in the different chapters, and Elias Bosch for his support locating online resources on Nazi Germany.

OpenAccess. © 2022, published by De Gruyter. This work is licensed under the Creative Commons Attribution 4.0 International License. https://doi.org/10.1515/9783110714692-012

Bondzio, Sebastian, and Christoph Rass. "Allmächtig, allwissend, allgegenwärtig: Die Osnabrücker Gestapo Kartei als Massendatenspeicher und Weltmodell." *Osnabrücker Mitteilungen* 124 (2019): 223–60.

The image of the Gestapo during the Nazi period was of an omnipotent, omniscient, and omnipresent police force, an image that was reproduced in postwar Germany for more than 50 years. Historians put in a significant research effort to dispel this image by the end of the twentieth century. In this paper, Bondzio and Rass investigate how this image of an all-powerful Gestapo came into being. They analyze the Gestapo's legal resources, actions, and presence to show why the Gestapo appeared to society in the way it did, and they highlight how the image of the Gestapo was a collective perception with deep psychological roots rather than corresponding at all closely to fact.

Busse, Dietrich and Wolfgang Teubert, "Using Corpora for Historical Semantics." In *The Discourse Studies Reader: Main Currents in Theory and Analysis*, edited by Johannes Angermuller, Dominique Maingueneau, and Ruth Wodak, 340–49. Amsterdam: Benjamins, 2014.

Twenty years after their seminal article "Ist Sprache ein diskurswissenschaftliches Objekt?," which paved the way for German linguistic discourse analysis (*Linguistische Diskursanalyse*), Busse and Teubert provide an update of their "language-oriented history of words and concepts that works with genuine linguistic methods" (p. 340).

Digital Holocaust Memory Project. https://reframe.sussex.ac.uk/digitalholocaustmemory/.

The *Digital Holocaust Memory Project* is led by Victoria Grace Walden from the University of Sussex and focuses on the application of digital methods and technologies by institutions dedicated to research about and remembrance of the Holocaust. It includes a blog which reflects on current developments like TikTok challenges, gamification of Holocaust memory, and online archives, among others.

Gänßbauer, Monika. "Digital Humanities in the German-Speaking World." In *Digital Humanities and New Ways of Teaching: Digital Culture and Humanities*, edited by Anna Wing-bo Tso. Singapore: Springer, 2019. Accessed August 10, 2021. doi: 10.1007/978-981-13-1277-9_1.

The article provides a useful historiographical review of projects in and debates about digital humanities in the German-speaking world over the last few decades.

Graham, Shawn, Ian Milligan, and Scott Weingart. *Exploring Big Historical Data: The Historian's Macroscope*. London: Imperial College Press, 2016.

The book is an introduction for historians on how to work with Big Data. It provides an overview of an emerging field, discussions, and hands-on examples of specific tools for textual analysis and introduction to network analysis.

Horan, Geraldine. "'Er zog sich die "neue Sprache" des "Dritten Reiches" über wie ein Kleidungsstück': Communities of Practice and Performativity in National Socialist Discourse." *Linguistik Online* 30, no. 1 (2007): 57–80. Accessed June 13, 2020. doi: https://doi.org/10.13092/lo.30.549.

Horan is another historian who uses the tools of digital discourse analysis to investigate, in this article, the extent to which social conditions under National Socialism were formed and established in various communities of practice through their discursive co-constitutions. In doing so, she highlights the interplay of sometimes completely divergent discursive practices that unfolded in Nazi Germany.

Kansteiner, Wulf. "Transnational Holocaust Memory, Digital Culture and the End of Reception Studies." In *The Twentieth Century in European Memory: Transcultural Mediation and Reception*, edited by Tea Sindbaek Andersen and Barbara Tornquist-Plewa, 305–43. Leiden: Brill, 2017.

This article emphasizes the importance of digital technology for future Holocaust memory. Kansteiner gives examples of both successful and failed digital Holocaust memory, and he considers the role of those working in the field of Holocaust memory in its transitioning into digital forms. Overall, the article urges—sometimes provocatively—much more reflection on the possibilities of digital Holocaust memory, especially concerning simulative and immersive technology.

Knoch, Habbo. "Das KZ als virtuelle Wirklichkeit: Digitale Raumbilder des Holocaust und die Grenzen ihrer Wahrheit." *Geschichte und Gesellschaft* 47 (2021): 90–121.

Starting from a Baudrillardian framework (imitation, production, simulation), Knoch examines the usage of digital tools by memorial sites at former concentration camps from a theoretical perspective. Of particular concern to Knoch are issues around immersion and authenticity when representing (or re-creating) spaces digitally. He worries that often digital media "remediate" without resolving issues that already existed in earlier presentations of history. This article, focusing on the context of Nazi Germany, is part of a special issue of *Geschichte und Gesellschaft* on digital history more generally.

Knowles, Anne Kelly, Tim Cole, and Alberto Giordano. *Geographies of the Holocaust.* Bloomington: Indiana University Press, 2014.

This book is an impressive exploration of the possibilities of combining historical, geographical, and digital methods. The researchers look at different aspects of spatial Holocaust history, which enables them to shed new light on various topics, such as the movement of Jews in the Budapest Ghetto or the construction process of Auschwitz and its ramifications for the concentration camp's inmates. The individual chapters are each complemented by a detailed methods section, while an accompanying website presents the book's research results in interactive forms (https://web.stanford.edu/group/spatialhistory/cgi-bin/site/project.php?id=1015).

McCullough, Kelly, and James Retallack. "Digital History Anthologies on the Web: German History in Documents and Images." *Central European History* 46, no. 2 (2013): 346–61.

The article discusses the origins and development of the website German History in Documents and Images, a project begun by the German Historical Institute in 2002. The article looks in detail at the project's goals, editorial decisions, and its audience, to offer a useful case study from which reflective insights into digital source editions emerge.

Menny, Anna, Miriam Rürup, and Björn Siegel, "Jüdische Geschichte im deutschsprachigen Raum." In *Clio-Guide. Ein Handbuch zu digitalen Ressourcen für die Geschichtswissenschaften*, edited by Laura Busse, Wilfried Enderle, Rüdiger Hohls, Thomas Meyer, Jens Prellwitz, and Annette Schuhmann, S. E.2 – 1 – E.2 – 56. Berlin: Clio-Online and Humboldt University Berlin, 2018.

This article provides a comprehensive overview of the various digital resources regarding Jewish history in the German-speaking region. The resources listed range from archives, museums, and reference works to study programs and online portals.

Nägel, Verena Lucia, and Sanna Stegmeier. "Lernen auf Entfernung: Digitale Angebote über Nationalsozialismus und Holocaust." *Bundeszentrale für politische Bildung (bpb)*, May 12, 2020. Accessed October 20, 2020. https://www.bpb.de/lernen/digitale-bildung/werkstatt/309719/lernen-auf-entfernung-digitale-angebote-ueber-nationalsozialismus-und-holocaust.

This article presents some of the online possibilities that can be utilized for teaching the history of Nazi Germany and the Holocaust (in German-speaking schools), especially in light of Covid-19 restrictions which, at the time the article was written and published, were making excursions to memorial sites and exchanges with witnesses difficult if not impossible.

Rass, Christoph, and Sebastian Bondzio. "Next Stop Big Data? Erfahrungen mit der Digitalisierung von Geschichte und Geschichtswissenschaft." In *Vergangenheit analysieren – Zukunft gestalten*, edited by Paul Thomes and Tobias Drewes, 15 – 50. Aachener Studien zur Wirtschafts-, Sozial-, und Technologiegeschichte 20. Düren: Shaker Verlag, 2020.

Rass and Bondzio reflect in this paper on their experiences with a historiography that is changing more and more due to digitization. Both authors consider themselves digital historians and work at the forefront of digital change. Yet their self-image as digital pathbreakers does not exclude the need to critically question their own work. In doing so, they develop a vision for the future of their academic discipline in which new sources will bring radical new perspectives but traditional practices will remain valid, so that fundamental discussions between the old and the new ways will arise, and established structures will soften up.

Sahle, Patrick. *Digitale Editionsformen. Zum Umgang mit der Überlieferung unter den Bedingungen des Medienwandels.* 3 volumes. Norderstedt: Books on Demand, 2013.

Patrick Sahle's three volumes provide a very useful and comprehensive overview of the development and publication of source editions as the state-of-the-art moves into digital form, including theoretical and methodological analysis of both traditional and digital practices when creating a source edition, complemented by overviews of terminology, processes, etc.

Schmale, Wolfgang. *Digitale Geschichtswissenschaft.* Vienna: Böhlau Verlag, 2010.

Schmale's short book provides a usefully concise introduction to "digital history" and its frameworks, possibilities, and challenges, especially in the German context. More recently, he has also edited a helpful volume of papers about digital humanities, including chapters with a focus on history: *Digital Humanities: Praktiken der Digitalisierung, der Dissemination und der Selbstreflexivität* (Historische Mitteilungen – Beihefte). Stuttgart: Frank Steiner Verlag, 2015.

Scholl, Stefan. "Für eine Sprach- und Kommunikationsgeschichte des Nationalsozialismus. Ein programmatischer Forschungsüberblick." *Archiv für Sozialgeschichte* 59 (2019): 409–44.

In his bibliographical review, Scholl gives an overview of older approaches and the more recent historiography of language use under National Socialism. He examines the extent to which language was a constitutive element of National Socialism. The article advocates a language-oriented historical analysis.

2 (Academic) Training Platforms for Digital Historians

Ranke.2 – Source criticism in the digital age: https://ranke2.uni.lu/.

This platform, maintained by the Luxembourg Centre for Contemporary and Digital History at the University of Luxembourg is a teaching platform targeting both students and professional historians. It offers information and tutorials about digital sources and digital source criticism. The website is available in English, French, and German versions. It also offers teaching aids, downloadable as pdfs.

The Programming Historian: https://programminghistorian.org/.

This collaborative, open-source website offers a range of tutorials that show historians how to apply different methods for both digital historical research and teaching. The predominant focus is on which software tools and packages are available, and how to use them, especially in the general area of data analysis, but tutorials are also available for programming (e.g., Python) and other digital skills. The tutorials are all peer-reviewed and regularly updated. The platform offers its widest range of tutorials in English but also includes content in French and Spanish.

3 Databases and Bibliographies

The Aufbau Indexing Project, by Alex Calzareth and Harry Katzman: http://www.calzareth.com/aufbau/.

The goal of the Aufbau Indexing Project is to index all the announcements of birth, engagement, marriage, death, and other special occasions that appeared in the pages of the *Aufbau* magazine for German-Jewish exiles and emigrants for the period of its New York publication, from 1934 to 2004. One of the goals of this project is to allow individuals researching their German-Jewish ancestry to discover relevant family information as represented in the pages of *Aufbau*.

Austrian Victims of the Holocaust, by the Documentation Center of Austrian Resistance (DÖW): https://www.doew.at/english/austrian-victims-of-the-holocaust.

The database includes more than 63,000 names of Austrian victims of Nazi persecution from 1938 to 1945. A search for victims by both first and last name is possible. People whose data was recorded by the Viennese Gestapo are also included in the database.

Bibliography of Key Documents of German-Jewish History, by the Institut für die Geschichte der deutschen Juden (IGdJ): https://jewish-history-online.net/bibliography.

The bibliography of the online source edition Key Documents of German-Jewish History lists research literature on all topics addressed in the edition. It is also a valuable resource for identifying scholarly literature that explicitly focuses on the digital conveyance of Jewish history in Germany.

Die Dabeigewesenen in Hamburg, by the Landszentrale für Politische Bildung Hamburg: https://www.hamburg.de/ns-dabeigewesene.

This database provides short profiles of individuals who in some way participated in Nazi crimes in Hamburg. The database can be searched by name and by address. An accompanying app—"NS-Dabeigewesenen Hamburg"—locates the names on a map or informs users of entries in the database linked to locations in their vicinity. The database went online in 2016 and is still growing; as of May 2020, 819 short profiles were available.

The Database of Jewish Businesses in Berlin 1930–1945, by Humboldt University Berlin: https://www2.hu-berlin.de/djgb/www/about?language=en_US.

This is an abridged version of a database containing information about more than 8,000 Jewish businesses in Berlin between 1930 and 1945 that were the targets of Nazi persecution.

Datenbank: Games and Erinnerungskultur, by the Stiftung Digitale Spielkultur: https://www.stiftung-digitale-spielekultur.de/games-erinnerungskultur/.

The Foundation for Digital Games Culture, established by the German games industry, runs this database in collaboration with historians from the Arbeitskreis Geschichtswissenschaft und Digitale Spiele (AKGWDS). It compiles computer games which take place in specific historical contexts, focusing on those which relate to German history, and especially to the periods of colonialism, the world wars, Nazi Germany and the Holocaust, as well as the periods of post-WWII-history and Germany's division. The database is primarily meant to provide guidance for museums and memorial sites, schools, universities, etc., when considering the use of games in educational contexts.

Digibaeck, by Leo Baeck Institute: https://www.lbi.org/collections/digibaeck/.

DigiBaeck enables users to search the digital collections of the Leo Baeck Institute. These collections include memoirs and manuscripts, works of art, books and periodicals, photographs, audio recordings, and archival material on German-Jewish history.

digital // memory, by the Stiftung "Erinnerung, Verantwortung und Zukunft": https://www.stiftung-evz.de/eng/funding/critical-examination-of-history/digital-memory.html.

This is the website for "digital // memory," the funding program of the Foundation "Remembrance, Responsibility and Future" which supports projects that "develop and test digital formats for historical-civic education." It provides descriptions of and links to the projects that have been funded, with foci including

AR and learning apps as well as serious games concerned with aspects of the history of Nazi Germany.

#everynamecounts, by the Arolsen Archives: International Center on Nazi Persecution: https://enc.arolsen-archives.org/en/.

The crowdsourcing project #everynamecounts aims to create the largest digital memorial and to encourage the active commemoration of the victims of Nazi persecution. The project is based on working digitally with original documents of the Arolsen Archives. Participants are asked to transfer names and other biographical information about victims' lives and persecution to the online archive, where they will remain permanently and can be researched. Since the launch of the project in January 2020, Every Name Counts has already gathered over 9,000 followers and recorded 1.5 million documents that are now available to the public.

Frank Falla Archive: https://www.frankfallaarchive.org.

This website provides a searchable online database on Channel Islanders who were deported to Nazi prison and concentration camps. Also provided are digital maps describing the location of these prisons and camps, and in some cases, background information about them.

Jewish Gen's Holocaust Databases, by the Museum of Jewish Heritage: https://www.jewishgen.org/databases/Holocaust.

This is an access point to a collection of databases containing information about victims and survivors of the Holocaust. More than 190 datasets can be simultaneously searched, affording access to more than 2.75 million entries.

Lost Art Database, by the German Lost Art Foundation: http://www.lostart.de/Webs/EN/Datenbank/Index.html.

The Lost Art Database provides access to data on artwork and cultural objects which were removed or relocated—either during the Nazi period or in its direct aftermath and as a consequence of World War II.

Memorial Archives, by the Concentration Camp Memorial Flossenbürg: https://memorial-archives.international.

The website includes a searchable database on victims of the concentration camp Flossenbürg. Also available are historical images of Flossenbürg, videos of survivors, and an extensive database of publications related to the history of the camp.

Memorial Book for the Victims of National Socialism at the University of Vienna in 1938, by the University of Vienna: https://gedenkbuch.univie.ac.at/index.php?id=435&no_cache=1&L=2.

A searchable database of students, staff, and faculty members of the University of Vienna who were victims of Nazi persecution after the annexation of Austria in 1938.

The Nazi Concentration Camps, by Birkbeck College, University of London: http://www.camps.bbk.ac.uk/overview.html.

This website, developed and authored by Nikolaus Wachsmann, provides an extensive collection of information about Nazi concentration camps, including introductory texts, interactive maps, timelines, teaching resources, short (historical) documentaries, and video testimonies, as well as testimonies in written and audio recorded form. The website offers a collection of historical documents, in English translation, relating to various aspects of the history of Nazi concentration camps.

4 Digital Mappings / GPS-Based Guided Tours

Danish Jews in Theresienstadt, by the University of Southern Denmark: https://www.danskejoederitheresienstadt.org/.

This project digitally maps the places mentioned in testimonies by Danish Jews who were deported to the Theresienstadt Ghetto between 1943 and 1945. This mapping, which involved fieldwork in Terezin in combination with digital methods, was carried out by graduate students as part of the project "Danish Jews in Theresienstadt: Topography and Memory" under the supervision of Therkel Straede, University of Southern Denmark, Odense.

Digitale Erinnerungslandschaft, by the Centrum für Jüdische Studien, Karl Franzens University Graz: http://www.zukunftsfonds-austria.at/projektinfo.php?pcode=P19-3462.

This is a project to create a digital and georeferenced map that will make memorials of Nazi persecution visible and accessible. The map, which is currently being developed, will provide background information on the memorials and is intended especially for use in schools.

Mapping the Lives, by Tracing the Past: https://www.mappingthelives.org/.

Tracing the Past is a Berlin-based non-profit organization which maintains this website presenting interactive, scalable maps with the addresses of those persecuted by the Nazi regime in Europe between 1933 and 1945.

Memory Loops, by Michaela Melián: http://www.memoryloops.net.

Memory Loops is a digital memorial for the victims of Nazi persecution in Munich, Bavaria. It is based on both historical and contemporary audio recordings of reports by Nazi victims and perpetrators, read by actors and children and set to music. The soundtracks (300 in German, 175 in English) have been produced and choreographed by artist Michaela Melián and are each linked to a specific location in Munich. They can be accessed via the website; additionally, there are information panels displayed at sixty-one sites in Munich's city center, which provide access to relevant Memory Loop soundtracks via URLs and phone numbers. Memory Loops was the 2008 winner of Munich's competition Opfer des Nationalsozialismus – Neue Formen des Erinnerns und Gedenkens and was also recognized by the 2012 Grimme Online Award.

NS Forced Labor in Leipzig – Digital Map, by the Gedenkstätte für Zwangsarbeit Leipzig: https://www.zwangsarbeit-in-leipzig.de/en/nazi-forced-labour-in-leipzig/ns-forced-labour-in-leipzig/digital-map/.

Leipzig's Memorial for Nazi Forced Labor provides via its website a digital map depicting forced labor camps located in Leipzig's metropolitan area during World War II. The map provides names, locations, and background information for more than 700 sites. It is continuously updated, reflecting the current level of research based on files held in Leipzig City Archive.

Politics of Remembrance, by the University of Vienna: https://www.univie.ac.at/porem/maps/#Place/11/1823373,6143598/all/1933-2018.

This website provides a digital map illustrating "Vienna's culture of remembrance." Its focus is the city's memorial landscape during the period of 1945 to 2018, focused on the eras of Austrofascism (1934–1938) and German occupation (1938–1945). Displayed are memorials on a timeline. A key aspect of the map are its filter tools which allow highlighting of the memorial's temporal, spatial, social, and thematic characteristics.

Sites in Mind, by the NS-Dokumentationszentrum München: https://apps.apple.com/de/app/sites-in-mind/id1062097278?l=en.

With this app, users can access background information, including images, biographies, and audio and video recording, about a selection of 120 locations in Munich that are related to the city's history during the period of Nazi Germany. The information is linked to a scalable map with GPS alerts. The app also offers guided tours and AR functionality.

Transnational Remembrance of Nazi Forced Labor and Migration, by the Arolsen Archives: International Center on Nazi Persecution: https://transrem.arolsen-archives.org/maps/.

This website offers an interactive map on which the migration of displaced persons and liberated forced laborers after World War II can be traced. Their movements are traceable, spatially and temporally, for the period from their birth until (re)migration.

Virtual Stolpersteine / Virtual Stumbling Stones, by Felix Flaig und Johannes Hebsacker: https://virtuellestolpersteine.wordpress.com/.

Since 1992, the artist Gunter Demnig has put small golden commemorative plaques with names of victims of Nazi Germany among the ordinary paving stones in front of the buildings they once lived in. These *Stolpersteine* (stumbling stones) are now to be found in many German and European cities. When the city council of Villingen-Schwenningen, however, blocked the installation of these stones, local high school students developed a virtual art project, providing information about Jewish victims deported from the city during World War II on a website and putting QR codes linking to this information on the houses they formerly inhabited. Similar projects creating such "virtual stumbling stones," have since been developed in other German cities—for example, Dortmund, Hohenlimburg, and Hagen (see https://www.rvkonline.de/digitale-stolpersteine/). In some places the virtual stumbling stones complement physical ones installed by Demnig—for example, in Nordhorn (https://www.nordhorn.de/portal/meldungen/qr-codes-fuer-stolpersteine-900000326-26710.html) or Offenburg (https://www.stadtanzeiger-ortenau.de/offenburg-stadt/c-lokales/app-liefert-infos-ueber-die-opfer_a42336). The pairing of real and virtual stones is sometimes done via apps, which enhance the information possible on the physical stones, and by linking audio and visual material.

Zwangsarbeit. Zeitzeugen App, by the Berliner Geschichtswerkstatt e.V.: http://www.berliner-geschichtswerkstatt.de/app.html.

This app provides several guided tours through Berlin focused on the experience of forced laborers during World War II. The tours are based on the testimonies of several forced laborers, and include historical documents and photographs of both victims and perpetrators.

5 Digital Teaching Material and Primary Source Collections

1938Projekt: Lesson Plans, by the Leo Baeck Institute: https://www.lbi.org/projects/1938projekt-lesson-plans/.

The Leo Baeck Institute offers eleven lesson sets for middle and high schools. They were developed in collaboration with teachers and are designed to introduce students to digital archival source material and historical research methodologies.

E-Learning Courses, by the Jewish Partisan Educational Foundation: http://www.jewishpartisans.org/elearning.

This website provides access to eleven video courses, offered by the non-profit organization Jewish Partisan Educational Foundation. The courses are between 10 and 60 minutes long and focus on different aspects related to the history of Jewish partisans during the Holocaust.

Education and E-learning, by Yad Vashem: https://www.yadvashem.org/education.html.

Yad Vashem provides an extensive educational platform via its website. It contains educational videos discussing important terms, events, and actors in the history of the Holocaust, lesson plans for the elementary, middle and high school levels, as well as a "Survivors Testimony Films Series."

Experiencing History: Holocaust Sources in Context, by the United States Holocaust Memorial Museum (USHMM): https://perspectives.ushmm.org/.

The website offers several collections of primary sources, organized by the themes "Jewish Perspectives on the Holocaust," "Americans and the Holocaust," and "Everyday Life: Roles, Motives, and Choices During the Holocaust." Digital copies of various forms of primary source are provided, with translations into English (when relevant) and transcriptions as well as texts providing historical contextualization and background information. The sources are also tagged, with categories such as "children and youth," "religious life," "music," to name a few, facilitating the exploration of interconnections and self-directed thematic exploration of the sources and the reflected history.

Forced Labor 1939–1945. Memory and History, by the Stiftung "Erinnerung, Verantwortung und Zukunft" in collaboration with the Freie Universität Berlin and the German Historical Museum: https://www.zwangsarbeit-archiv.de/en/index.html.

This website contains a collection of over 600 testimonies of people from twenty-six countries who were forced to work in Nazi Germany. The interviews, provided in video or audio format, are available in German, Russian, and English. The website also includes transcripts and translations as well as photos and short biographies of forced laborers. Seven of the video interviews have been integrated into lesson plans (in German only), augmented with transcripts, background material, exercises, timelines, and more.

Fundamentals of Teaching the Holocaust, by the United States Holocaust Memorial Museum (USHMM): https://www.ushmm.org/teach/fundamentals.

This website hosted by the USHMM provides general guidelines for teaching the Holocaust, a collection of lesson plans and teaching materials on the Holocaust (organized by different topics that include "Antisemitism and Racism," "Propaganda," "Roles of Individuals," etc.)

German History in Documents and Images, by the German Historical Institute: http://german historydocs.ghi-dc.org/Index.cfm?language=english.

This website gives access to a collection of primary sources related to Germany's history from 1500 to the present. The sources are provided in both German and English translation and are thematically organized in ten large chronological chapters, including one on the history of Nazi Germany. Each chapter contains an introductory essay and several sub-chapters, providing documents, maps, and images. For a review and documentation on this online edition, see the text by McCullough and Retallack discussed above in the section on academic scholarship.

Holocaust Encyclopedia: Identification Card, by the United States Holocaust Memorial Museum (USHMM): https://encyclopedia.ushmm.org/landing/en/id-cards.

This website is a collection of digital identification cards created by the USHMM. Each card contains biographical information and a photo of an individual Holocaust survivor or of a person who was killed during the Holocaust, and a description of their experiences during the years 1933 until 1939 and during World War II, and of the circumstances of their survival or death (if known). The identification cards were developed based on interviews with 130 Holocaust survivors. The website allows browsing the 600 cards and filtering them by last name. These cards are a digital version of those given to visitors to the museum in Washington DC.

The International Military Tribunal for Germany, by Yale Law School: https://avalon.law.yale.edu/subject_menus/imt.asp.

As part of Yale Law School's Avalon Project, which publishes digital historical documents in the areas of law, history, and diplomacy, this website makes accessible proceedings and documents produced during the International Military Tribunal for Germany as well as key documents related to the Nuremberg Trials, and texts of historical documents which were cited in the tribunal's official record.

Visual History of the Holocaust: Rethinking Curation in the Digital Age, by the Ludwig Boltzmann Institute for Digital History (Vienna): https://www.vhh-project.eu/.

This EU Horizon 2020 project focuses on the digital curation and preservation of film records related to the liberation of Nazi concentration camps and other sites of Nazi crimes. As part of the project, which began in January 2019, the film records will be further contextualized by linking them to photographs, audio, and texts. The aim is to devise new forms of user interaction with digital data and learning experiences that can be employed by museums, libraries, and archives, but also in the fields of cultural tourism and education.

World War Two, by the BBC: http://www.bbc.co.uk/history/worldwars/wwtwo/.

This website includes summaries as well as introductory texts by historians on several aspects related to the history of World War II. Also available are some animated maps and short videos.

6 Models of Historical Sites in 3D, Online and 3D Exhibitions, and Virtual and Augmented Reality Applications

1943 Berlin Blitz in 360, by the BBC: https://www.bbc.com/historyofthebbc/100-voices/ww2/360berlin.

This short movie provides an immersive VR / 360° experience of a report from an air raid over Berlin during World War II. It is based on original archive recordings taken during a night flight in September 1943 by BBC war correspondent Wynford Vaughan-Thomas and recording engineer Reg Pidsley. The video simulated being inside the plane with them.

Die Befreiung / The Liberation, by Bayrischer Rundfunk (BR): https://diebefreiung.br.de/.

This is an audio-visual tour of the history of the liberation of Dachau concentration camp in 1945, available directly via the website or through an app with an AR component. Provided by the German public broadcaster Bayrischer Rundfunk, the tour includes historical photographs and testimonies of witnesses to this history.

Bergen-Belsen on Site with Augmented Reality, by the Synthetic, Perceptive, Emotive and Cognitive Systems (SPECS) research group, Barcelona: http://www.belsen-project.specs-lab.com/the-tablet-application/.

Since 2014, tablets with an app with geo-localization can be used at the Bergen-Belsen memorial site. The app has been created to guide and enhance visitors' exploration of the site by providing an AR visualization of Bergen-Belsen concentration camp buildings that no longer exist.

Courtroom 600, by Greenhouse Studios, University of Connecticut: https://greenhousestudios.uconn.edu/projects/courtroom-600/.

This project aims to create a 3D VR experience that will afford users an interactive exploration of the history of the Nuremberg Trials. It is based on primary sources available in open-access digital collections, including papers of the Executive Trial Counsel Thomas J. Dodd, which are held by the University of Connecticut.

Future Memory App, by the Falstad Center and Synthetic, Perceptive, Emotive and Cognitive Systems (SPECS) research group Barcelona: https://falstadsenteret.no/en/hva-skjer/exhibition/digital-reconstruction.

As part of the EU-funded HERA research project IC_Access: Inclusive Strategies for European Conflicted Pasts, the Future Memory App has been developed, offering a digital model of the Falstadt Concentration Camp (SS Strafgefangenenlager Falstadt) in Norway. It combines data from historical primary sources with geo-localized information. Since 2018, visitors to the Falstad museum can borrow iPads with this app, allowing them to explore the site of the former camp in an immersive and interactive manner, based on XR technology.

Litzmannstadt Ghetto Model, by The Museum of Independence Traditions in Łódź: http://radegast.pl/en/information/about-the-project,9.html.

This interdisciplinary project, launched in 2015, aims to create a 3D-model of the Ghetto in Łódź, Poland.

New Dimensions in Holocaust Testimony, by the USC Shoah Foundation: https://ict.usc.edu/prototypes/new-dimensions-in-testimony/.

The USC Shoah Foundation has created video exhibits of testimonies by Holocaust survivors that allow dialogue-like interaction with 3D visualizations ("hologram-like") of individual survivors. To create these complex exhibits, Holocaust survivors were filmed in a special green room and their recorded testimonies processed with methods from computational linguistics. One of the motivations behind this project was to preserve human-style interactivity with Holocaust survivors in the (coming) "era without witnesses."

Online Exhibitions, by the United States Holocaust Memorial Museum (USHMM): https://www.ushmm.org/information/exhibitions/online-exhibitions.

The USHMM provides access to various online exhibitions dealing with a wide array of topics related to the history of Nazi Germany and the Holocaust.

Secret Annex (Anne Frank's Hiding Place), by the Anne Frank House: https://www.annefrank.org/en/anne-frank/secret-annex/.

As part of the material and information it provides online, the Anne Frank House in Amsterdam presents a virtual exhibition of Anne Frank's hiding place. Visitors can "see" the place where she wrote her famous diary through a 360° virtual model.

Synagogen in Deutschland: Eine virtuelle Rekonstruktion, by the Technical University Darmstadt: https://www.dg.architektur.tu-darmstadt.de/forschung_ddu/digitale_rekonstruktion_ddu/synagogen/index.de.jsp.

One of the earliest undertakings in digital modeling of Nazi history, this project at the Technical University Darmstadt uses digital tools to re-create historical buildings destroyed during the Nazi period. The project began by generating digital images of synagogues in Frankfurt that had been destroyed in Nazi pogroms or during World War II. Later, this extended to synagogues in the German cities of Berlin, Dortmund, Dresden, Düsseldorf, Hamburg, Hannover, Kaiserslautern, Cologne, Leipzig, Munich, Nuremberg, Plauen, and Stuttgart. As the project has developed, it has also incorporated 3D and VR technology as well as digitally enabled rapid prototyping (3D printing) to create physical models of destroyed buildings.

Similar efforts to digitally reconstruct synagogues have been undertaken, for example, for Breslau by the Hochschule Mainz (https://architekturinstitut.hs-mainz.de/projekte/digitale-rekonstruktion-der-breslauer-synagoge), and for Linz (by René Mathe as part of his Diplomarbeit at Technical University Vienna: https://ars.electronica.art/aeblog/de/2016/11/10/linz-synagogue).

The Last Goodbye, by the USC Shoah Foundation: https://www.oculus.com/experiences/rift/1973329179388804/.

The Last Goodbye is a 20-minute virtual reality testimony experience, based on the testimony of Holocaust survivor Pinchas Gutter when touring the site of the Majdanek concentration camp. It has been displayed in various exhibitions and museums (currently at the Museum of Jewish Heritage, New York; https://mjhnyc.org/exhibitions/the-last-goodbye/) and is now also available for free via oculus.com.

Virtual Tour, Auschwitz-Birkenau, by the Auschwitz-Birkenau State Museum: http://panorama.auschwitz.org/.

Virtual Tour, Neuengamme, by the KZ-Gedenkstätte Neuengamme: https://www.kz-gedenkstaette-neuengamme.de/360tour/.

These memorials at the former concentration camps Auschwitz and Neuengamme offer 360° photographic or virtual tours of their sites. Both mostly use present-day footage for their tours. Visitors can move with relative freedom throughout the site, somewhat similarly to Google Street View. Background information on various buildings and areas can be accessed.

Visualizing the History of the Janowska Camp and the Holocaust in Lviv, by Northumbria University: https://www.northumbria.ac.uk/about-us/academic-departments/humanities/institute-of-humanities/projects/visualizing-the-history-of-the-janowska-camp-and-the-holocaust-in-lviv.

This project, led by Waitman Wade Born at Northumbria University, develops a digital 3D-model of the Janowska concentration camp, located near Lviv, to further explore the camp's history. The 3D mapping is complemented by a social network analysis of individuals linked to the camp, with the aim to create a GIS visualization depicting their movements over space. (See also https://waitmanbeorn.wixsite.com/holocaustvisualized/janowska-3d-mapping-project and https://waitmanbeorn.wixsite.com/holocaustvisualized/janowska-camp-social-network-analys)

WDR AR 1933–1945, by the West-Deutscher Rundfunk (WDR): https://www1.wdr.de/fernsehen/unterwegs-im-westen/ar-app/ar-app-info-100.html.

This app from the German public broadcaster WDR is based on digitalized reports by contemporary witnesses of their experience in Germany during the years 1933–1945. Using AR technology on smartphones, these reports can then be seen—virtually—in the room of the user. Schools are one of the main target audiences of the app, which can simulate real-life visits by witnesses to classrooms.

7 Online Talks by Historians and Other Experts

Several academic institutions, museums, and archives have begun to provide online access to recorded talks and lectures on aspects related to the history of Nazi Germany; the 2020 Covid-19 pandemic has further accelerated this trend. Audio recordings of talks and panel discussions hosted by the museum Topographie des Terrors, Berlin, can be found here: https://www.topographie.de/digitale-angebote/. Book talks and lectures hosted by the Wiener Holocaust Library can be accessed via the library's YouTube channel: https://www.youtube.com/thewienerlibrary. Yad Vashem's website provides access to a "Video Lecture Series": https://www.yadvashem.org/holocaust/video-lectures.html. The United States Holocaust Memorial Museum has started to stream their live talks as virtual events: https://www.ushmm.org/online-calendar.

Contributors

Dr. Andreas Birk is Professor of Electrical Engineering and Computer Science at Jacobs University Bremen where he leads the Robotics Group. He is the Principal Investigator for the BMBF-funded project 3D Erfassung der Gedenkstätte U-Boot Bunker Valentin durch Luft-, Boden- und Unterwasserroboter (Valentin 3D). He started at Jacobs University in 2001 (turning down an offer for a professorship at the Universität Rostock). Previously, he was a professor at the Vrije Universiteit Brussel (VUB) and a Fellow of the Flemish Society for Applied Research (IWT) at VUB's Artificial Intelligence Lab, where he had earlier held a postdoctoral position supervising a research group. Birk has also been a visiting professor at the Universität Koblenz-Landau. He studied Computer Science at the Universität des Saarlandes, Saarbrücken from 1989 to 1993, and then received his doctorate there in 1995.

Dr. Sebastian Bondzio is a digital historian who studied history, philosophy and Latin philology at Osnabrück University, where he wrote his MA thesis on the social profile of German war volunteers during the First World War. From 2013–2018, he was a member of the research project Gefallene in der Gesellschaftsgeschichte at Osnabrück University, and in 2018 completed his dissertation (published as *Soldatentod und Durchhaltebereitschaft. Eine Stadtgesellschaft im Ersten Weltkrieg*. Paderborn: Ferdinand Schöningh, 2020). Since 2018, he has worked on the DFG-funded research project Überwachung. Macht. Ordnung, an in-depth study of the Gestapo's practices of power based on an analysis of historical big data. In 2020, he also became a senior researcher in Osnabrück University's workgroup *Data Driven History*, and was awarded the Gerda Henkel Fellowship for Digital History, which supported him as a visiting fellow at the German Historical Institute in Washington, D.C. and the Roy Rosenzweig Center for History and New Media at George Mason University (Fairfax, VA) in 2021.

Frederike Buda, M.A., studied History and German Studies at the University of Bremen, receiving a master's degree in Public History in 2017. Since 2018, she is a research associate at Jacobs University Bremen. She is part of the interdisciplinary project Valentin3D, that digitally maps Bunker Valentin, a former submarine pen built by forced laborers during World War II. Since 2020, she has also been working in the project Digital Contingency – Prospects and Limitations of Technology in Digital Humanities, led by Andreas Birk and Julia Timpe. She is working on her PhD dissertation at Jacobs University: her research explores the history of the circle of industrialists known as the Freundeskreis Reichsführer SS. Together with Julia Timpe, she organized the workshop Zeugnisse des Nationalsozialismus, digital – Projekte, Methoden, Theorien at Jacobs University in December 2019.

Dr. Heiko Bülow is a Postdoctoral Fellow at Jacobs University and a member of the Robotics Group. His research interests include multidimensional signal processing (in particular spectral registration and array processing), machine vision, pattern recognition and autonomous systems.

Daniel Burckhardt, Dipl. Math., M.A., has been a Research Associate at the Institute for the History of the German Jews since 2015. He studied mathematics in Zürich and the history of science and technology in Berlin. He has worked as a research assistant in various Digital History projects at the Humboldt University of Berlin's Department of History, at the Leibniz Centre for Contemporary History Potsdam and at the German Historical Institute Washington. In addition, he is a member of the editorial board and steering committee of H-Soz-Kult.

Arturo Gomez Chavez, M.Sc., received his B.Sc. in Electronic Systems and Engineering from ITESM-CCM in Mexico in 2013 and his M.Sc. in Robotics and Cognitive Systems from Jacobs University Bremen in 2016. He is currently in the final phase of his Ph.D. studies at the latter institution. He is a research associate in Jacobs University's Robotics Group, where he has been involved in several EU projects focused on the development and application of robotic systems in challenging scenarios, specifically in the areas of machine learning and computer vision. His goal is to contribute to societal challenges through his knowledge artificial intelligence and robotics.

Dr. Mark Dang-Anh studied German philology, political science and psychology at the RWTH Aachen. He was a research associate at the University of Bonn and the University of Siegen, where he received his PhD in Media Studies in 2018 (published as: *Protest twittern. Eine medienlinguistische Untersuchung von Straßenprotesten.* Bielefeld: Transcript, 2019). He is currently working as a research associate in the project Social History of Language under National Socialism at the Leibniz-Institute for German Language, Mannheim. He is co-editor of the *Journal for Media Linguistics.* His main research interests are media linguistics, discourse analysis, political discourse, sociocultural linguistics, interactional linguistics, and media semiotics.

Dr. Sonja Dickow-Rotter has been a research associate at the Institute for the History of the German Jews since 2019. She studied literature and cultural anthropology in Hamburg. Her doctoral thesis was published as *Konfigurationen des (Zu-)Hauses. Diaspora-Narrative und Transnationalität in jüdischen Literaturen der Gegenwart.* Berlin: J.B. Metzler, 2019. She has been a Visiting Research Fellow at *Da'at Hamakom: Center for the Study of Cultures of Place in the Modern Jewish World* at the Hebrew University Jerusalem, and is an alumna of the Ernst Ludwig Ehrlich Studienwerk.

Christian Günther, M.A., is a researcher at the Department of Digital Humanities at the University of Wuppertal. He studied history and philosophy at the University of Bonn and is currently pursuing his PhD at the University of Cologne, writing a dissertation on digital education methods at memorial sites. His research focusses on the history of National Socialism, especially on the topics of the Gestapo, resistance under National Socialism, and forced labor, and on the history education in the digital sphere. Prior to his position at the University of Wuppertal, he worked for numerous museums and memorial sites, including the NS-Documentation Center of the City of Cologne. He was involved in several research projects that generated publications and exhibitions such as *Trumpf* (Streb, Joachim. *Trumpf: Geschichte eines Familienunternehmens.* Munich: Carl Hanser, 2018), Opposition und Widerstand in Köln 1933–1945 and Gestapo Köln.

Dr. Christian A. Müller received his B.Sc. in Computer Science in 2007 and his M.Sc. in Autonomous Systems in 2012, both from the Bonn-Rhein-Sieg University of Applied Sciences. From 2012 until January 2020, he was part of the Robotics Group at Jacobs University Bremen where he obtained his doctorate in 2019 and contributed to BMBF- and EU-funded projects. In 2020, he became a project cordinator at the Institute for Artificial Intelligence, University of Bremen. His interests include artificial intelligence, in particular machine learning, data mining and computer vision related to robotics.

Jannik Sachweh, M.A., is a historian working on the regional and contemporary history of north-western Germany, focussing on the history of National Socialism and science. He studied history at the University of Bremen, where he worked in the research project Vorgeschichtsforschung in Bremen unterm Hakenkreuz (Prehistorical archaeology in Bremen under the Swastika). He has worked as a student assistant for Bremen's archaeology department and wrote his master's thesis about the archaeologist and art historian Helen Rosenau, who was persecuted by the National Socialists. As a curator and researcher, he has worked for several museums, memorial places and research institutions. From 2018 to 2020, he was a member of the Lower Saxony Memorials Foundation's research staff, working on a project on the visibility of National Socialist judiciary crimes at the Wolfenbüttel memorial.

Dr. Stefan Scholl studied history at the Universities of Bielefeld and Paris 7. In 2014, he received his PhD in History from the University of Bielefeld (dissertation published as: *Begrenzte Abhängigkeit. 'Wirtschaft' und 'Politik' im 20. Jahrhundert*. Frankfurt am Main: Campus, 2014). From 2012 to 2017, he was a lecturer at the University of Siegen and worked on European sports history and biopolitics. Since 2018, he is a research associate in the project Social History of Language under National Socialism at the Leibniz-Institute for German Language, Mannheim. His main research interests include history of petitions during National Socialism, history of National Socialism as a communicative space, history of biopolitics and sport, and the history of liberal economic discourse.

Dr. Julia Timpe is University Lecturer for Contemporary History at Jacobs University Bremen. She studied history and German literature at Humboldt University of Berlin and Brown University, and received her PhD from Brown for a dissertation on the Nazi leisure organization *Kraft durch Freude* (published as: *Nazi-Organized Recreation and Entertainment in the Third Reich*. London: Palgrave Macmillan, 2017.) After completing postdocs at Harvard University and the United States Holocaust Memorial Museum in Washington D.C., and serving as Lecturer at the University of Bremen, she joined Jacobs University Bremen in 2016. Her research focusses on the everyday history of Nazi Germany. She is an affiliated member of the Jacobs Robotic Group's BMBF- funded project Valentin3D. Together with Frederike Buda, she organized the workshop Zeugnisse des Nationalsozialismus, digital – Projekte, Methoden, Theorien at Jacobs University in December 2019.

Christiane Charlotte Weber, M.A., studied medieval and modern history, German literature, and British and American literature and culture at Justus Liebig University Gießen. After ten years at the Arbeitsstelle Holocaustliteratur, a research institution at the University of Gießen that examines fictional and non-fictional texts about the Holocaust from a literary perspective, she started working for the International Tracing Service (ITS)/Arolsen Archives in 2017. Her responsibilities there include developing the e-Guide, a digital tool that contextualizes documents about the Holocaust, forced labor, and the life of Displaced Persons after the Second World War.

Index

3D model / 3D-mapping   8, 23–24, 133–136, 141–166, 218–222

Algorithms   65–66, 91–92, 144–146, 152
Allied Forces   5–6, 41–42, 136–140, 176
– American Air Force   135–140, 162–165
Annotation   10, 101, 104, 108, 123–125, 141–146, 152, 154–155, 159, 165
Antisemitism   24, 32, 216
Apps (Applications)   3–4, 19, 26, 35, 192–194, 196, 209, 211, 214–215, 218–222
Arbeitsamt (Labor Office)   76–77
Arbeitserziehungslager (AEL; Labor Education Camp)   76–77
Archives   4–6, 11, 12, 22, 28, 39–53, 66, 134, 189, 198, 207, 211–214, 218, 222
– Online Archives   40–41, 44–53, 211
Arolsen Archive (International Tracing Service; ITS)   5, 39–53, 189, 198, 211, 214, 225
Artificial Intelligence (AI)   65, 91, 223, 225
Augmented Reality (AR)   3, 171, 179, 182–184, 190, 211, 214, 218–219, 222
Authenticity   9, 181, 185–186, 189–197, 206

Beutelsbach Consensus   184
Big Data   4, 6–7, 57, 66, 68, 141, 205, 207, 223
Bunkers   8, 133–166, 181, 223

Card Files   42, 45–46, 203–204
Codes   27, 29–30, 36,43, 195, 198, 213–215
Covid-19   35, 163, 198, 207, 222
Collocation   7, 105, 111–113
Computer Sciences   91, 224
Concentration Camps   41–44, 51, 73–74, 76–77, 84, 89–90, 137–138, 170, 174, 175, 176, 177, 179, 206, 211–212, 217, 221
Concordances   108–109, 111, 113, 117, 125
Commemoration   8, 188, 211

Corpora   68, 99, 100, 101, 103–108, 111, 113, 115–116, 119, 124–125

Data Driven History   6, 65–67, 203, 223
Databases   4, 7, 44–46, 66–68, 79, 87, 91, 189–190, 198, 210–212
Death Marches   45
Denunciations   59, 75
Digital Exhibitions. *See* Exhibitions.
Digital History   1–14, 17–18, 29, 67, 203–206, 223–224
Digital Maps   8–9, 169–179, 178–179, 211, 213, 214
Digital Methods   4, 6, 204, 206
Digitization   1, 5–12, 18, 27, 28, 36, 44–46, 51, 65, 91, 92, 117, 124, 133–135, 141, 144, 148, 151, 156, 164, 166, 188–189, 191, 197, 198, 203, 207, 222
Discourse Analysis   6–7, 10, 99–125, 204–205, 224
Dispersion   105, 107, 108, 115,
Displaced Persons (DPs)   5, 40, 42–44, 50, 225

e-Guide   5, 39, 41–43, 48–52, 225
Education   2, 4, 8, 11, 18, 26, 28, 32, 34–36, 48, 59–60, 69, 72, 77, 89, 134, 137–138, 151, 181, 184, 188, 190, 196–197, 207, 210, 213–216, 218, 222, 224
Ethics   2, 3, 4, 5, 192, 196–197, 203
Exhibitions   3, 8–9, 26, 30, 35, 140, 170, 172, 179, 186–187, 218, 220–221, 224
– Museums   2, 4, 11–12, 19, 171, 189–191, 196, 198, 207, 210, 218, 221–222, 224–225
– Online/Digital Exhibitions   2, 8–9, 26, 30, 35, 170, 172, 179, 218, 220–221, 224

Forced Labor   69, 75, 77, 82, 84, 87–88, 134, 175–177, 213, 214, 216, 224–225
Fourier Mellin SOFT (FMS)   145, 147, 153, 156
Frequency   71, 75, 83, 86, 93, 107, 112

Game Studies 181, 183, 192, 193, 197
Gatekeepers 197–198
Gestapo. See Police.

Hermeneutics 67, 101–104, 115
Holocaust 2–6, 20–21, 44–45, 190–191, 195, 197, 199, 204–207, 210–211, 215, 216, 217, 220–222, 225

Ideology 6, 93, 170
Immersion 183, 206
Index 6–7, 24, 41, 44–46, 51, 58–59, 60–93, 106, 113, 198, 209, 212, 216–217, 220
Interactivity 9, 24, 52, 103, 147, 151, 153, 170–172, 182–183, 190, 192–193, 195, 212–214, 219–220
Interdisciplinarity 135, 166, 219, 223
International Refugee Organization (IRO) 41, 45
International Tracing Service (ITS). See Arolsen Archives.
Internet 5–6, 11, 17, 25–27, 29–31, 33, 40, 75, 151–152, 147, 154, 155, 188–189, 198–199, 206, 208, 210–218, 222
– Search Engines 47
– Websites 25–26, 147, 188–189, 198–199, 206, 208, 210–218, 222

Jews 4–5, 17–36, 45, 109–110, 118, 121–122, 206–207, 209–224
Judiciary System 173–174
– *Volksgerichtshof* (People's Court) 174

Keywords 99, 106–111, 113, 115, 117

Laser Range Finder (LRF) 134, 142, 144, 146–149, 151, 153
Lebensraum 7, 99, 104, 107–108, 110, 113, 115, 125
Letters of Complaint 7, 104, 116
Letters of Request. See Letters of Complaint.
Linguistics 99, 101, 102–103, 105–107, 111–113, 115, 125, 220, 224

Manipulations 12, 196

Memorial Sites 2–4, 8–9, 19, 22, 140, 170–172, 181–199, 206–207, 210–225
Metadata 5, 18, 27–28, 31, 36, 46, 51, 198
Micro Aerial Vehicles (MAVs) 134, 143, 153–155
Migration 17–18, 21, 24, 32, 46, 214
Mixed Reality (MR) 182, 190
Museums. See Exhibitions.

National Socialist German Workers' Party (NSDAP) 90, 109–110, 116, 122
Nazi Persecution 5, 36, 40, 45, 47, 50, 52, 75–78, 210–214
Networks 34, 121, 189
Nodes 111–115
Normed Data 19

Online. See Internet.
Online Archives. See Archives.
Online Exhibitions. See Exhibitions.
Optical Character Recognition (OCR) 117
Organisation Todt 139, 176

Photogrammetry 143, 153
Pogroms 20, 22, 220
Point Clouds 143, 146, 149, 152,
Police 6, 41, 58–93, 138, 170, 174, 177, 179, 204
– *Abwehrpolizei* (Defense Police) 62–63
– Gestapo (*Geheime Staatspolizei*; Secret State Police) 6, 7, 10, 57–69, 70–97, 125, 137, 138, 167, 170, 174–178, 203–204, 223–224
– *Politische Polizei* (Political Police) 62–63, 69–70, 72, 74, 78–79, 81–86, 92, 170, 179
Political Opponents 83, 85, 170, 179
Political Speech 104, 106, 124
Post-War Period 22, 100, 177, 186
Prisons 8–9, 44, 71–90, 139, 169–179, 211
– *Kreisgefängnis* (district prison) 173
– *Landesstrafanstalt* (state prison) 173
– (prison) sentence 71–72, 74, 81–85, 89, 172, 174

– Prisoners   2, 40, 42, 44, 46, 48, 50, 72, 74, 90, 139, 173–177
– Prisoners of War (POWs)   2, 139, 175–176
Propaganda   68, 78, 94
Provenance   42, 186
Public History   2, 17, 19, 203, 223

Reichssicherheitshauptamt (RSHA)   63, 73, 89
Remembrance   2–3, 5, 11, 47, 140, 189–190, 195, 197–198, 204, 210, 214
Remote Operated Vehicle (ROV)   133–134, 143, 158–159, 163, 165
Remote Sensing   141
Rhetoric   7, 100, 117

Samples   178
Sanctions   6, 60–94
Schutzhaft (Preventive Custody)   62, 70–73
Search Engines. *See* Internet.
Second World War. *See* World War II.
Semantics   27, 102–104
Shoah. *See* Holocaust.
Smartphones   26, 35, 52, 182, 222
Simulation   6, 57, 183, 192–193, 196, 206
Social Media   31, 51, 190, 192, 194, 197, 199
Sources   1–13, 18–19, 22–36, 41–53, 59–60, 63–68, 76, 81, 92–93, 99, 101, 104, 117–118, 136, 137, 139, 144, 152, 153, 157, 164–165, 171, 173, 184, 189, 196, 198, 199, 203–209, 212, 215–219
– Analog Sources   8–9, 35, 41, 50–52, 66, 188, 203
– Audiovisual Sources   23–24
– Audio Recordings   210, 213, 218, 222
– Digital Sources   2, 4–6, 8–12, 18–19, 22, 24, 26, 206, 208
Serial Sources   6, 50, 66, 92, 203

Stolpersteine (Stumbling Stones)   22, 214–215
Structure from Motion (SfM)   154–155
Synagogues   20, 22, 220, 221

Tag   7–8, 36, 107, 119, 123–124, 216
Technology   3, 9, 13, 39, 92, 101, 125, 135, 182, 190, 192–193, 205, 219, 220, 222–224
Testimonies. *See* Witness (reports/testimonies).
Tokens   105, 107–108, 111
Touch Screens   171, 173

United Nations Relief and Rehabilitation Administration (UNRRA)   41
United States Holocaust Memorial Museum (USHMM)   216–217, 220, 222, 225
USC Shoah Foundation   90, 220–221

Virtual Reality (VR)   3, 9, 171, 179, 181–184, 186, 191–194, 196–198, 218–221, 223
Visualization   2, 4, 135, 143, 147–148, 151, 153–154, 164, 203, 219–221
Volk   60, 106, 109–110, 113–124
Volksgemeinschaft   7, 57–64, 73, 76, 79, 81, 86, 88–94, 117, 170, 179

Web Graphics Library (WebGL)   152
Witness (reports/testimonies)   9, 18, 20, 31, 33, 70, 84–85, 89, 125, 157, 165, 177, 185–187, 190–196, 207, 213, 216, 218, 220–222
Wehrmacht   169, 172, 175
World War II   2, 4–8, 20, 22, 32, 41, 47, 61, 67, 110, 134, 136, 137, 141, 156–158, 170, 175, 177, 181, 210–220, 223
World Wide Web. *See* Internet.

Open-Access-Transformation in History

Open Access for excellent academic publications in the field of history: Thanks to the support of 32 academic libraries and initiatives, 9 frontlist publications from 2022 can be published as gold open access, without any costs to the authors.

The following institutions and initiatives have contributed to the funding and thus promote the open access transformation in German linguistics and ensure free availability for everyone:

Dachinitiative "Hochschule.digital Niedersachsen" des Landes Niedersachsen
Universitätsbibliothek Bayreuth
Deutsches Zentrum für Integrations- und Migrationsforschung (DeZIM)
Staatsbibliothek zu Berlin – Preußischer Kulturbesitz
Universitätsbibliothek Bern
Universitätsbibliothek Bochum
Universitäts- und Landesbibliothek Bonn
Staats- und Universitätsbibliothek Bremen
Universitäts- und Landesbibliothek Darmstadt
Universitätsbibliothek Duisburg-Essen
Universitäts- und Landesbibliothek Düsseldorf
Albert-Ludwigs-Universität Freiburg – Universitätsbibliothek
Niedersächsische Staats- und Universitätsbibliothek Göttingen
Universitätsbibliothek der FernUniversität in Hagen
Staats- und Universitätsbibliothek Hamburg Carl von Ossietzky
Gottfried Wilhelm Leibniz Bibliothek – Niedersächsische Landesbibliothek, Hannover
Universitäts- und Landesbibliothek Tirol, Innsbruck
Universitätsbibliothek Kassel – Landesbibliothek und Murhardsche Bibliothek der Stadt Kassel
Universitäts- und Stadtbibliothek Köln
Universitätsbibliothek der Universität Koblenz-Landau
Zentral- und Hochschulbibliothek Luzern
Universitätsbibliothek Magdeburg
Universitätsbibliothek Mainz
Bibliothek des Leibniz-Instituts für Europäische Geschichte, Mainz
Universitätsbibliothek Marburg
Universitätsbibliothek der Ludwig-Maximilians-Universität München
Universitäts- und Landesbibliothek Münster
Universitätsbibliothek Osnabrück
Universitätsbibliothek Vechta
Herzog August Bibliothek Wolfenbüttel
Universitätsbibliothek Wuppertal
Zentralbibliothek Zürich

OpenAccess. © 2022, published by De Gruyter. This work is licensed under the Creative Commons Attribution 4.0 International License. https://doi.org/10.1515/9783110714692-015

www.ingramcontent.com/pod-product-compliance
Lightning Source LLC
Chambersburg PA
CBHW050523170426
43201CB00013B/2064